By Donald Lambro

WASHINGTON — CITY OF SCANDALS: INVESTIGATING CONGRESS AND OTHER BIG SPENDERS

FAT CITY: HOW WASHINGTON WASTES YOUR TAXES

THE FEDERAL RATHOLE

WASHINGTON —
CITY OF
SCANDALS

WASHINGTON— CITY OF SCANDALS

Investigating Congress and Other Big Spenders

Donald Lambro

LITTLE, BROWN AND COMPANY · BOSTON · TORONTO

FIRST EDITION

Library of Congress Cataloging in Publication Data

Lambro, Donald.
    Washington—city of scandals.

    Includes index.
    1. Waste in government spending—United States.
I. Title.
HJ2052.L35   1984   353.0072   84-12548
ISBN 0-316-51288-5

MV

Designed by Dede Cummings

*Published simultaneously in Canada
by Little, Brown & Company (Canada) Limited*

PRINTED IN THE UNITED STATES OF AMERICA

To the American Taxpayer

Acknowledgments

So many people contributed to the production and completion of this book. I am especially indebted to Edwin J. Feulner, Jr., president of The Heritage Foundation, for generously providing the research support needed to conduct my investigation. I remain equally indebted to M. Stanton Evans and the highly successful National Journalism Center he has established to bring bright, young prospective journalists into the Washington arena to practice their craft.

Thanks to the support of these two organizations, a small band of resourceful and very talented people helped me to track down facts, figures, internal memoranda, studies, audits, and assorted documents, and to question a vast array of government officials and other sources. Their inexhaustible energy and curiosity left few stones unturned, not to mention more than a few bureaucrats muttering about "pestering reporters."

My thanks to Martha Dawson who, fresh out of the University of Virginia, fulfilled every research challenge thrown at her with intelligence, dogged determination, unfailing good humor, and a characteristic thoroughness; Martin Cohen, a Harvard student bright beyond his years, who helped me dig into several government programs in his usually methodical and diligent way, leaving him, he says, with a "different perspective" about Washington, one that I suspect is not being taught at Harvard; Kenneth M. Scheibel, Jr., a De Paul University law student, who jumped into our paper chase with his customary enthusiasm, scholarship, and lawyer's eye for detail; and to Washington writer Greg Rushford for his extra research assistance.

I am also indebted to the editors of the monthly magazine *Inquiry*, the Heritage Foundation's quarterly journal *Policy Review*, and *Barron's*, the financial weekly published by Dow Jones, for giving me permission to include a few previously published excerpts.

My thanks also to television producer Neal Freeman, who has dedicated himself to getting people to do more than just think about doing things, for getting the creative wheels turning a little faster; Washington speechwriter William Gavin for his always professional advice; Roberta Miller, literary properties director at United Media Enterprises, for her invaluable guidance and encouragement; and especially to senior editor Ray Roberts, Ann Sleeper, and Mike Mattil of Little, Brown and Company, whose editing skills have made this a much better book. Thanks also to Herb Berkowitz and Hugh Newton of The Heritage Foundation for their special assistance, to Don Caldwell for a fine index, and to someone who wishes to remain anonymous for his additional research support.

Finally, a very special note of thanks to my wife, Jackie, for all her inspiration, patience and help, as well as to my son, Jason, who, when a brief respite from the labors of writing was absolutely crucial, took every advantage of my fatigue on the tennis court, for which I intend to get even at the first opportunity.

Contents

BOOK I

CONGRESS

1

Potomac Myths

"You know, the longer I cover this town, the more I realize that a lot of what goes on here is a crock," the chief congressional correspondent for one of the three major television news networks confessed to me in the Senate Press Gallery.

It was an observation made during one of those slow news days that motivates one to consider weightier matters than the dreary debate droning on in the Senate chamber. He was not, he hastened to add, talking about matters of major importance, either foreign or domestic, whose direction and outcome Washington legitimately, though often vainly, struggles to influence. Rather, he was talking about a lot of other things that consume so much of the government's finite resources and energies. "Congress spends so much of its time dickering over programs and agencies that do essentially nothing of importance," this veteran reporter said. "If some of them disappeared tomorrow, no one would ever notice."

Had he ever thought about doing a piece exposing this to his viewers? I inquired. "Good God, no," he replied, "it would never get on the air."

The national news media's reluctance to reveal the real government in Washington is a major reason why so many of the nebulous and unworkable activities of government have continued to exist and to grow for so many years. Yet this reluctance alone does not begin to explain why, despite millions of words written and spoken about the growth of government and its impact for good and for ill on our society, so much of what official Washington does remains deeply misunderstood by the people it is elected to serve. The reasons for this misunderstanding are many and complex.

There are, at least in a perceptive sense, two governments in Washington.

There is the government that is taught in our institutions of learning, reported by the Washington news media, and aggressively promoted and hyped by Uncle Sam's vast billion-dollar-a-year, media and public information apparatus. It is the government portrayed in charts and organizational diagrams, showing the systematic way the legislative process works; how the executive branch administers Congress's programs; and how the judiciary ensures that the entire structure and process stay within the letter of the law. It is a government of conscientious political representatives and honest, hardworking civil servants who are striving to deal with monumental national problems and responsibilities within our constitutional system of checks and balances. It is the government we praise on the Fourth of July and the one to which we pledge our allegiance.

At the same time, there is another government, one that is far less visible and much less understood, one that we hear about only occasionally and incrementally. This is not the government that we read about in our civics textbooks and were taught about in Government I classes. Nor is it the government usually portrayed on television's nightly news shows or reported in our weekly news magazines and major daily newspapers.

It is a government that too often does too much of what it should not do and not enough of what it should do.

It is a government made up of a jumble of conflicting laws and programs whose performance and effectiveness most of us, and most of our representatives as well, know about only vaguely. This vague knowledge is due to their prolific number. But it is also due to the frequently exaggerated, and in many cases dishonest, salesmanship, both by lawmakers who create, enact, fund, and often politically exploit these laws and programs, and by the bureaucracy and special interests who protect and promote them.

It is a government in which members of Congress deeply abuse their privileges and hypocritically refuse to abide by the same laws and rules they set for the rest of us.

It is a government in which lawmakers have enacted complex and costly agencies and programs, but often show little or no interest in what happens to them afterward.

It is a government whose swollen yearly legislative branch budget took a full ten years to rise from $282 million to $1 billion, but in the succeeding five years shot up by another half-billion dollars.

It is a government that has grown to nearly two thousand departments, divisions, agencies, administrations, boards, commissions, councils, quasi-government corporations, and other assorted bureaucratic conglomerations — concerning themselves with virtually every form of human endeavor, from producing news and musical programming for local radio stations to promoting stamp collecting.

It is a government whose annual expenditures have ballooned by an additional $200 billion during the past four years of so-called austerity budgets — from $728 billion in fiscal 1982 outlays to an estimated $925 billion in fiscal 1985.

Despite complaints that the Reagan administration has cruelly cut federal spending, the total annual budget, both on- and off-budget expenditures, will easily surpass the unprecedented $1 trillion mark by fiscal 1986, which begins October 1, 1985. Such a budget would be an awesome $340 billion above the budget President Ronald Reagan inherited from President Jimmy Carter in January 1981.

At the same time, because federal spending far exceeds federal revenues, the government's deficit over the last three years has mushroomed by $500 billion, pushing the gross national debt to nearly $2 trillion. Meanwhile, the full taxpayer liability for the government's present and future income transfer costs, including federal pensions and social security, has become a $12.1 trillion debt that is owed by every man, woman and child in America, and those who come after them.

It is a government whose agencies and programs, no matter how scandal ridden or ineffective, are rarely if ever eliminated or significantly scaled back. It is a government that has instead piled bureaucracy upon bureaucracy, law upon law, and regulation upon regulation, in an indiscriminate extravaganza of program expansion, duplication, regulatory chaos, and bureaucratic red tape.

It is a government that officially admits to employing a civilian and military workforce of nearly five million people, at a cost of over $100 billion a year — but which in truth is paying a hidden workforce of at least ten million additional workers, researchers, consultants and contractors who support, deliver, or administer federal programs and services on the federal, state and local level.

Today, for every five workers in the private sector, there is one person working for the government at one level or another, many of whose jobs are either financed or mandated by federal laws and programs.

It is a government that owns 744.1 million acres of property, or nearly one out of every three acres of land in the United States, in addition to possessing $316 billion in buildings, structures and other facilities, many of which auditors say are unused and unneeded.

It is a government that has grown so enormous that no single institution — least of all the United States Congress which created and funds every bit of it — is monitoring and overseeing its activities, except in only the most irresponsible, haphazard and cursory way.

It is a government in which a presidential task force, when asked to identify areas where budget savings can be made, uncovered a staggering $100 billion a year in wasteful or unnecessary spending and lost revenues — though they admit they examined only "the tip of the iceberg."

It is a government that in the last twenty years has wasted hundreds of billions of hard-earned tax dollars on programs that have become colossal yet quickly forgotten failures.

It is a government that squandered nearly $8 billion between 1968 and 1981 on a misguided and abuse-ridden attempt to try to fight crime from Washington, while the crime rate skyrocketed by 72 percent during this period, according to the FBI's Office of Uniform Crime Reports.

It is a government that spent $246.2 billion in direct federal aid to education between 1971 and 1982 — representing a 195 percent increase in aid — while educational achievement scores fell to all-time lows.

It is a government that mounted the biggest and most wasteful housing and urban renewal program in history — spending more than $134 billion in actual outlays on the Housing and Urban Development Department (HUD) since 1968. Had this money been spent solely on housing for America's poorest families, it could have provided $50,000 single-family homes for more than 2.7 million poor families — instead of the slum housing in which many now needlessly live.

It is a government that through the years mounted costly "urban renewal," "model cities," and "new communities" programs for America's ill-housed poor, and sent federally funded bulldozers to destroy old but stable inner-city neighborhoods. In their place the government erected poorly designed, badly supervised, rent-subsidized high-rise projects that became a breeding ground for crime and quickly deteriorated into some of the worst ghetto slums this nation has ever seen. At the same time, billions of dollars were paid out in housing loan defaults that ended up enriching the banks, while the poor got little or nothing in the way of decent housing.

This is why Uncle Sam is the nation's biggest slumlord, owning 1.2 million public housing units in which approximately five million poor people live.

It is a government that, with the start of the War on Poverty programs in 1964, proceeded to spend tens of billions of dollars on antipoverty programs of one sort or another, only to see the number of poor people increase significantly.

Taxpayers spent twice as much on direct cash income transfer payments to the poor in 1980 as in 1970 — and fourteen times more than in 1950 — yet by 1980, in cash income alone, there were actually more poor people in the United States than there were in 1968.

It is a government whose annual budget contains half a trillion dollars in nondefense spending exclusive of interest, $424 billion of which goes into transfer payments and social programs of one kind or another — over $86 billion of which in 1982 went to the poor in means-tested entitlement programs.

Nevertheless, the 1982 Census Bureau statistics revealed there were 34.4 million people in the United States still living at or below the poverty level, which, according to the government, was $9,862 a year for a family of four in 1983.

Rarely acknowledged is the tragic reality that much of the government's poverty assistance never reaches the poor. Instead, it is siphoned off by poverty consultants, poverty surveys and research, paperwork, and other administrative costs associated with maintaining a huge social welfare bureaucracy.

If the $86 billion spent in behalf of the poor in means-tested programs during fiscal 1982 — which does not include social security for the elderly poor, or billions of dollars in other social service programs — had been simply divided among the 7,512,000 families classified as poor, each family could be receiving $11,493.33 a year, placing them significantly above the poverty income level.

It is a government that says it cannot afford to improve its assistance to the poor, the elderly and the ill, yet it continues to distribute billions of dollars in block grant or categorical grant aid to thousands of wealthy and solidly middle-class cities and towns year after year.

Moreover, it is a government that continues to spend approximately $30 billion a year on what a confidential analysis within the Office of Management and Budget calls "corporate welfare," a panoply of budget and off-budget programs that are pouring direct and indirect subsidies into America's richest multinational corporations. And so it goes. . . .

Harry Truman once said, "The buck stops here," suggesting that all major problems in government eventually end up at the White House. However, the aim of this book is not to find out where the problems of government end up, but where they start. In truth, the buck literally and figuratively starts and stops in Congress. And this is where our story begins.

2

Congressional Oversights

WHEN John Breen, a young, conscientious yet deeply troubled employee of the Treasury Department's U.S. Savings Bond Division, went to the House Appropriations subcommittee that funds his agency, he was convinced the scandal he had kept locked away for several years would at last be exposed to public scrutiny and cleansed away by an outraged Congress.

Folded neatly in his wallet was a well-worn copy of the "Code of Ethics for Government Service," enacted on July 3, 1980, by the 96th Congress, and displayed by law in every federal building throughout the government. Its provisions require all civil servants to "put loyalty to the highest moral principles and to country above loyalty to persons, party, or Government department." It demands that all federal employees "uphold the Constitution, laws, and regulations of the United States and of all governments therein and never be a party to their evasion." It insists that each public servant "give a full day's labor for a full day's pay; giving earnest effort and best thought to the performance of duties." And it further requires that all federal workers "expose corruption wherever discovered."

John Breen devoutly believed in these words, believed they meant exactly what they said, and believed that he was required to follow them to the letter. But the people with whom he worked very often chose not to abide by them, to look the other way, to ignore the abuses he had witnessed for too long. Now, after months of mental anguish over the idea of "ratting" on his fellow workers, Breen finally decided that the time had come to blow the whistle on himself and on his agency.

Surely, he thought, when the Treasury subcommittee, which provided the yearly appropriations to run his little agency, learned of the waste, mismanagement, abuse and bureaucratic make-work, it would take action. An investigation would be launched. The General Accounting Office would be asked to conduct a full-scale audit. The Treasury Department's Office of Inspector General would begin an internal inquiry. Congressional hearings would be held. Why, he might even be called to testify as the lead witness. Congress would give his agency a tough going over and, he imagined, completely reevaluate the very basis for this bureaucratic vestige of the war bonds era in today's modern, investment-conscious economy.

But nothing of the sort happened. When Breen, a bond sales promotional representative in the division, told his story to Tex Gunnels, the subcommittee's chief counsel, Gunnels suggested that he take his allegations elsewhere or look for another job. Breen was, to put it mildly, crushed.

What he had admitted, after years of painful deception, was that he had been deliberately padding and falsifying his bond sales performance reports because of unrealistic and often nonsensical work quotas set by the program. Among other things, he recorded promotional sales visits that were never made. He reported that he had met with corporate executive officers in order to promote bond sales to company employees when, in fact, he had not. He said that large numbers of workers attended his bond promotion meetings when the meetings were poorly attended. But Breen was by no means alone. Other bond sales promoters in the agency were similarly filling out their call sheets with fictitious information, he said. He charged that the voluminous performance records of the agency's two hundred employees were, to a large degree, a tissue of deceptions and distortions.

Unimpressed, Gunnels suggested that Breen take his story to the Merit Systems Protection Board, created by Congress to protect whistle-blowers such as himself. He said the subcommittee had no other choice but to believe agency officials when they told the panel during annual oversight hearings that the program was in tip-top shape and doing a gangbusters job of selling U.S. Savings Bonds. "We have to take them at their word," Breen said Gunnels told him.

Frustrated, but persistent, Breen carried his story to other House and Senate oversight subcommittees, trying to sell his scandal as persuasively as he had sold the U.S. Savings Bond program to corporate executives. Unfortunately, the disinterested responses that the mild-mannered, forty-year-old bureaucrat received from the committees were all too typical of Congress's anemic concern for oversight. Breen "went public" with his allegations and managed to stir up a hornets' nest at the agency. Treasury officials at first vehemently denied any wrongdoing. Later, however, after the ugly details unfolded, they were forced to conduct their own inquiry, an examination that largely whitewashed the agency's inherent problems. Yet during this time Congress never, in any significant oversight sense, got involved. (I will examine this little-known scandal in a later chapter.)

John Breen's experience illustrates dramatically, and accurately, how Congress fails all too often to fulfill its primary function and responsibility as guardian of the government's purse strings. His story vividly reveals what very few people in Washington realize or are willing to admit: namely, that Congress, as the legislative branch of our government, has largely abdicated its role and responsibilities for monitoring and controlling the bureaucracy it has so painstakingly and excessively created, layer by layer, over many decades. Not only does Congress lack the time and the interest to conduct its myriad oversight functions regularly, but there is serious question of whether, with all of its resources, it has even the capacity to regularly and adequately evaluate and control everything under its vast legislative domain.

Equally alarming is the fact that so little attention has been paid to Congress's negligence by our best scholars, our brightest journalists, or our most principled political leaders. An examination of public policy research and analysis over the past forty years reveals an overwhelming preoccupation with Congress's legislative creations, its great acts, its super departments, its landmark laws, its regulatory achievements. Very little attention, on the other hand, has been paid to Congress's failure to look back at what it has wrought over many decades, to reevaluate and to repair its mistakes.

Much of this failure to expose and chastise Congress for its abysmal oversight negligence rests with the Washington news media. They, to a very large extent, have fostered the popular myth that Congress is continually engaged in hard, probing, meticulous oversight of government programs and agencies. Don't we read in our newspapers and see on the nightly television news programs seemingly nonstop congressional hearings which tediously and untiringly explore every nook and cranny of the federal bureaucracy? Are not all agencies and programs constantly being screened through the authorization and annual appropriations process — an ongoing inquisition through which lawmakers fire tough questions at cringing agency heads about what they have been doing with our tax dollars? Isn't this picture, presented through the news media, an entirely accurate one? Sadly, the answer to all of these questions is an unequivocal no.

Of course, few members of the Washington news media would be willing to admit it, particularly those who make their living covering Congress. But the media bear much of the blame for covering up Congress's institutional neglect and misfeasance by giving its oversight system the appearance of accountability and action that it does not deserve. Indeed, instances where congressional hearings are well attended by lawmakers are very often the rare exception. One of the reasons for this deception is pack journalism. Reporters tend to cover stories in herds. They go where the major stories are, and this, of course, is where the television cameras go, too. When such stories occur in congressional hearing rooms, this is where you will find that rarest of congressional phenomena: 100 percent attendance by a committee's or subcommittee's members.

Such events, though, are generally the exceptions to the dozens of committee hearings that may be held by Congress on any given day. The deeply distorted picture Americans get of their senators and representatives on television, seemingly busy at work in packed, overheated hearing rooms, grilling nervous government bureaucrats, is a figment of the television age. The congressional committee, in most cases, is in full attendance only because the cameras are there, news reporters are there, and they have an opportunity to ask questions, make statements, and hurl charges that will get them on the evening network news, or quoted in their newspapers back home.

Frank Silbey, a veteran congressional investigator who spent nearly seventeen years on various House and Senate oversight staffs, believes Congress performs its oversight responsibilities "very, very poorly."

Silbey, who left Congress in 1983 for a job in the private sector, built his reputation as a tough, aggressive investigative gunslinger who frequently enraged bureaucrats with his blunt persistence. Occasionally, he also made headlines for his bosses — among them former California Congressman John Moss and Senator Orrin Hatch of Utah. Now on the outside looking in, and with no political considerations to muzzle him, Silbey confesses that Congress's many oversight failures are "a scandal."

"Congress tends to think more in terms of legislating, than oversight," he says. "Legislating is a higher-visibility activity. It gets a lot of public attention, a lot of media attention. Oversight is a thankless persuasion. It's an orphan. It doesn't get a lot of attention from members because it doesn't win a lot of votes back home.

"Oversight involves a lot of tedious drudgery." Silbey continues. "It is very controversial, it often involves a lot of very nasty digging around. The bureaucracy will fight back, delay, hold back documents, or go to other members of Congress and try to get [the subcommittee chairman] to pull away" and stop the investigation.

He especially blames the Washington media for oversight's back-burner status in Congress. The media are willing to invest their resources in covering the few major scandals, the sexy stories that will sell newspapers and win broadcast ratings, but such hearings are rare on Capitol Hill. "It's almost impossible to get a lot of media interest unless it involves someone being caught in bed with a live man or a dead woman," he says. "As a result, your hearing falls on sterile ground. Nobody finds out about it. A few insiders say, 'Gee, that was a nice piece of work,' but the chairman didn't get any publicity, nobody back home finds out about it, and it doesn't translate into votes or high publicity for the chairman. And let's face it, that is a payoff that a lot of members want."

So, says Silbey, "If there isn't a publicity payoff, there is a lot of frustration and a lot of members sort of lose enthusiasm for [oversight] and say, 'What the heck, why shouldn't I just go with the flow and pay attention to legislation, make sure the people who need something from the federal government in my district get it, instead of spending a lot of my time on something that isn't going to have any substantive payoff.' "

Michael J. Malbin, an expert on congressional operations, essentially agrees with Silbey's charges. "There is no incentive for members of Congress to do [oversight investigation]," he says. "More important, typically the subcommittee chairman who has to do the oversight is the person who most supports the program in question. That's a strong incentive not to do it."

What about formal evaluation of government programs, inquiring whether they are working, or even still needed? "Well, that doesn't go on very much," Malbin says. And even when it does go on, it does not result in a searching analysis and evaluation of a program or agency. "Typically, agencies go through one or two days of hearings," Malbin says, "but you just don't find out very much" in that amount of time.

Malbin created something of a stir in Congress when he published his book, *Unelected Representatives*, which reveals the extent to which Congress's committee staffs run the legislative branch of government. As a resident scholar at the American Enterprise Institute, a Washington-based think tank, Malbin spends his time analyzing and studying Congress. And what he has concluded about Congress and government does not find its way into high school and college civics books. "Congress has chosen to create a government that's larger than it can oversee," he says. "If there is a fault, it is for having a government it cannot manage. The president can't manage it. The Office of Management and Budget can't manage it. The Cabinet secretaries who head the various departments can't manage it. We have created a bureaucracy that is too large to oversee."

While conducting an investigation in the late 1970s into what I then dubbed the government's "forgotten agencies," I went to the Senate Foreign Relations Committee to secure some details on their oversight of the Foreign Claims Settlement Commission. What I discovered was an extraordinary lack of knowledge about the agency, as well as a total reluctance even to question whether this agency was still needed. The commission no longer exists today as an independent agency, but at the time it was staffed by thirty employees, plus three $50,000-a-year commissioners, with an annual budget of $1 million. Most of this agency's work had been completed and there were legitimate questions as to its continued value as an independent commission. But the Foreign Relations Committee had never seriously raised such questions.

"Look," one of the committee's top staff officials told me at the time, "we just don't have time to look at agencies like this. We have to invest our energies in much larger subjects like the Panana Canal or the SALT treaties. We have to let agencies like this go by the board." (Eventually, Congress eliminated the commission and merged its functions into the State Department.)

As I probed deeper into the layers of forgotten agencies that were gathering dust in the farthest corners of the bureaucracy, with names like the Joint Mexican–U.S. Defense Commission and the Overseas Private Investment Corporation, it became clear that many lawmakers, and even their considerable oversight staffs, were totally unaware that some of these programs even existed.

"Congress doesn't have the time or even the desire to examine tiny agencies like these," says a veteran Senate investigator. "We don't have time to even examine the big agencies except in a very cursory way. This isn't something that a member of Congress would ever admit publicly, but most of the government gets very little attention from Congress. It's too big. It's too complex. To be perfectly frank with you, Congress as an institution has created a monster it can no longer control. In many respects we just go through the motions."

"Sure," he continued, "we hold lots of hearings. We ask questions. We come up with the overall figures for new appropriations and authorizations. But we are no longer in total control of either the agencies' actions or their spending. It's sad to say, but we spend most of our time putting out brush fires and chasing the next scandal. We're in charge of watching the store, but there are too many stores to watch."

Nothing more epitomizes what this very frustrated Senate official is saying than the scandal that rocked the General Services Administration, the government's $5-billion-a-year building and supply agency. The exposé of corruption, abuse, waste and mismanagement — which included everything from bribery to outright thievery — was broken by *Washington Post* reporter Ronald Kessler. His startling series of articles led to Senate hearings by the Government Operations Subcommittee on Federal Practices, then chaired by Senator Lawton Chiles of Florida. More important, perhaps, than the sordid details themselves was the question of how such a massive scandal could have festered for so long without Congress's doing something about it. Why, for example, had Congress allowed GSA to purchase annually for years a quarter of a billion dollars' worth of office furniture and equipment while government warehouses were bulging with the stuff? Why did Congress let GSA pay two to three times more for various supplies, materials and equipment from contractors than "off the shelf" stock would have cost?

The answer, in part, is that most of Congress did not know about these and many other abuses at GSA, and what is worse, made no effort to find out.

GSA, long the proverbial dumping ground for political hacks, had rarely, if ever, been seriously examined or evaluated by Congress during the 1960s and early 1970s when this agency's incestuous abuses and corruption began to grow and flourish. On the contrary, members were far more interested in GSA's plans to construct or lease an office building in their state or district than they were in what was going on behind the dingy, gray walls of GSA.

Moreover, if members of Congress could angelically express ignorance over outright corruption at GSA, how could they plead ignorance about the waste, abuse and mismanagement in its purchasing programs? Why didn't Congress know about these things sooner? Lawton Chiles asked Elmer Staats, then the comptroller general of the General Accounting Office (GAO), Congress's investigating and auditing arm.

Mr. Staats, a portly, distinguished-looking, white-haired gentleman who looked more like a diplomat than Congress's chief auditor, must have found it difficult to disguise his incredulity over such a question. Over the last six years, he told the subcommittee, GAO had provided Congress with over two hundred reports on GSA, which detailed much of the waste and mismanagement the subcommittee was now getting around to investigating.

The question, then, is why didn't Congress heed GAO's reports? Why did it ignore the disclosures of its own $243-million-a-year auditing agency?

The sad truth is that many of the findings uncovered by GAO audits, and their recommendations for dealing with them, are ignored by Congress. In the words of a House committee staffer, who has initiated numerous GAO inquiries for his boss, "Very few members read their reports. All too often they are used to come up with some sexy revelation for a good press release for the papers back home. [GAO's] recommendations for saving money are not being heeded by the oversight committees. For all the money we put into GAO, and the worthwhile investigative work they do, I'm afraid Congress just doesn't put the agency to good use."

How is it possible, then, that with an operating budget of $1.5 billion a year, with personal and committee staffs numbering nearly 18,000 employees, and with an additional 6,379 auditors, researchers and budget analysts, Congress performs its chief responsibility of oversight so poorly?

Once again, as both Silbey and Malbin make clear, much of the problem is that the members have little interest in the task of oversight, even though it is, next to lawmaking, Congress's primary job. Go to any of the committee or subcommittee hearings on any given day on Capitol Hill and you will find them very poorly attended by their respective members. The chairman of the committee will be there, possibly the ranking minority member. A few other members may occasionally drift into the hearing room, ask a few questions, and then leave. "Attendance is terrible at most hearings," a top Senate Appropriations Committee official told me, a frequently voiced complaint of many committee staffers.

Even the members who do attend oversight hearings do not come properly prepared to interrogate agency and department heads about how they have been spending their appropriations; or to ask why specific programs, whose goals remain dubious at best, continue to exist; or to demand that agency officials justify their activities and expenditures. "Oversight is tedious, dull work," observed a House Agriculture Committee staffer, "and those guys have no appetite for it. Very often questions are simply submitted in writing and the answers are placed in the [hearing] record weeks later, but no one ever bothers to read them."

In the last decade there has been substantial growth in personal congressional staffs and in committee and subcommittee staffs, giving the false impression that Congress has been improving its oversight machinery. Congress's personal staffs, as well as their committee staffs, have expanded by nearly 50 percent since the late 1970s, and have virtually doubled since the late 1960s. In 1970, congressional committee and subcommittee staffs alone numbered 1,600, more than four times their number in the late 1940s.

The staffs of House and Senate standing committees shot up from 1,751 in 1973 to nearly 3,000 in 1983. In this same period, the personal Washington office staffs of lawmakers leaped from 7,706 to 11,125. But this failed either to improve or to strengthen Congress's ability to monitor its authorizations and appropriations; if anything it has made it worse. "We've set up so many centers of power in the subcommittees that it's become nearly impossible to get anything coherent done," complained Congressman Henry Reuss of Wisconsin, a twenty-eight-year veteran of the House before his retirement in 1982.*

Arguing that as government grew, Congress had to grow, too, in

* "How Congress Collapsed: A Depressing Guide to Governmental Paralysis," by Gregg Easterbrook, *The Washington Post, Outlook*, December 12, 1982.

order to maintain some semblance of control over what it has created, lawmakers industriously set about turning a Byzantine committee system into a Rube Goldberg legislative contraption that defies comprehension. By 1983 this tangled oversight structure, in which the work of Congress is supposed to be done, was composed of 22 full or "standing" House committees and 141 subcommittees and "task forces"; 15 full Senate committees, and 101 subcommittees; plus 16 "special," joint and "select" congressional committees, including 31 subcommittees.

These committees and subcommittees provide lawmakers with one of the chief rewards the legislative branch has to offer: chairmanships. There are now 298 chairmanships in Congress, apportioned according to seniority. Once they were a rare and highly prized plum in Congress, held by only the most seasoned veterans. Now, about half of Congress's 535 members hold chairmanships. (Some hold more than one.) And with each chairmanship comes increased staffing, budget allowances, travel authority and the prestige and power that accompanies the title "Mr. Chairman."

But, instead of allocating the staffs of the major oversight committees to reflect the growth and complexity of government agencies and programs, Congress chose to create a panoply of panels — many with titles so amorphous and esoteric they allow their members to engage in virtually anything under the sun. This in turn has resulted in a ponderous and more chaotic Congress, one that is incapable of dealing intelligently and efficiently with the management and oversight of government. As a result, "The handicaps of Congress have become much greater in recent years," Reuss believes. "The institution has become much more rickety."

Congress's maddening legislative maze was vividly exposed by Washington journalist Gregg Easterbrook* when he asked who in the House has jurisdiction over an energy issue like hydroelectric power dams.

The Energy Committee's Subcommittee on Energy Conservation and Power? Or the Science Committee's Subcommittee on Energy Development and Application, or maybe its Subcommittee on En-

* Ibid.

ergy Research and Applications? Perhaps jurisdiction should go to the Interior Committee's Subcommittee on Energy and the Environment, or maybe its Subcommittee on Water Power and Resources.

Then again, why not the Public Works Committee's Subcommittee on Water Resources? Or the Agriculture Committee's Subcommittee on Forests, Family Farms and Energy (a natural combination if ever there was one)?

Or the Energy and Water Subcommittee of Appropriations, or the Energy and the Environment "task force" (equivalent of a subcommittee) of the Budget Committee, or the Energy, Environment and Natural Resources Subcommittee of the Government Operations Committee, or the Energy, Environment and Safety Issues Affecting Small Business Subcommittee (that's a real name) of the Small Business Committee.

And let's not forget the Senate, where we find the Energy Committee with its separate subcommittees on Energy Research and Development; Energy Conservation and Supply; Energy Regulation; Energy and Mineral Resources; Water and Power, and Public Lands and Reserved Water. Or the Water Resources Subcommittee of the Senate Environment and Public Works Committee; the Forestry, Water Resources and the Environment Subcommittee of the Agriculture Committee; the Energy, Nuclear Proliferation and Government Processes Subcommittee of the Government Affairs Committee; or the Energy and Water Development Subcommittee of the Appropriations Committee.

"So which of these 21 subcommittees has jurisdiction over a power dam?" Easterbrook asks. Potentially, all of them deal in some shape, manner or form with this subject. But is this any way to run the government of the United States?

It is true that the growth in committee staffs has in turn led to a concomitant growth in congressional hearings — almost twice as many hearings in 1982 as there were ten years ago. However, there is little evidence that this has led to improved congressional oversight. "A lot of hearings are called oversight but they aren't really oversight," says Silbey. On the contrary, the disorganized and chaotic nature of the congressional subcommittee system often produces hearings that overlap or duplicate each other or work at cross purposes. For example, as the allegations of political manipulation of the Environmental Protection Agency's $1.6 billion "Superfund" to clean up the nation's hazardous waste dumps reached a feverish pitch in early 1983, no less than six congressional subcommittees were conducting separate investigations into EPA. "When you have six different committees taking testimony [on EPA], that shows up on any quantitative measure as increased oversight," said Malbin. "But I think that kind of activity would be more accurately described as increased headline grabbing, not increased oversight." Congress's response to the EPA scandal resulted in little or no oversight coordination, wasted resources, and excessive demands on executive branch agencies. "Oversight committees are more likely to pursue a lead about a scandal than about a law that's working badly," said Malbin. "The scandal will get you a better headline."

The congressional hysteria over the EPA scandal, as with so many other highly visible inquiries, allowed the media to create the mistaken impression that congressional committees were combing the bureaucracy and really doing a lot of work. It is a myth. "Most committees don't do a lot," said Silbey. Indeed they don't.

A continuing survey I have been conducting of congressional subcommittees since 1980 reveals how little they actually do. Many, I have discovered, spend their time dealing with trivial matters better left to administrative employees. In one instance, the House Subcommittee on Libraries and Memorials held a hearing on a bill to regulate the flow of pedestrian traffic through the Capitol. Consider these additional examples:

During 1980 the House Interior and Insular Affairs Subcommittee on Pacific Affairs held only three hearings, and handled no legislation. It issued one report, financed one trip to the Pacific by its members, and sponsored seven staff trips. That was it for the year.

The Senate Judiciary Committee's Limitations and Contracted and Delegated Authority Subcommittee, with a staff of eight, acted on no legislation and held only eleven days of hearings over this period.

Similarly, the Senate Finance Committee's Subcommittee on Tourism and Sugar never met and did not hold any hearings that year. The Finance Committee's Subcommittee on the Internal Revenue Service also "didn't do much" in terms of oversight, nor did it "issue anything" in the way of reports or legislation, an aide said. Moreover, the committee's Subcommittee on Revenue Sharing, Intergovernmental Revenue Impact and Economic Problems held only four days of hearings and issued only two reports for the entire year.

During this same time, the Senate Select Committee on Small Business's Subcommittee on Governmental Regulations and Paperwork did not review any legislation, even though both problems — regulations and paperwork — have seriously burdened the private sector.

Even in cases where there were serious instances of legislative oversight, they were generally unrepresentative of Congress as a whole.

During 1982, for example, the Senate Labor and Human Resources Committee's Subcommittee on the Handicapped held only two hearings. Although it has a permanent staff of five, the subcommittee reviewed no legislation and issued no reports. In case you're wondering, there were no handicapped people on its staff.

The Senate Government Affairs Committee's Subcommittee on Oversight of Government Management, with a staff of thirteen, held only four hearings in 1982 and acted on only two minor pieces of legislation.

Additionally, the House Administration Committee's Services Subcommittee, with three staff people, acted on no legislation and held all of two hearings in 1982. The burning issue they reviewed: improving the service in the congressional barbershops.

The House Agriculture Committee's Tobacco and Peanuts Subcommittee, considered only one bill in the entire 97th Congress (1981–1982) and issued no reports. It has a staff of three.

The House Government Operations Subcommittee on Government Information, Justice and Agriculture, like many subcommittees, is a prolific publisher. Its staff of six professionals and two clerical assistants issued twelve reports during 1981 and 1982, but handled no legislation.

Some subcommittee chairmen, of course, tend to take oversight more seriously than others. William Proxmire chaired the Senate

Appropriations Subcommittee on Housing and Urban Development, the Veterans Administration, NASA, and other independent agencies when the Democrats controlled the Senate. A rare exception among his colleagues, Proxmire carved out a record as a tough overseer, putting agencies under his jurisdiction through lengthy questioning over their expenditures.

Jake Garn of Utah took over as chairman of the subcommittee when the Republicans assumed control of the Senate in 1981. The comparisons between the two are startling.

In 1980, the last year of Proxmire's chairmanship, his subcommittee conducted over thirty-seven hours of hearings, excluding testimony from public witnesses, at which agency heads submitted to questioning and examination. During 1981, under Garn, the number of hours for such oversight decreased to thirty-four, and then in 1982 dropped precipitously to a meager eighteen hours. That is hardly much time to examine seriously departments and agencies whose collective budgets total $54 billion a year. Why does Congress, with its bloated committee system, do such a pitiful job of overseeing our government? A Senate Appropriations Committee official pointed out a few structural reasons for this sad state of affairs:

"First of all, the authorizing committees tend to become advocates for the programs they are authorizing," he said. "If it's the Banking Committee, it's the homebuilders. If it's the Labor and Human Resources Committee, it may be the labor unions or the cities looking for more welfare money.

"In other words, these special interest groups want more funds to deal with their problems, and the authorizing committees are concerned only with deciding how much money do they need to deal with it. It's a little unusual for them to then go back and decide that the money is not being well spent. They are usually trying to find new ways to spend money, not ways to control expenditures."

The authorizing committees of Congress — Judiciary, Ways and Means, Labor, Energy, etc. — are responsible for establishing government programs, agencies and laws, and they in turn are required to reauthorize them periodically and change them if needed. This is where one would expect the kind of tough, searching, critical evaluation and oversight to take place in Congress. More often than not, however, these committees have found it much easier over the years, and politically more profitable, simply to reauthorize existing laws and programs and to enlarge them.

Ironically, the House and Senate Appropriations committees, which are empowered solely to approve the level of funding for all federal agencies and programs, have to a large extent assumed more of the oversight responsibilities than the legislative committees who created the programs in the first place. Yet all too often the various appropriations subcommittees have been severely ill-equipped to thoroughly examine the agencies and programs they are funding and evaluate how well or how poorly they are performing. Moreover, they are unable to reform the programs they must finance, since this authority is possessed only by the legislative committees.

Still, the Appropriations committees annually approve hundreds of billions of dollars to fund the government. Yet each panel is woefully understaffed. An all-too-typical example of the scandalously inadequate resources Congress gives its Appropriations subcommittees can be seen in the Senate Appropriations Subcommittee on Housing and Urban Development and Independent Agencies.

This one subcommittee is responsible for approving funding for the $14 billion Department of Housing and Urban Development, the $24 billion Veterans Administration, the $7 billion National Aeronautics and Space Administration, the $1 billion National Science Foundation, and almost a dozen other agencies. It must evaluate and approve budgets totaling more than $33 billion a year in outlays. The shocking and little-known truth is that this subcommittee has only three people — two on the majority (Republican) side and one on the minority (Democrat) side — to examine all the budget requests under its jurisdiction, review programs, conduct investigations, and prepare oversight questions for each of the agencies at its annual budget review hearings. (And actually, one can count only the majority side of the staff, which alone has responsibility for preparing the annual hearings and conducting the formal oversight process.) In other words, only the most cursory examination of these agencies and all that they do can possibly be made, despite the often heroic efforts of its meager staff.

This is not unusual among Congress's Appropriations subcommittees. The Senate Defense Appropriations Subcommittee, for example, which has oversight responsibility for $245 billion in expenditures, has only six staffers to examine the entire Pentagon establishment. The Labor, Health, Human Services, Education and Related Agencies Subcommittee, which oversees more than $100 billion in spending, has six majority-side staffers. The Transportation Subcommittee has three majority staffers to review and evaluate $26 billion in programs. The Agriculture Subcommittee, responsible for $25 billion in expenditures, has only two majority staffers.

Moreover, there is no apparent logic to Congress's allocation of staff resources. While the Transportation Subcommittee has only two majority staffers to oversee $26 billion, the Treasury, Postal Service and General Government Subcommittee, which is concerned with a budget less than half that size, $12 billion, has the same size staff.

The District of Columbia Subcommittee, which oversees $361 million in appropriations, employs two professional staffers, the same number as the Military Construction Subcommittee, which monitors $7.2 billion in programs. The Energy and Water Development Subcommittee, with $14.5 billion a year in funds to monitor, has only three staffers, the same number as the Legislative Branch Subcommittee, which oversees a far smaller $1.4 billion budget.

The point is there is no possible way for staffs of such minuscule numbers to perform the kind of serious investigation and oversight that is commensurate with Congress's responsibility as guardian of the nation's purse strings. Employing two majority staffers, in the case of the HUD Subcommittee, to examine and oversee appropriations of tens of billions of dollars can by no stretch of the imagination be called oversight. It is a joke, and a cruel one that is being played at the expense of the American taxpayer.

If this is not disturbing enough, attending a full Appropriations Committee "markup" of its funding bills is a case study in how not to run a government. If the American people were able to watch what goes on inside these markup meetings, where the money bills are cleared for House and Senate action, what little faith they have in how Congress spends their money would be quickly dissipated. There is little time allowed to weigh and evaluate thoroughly each proposed agency or departmental budget. Members wander in and out midway through consideration of specific spending provisions. Most lawmakers are more interested in protecting — i.e., expanding — the budgets of agencies under their respective subcommittees. All too often legislators vote billions of dollars for programs when they haven't the slightest idea where the money is going, or if its expenditure is accomplishing the objectives Congress set out to achieve. Frequently, figures are arbitrarily tossed out by members, with little idea as to whether the agency or program should even be funded at all, let alone have its budget raised. And most of the groundwork on funding bills, including most of the budget numbers, is handled not by our lawmakers but by staff. "It's all staff," said a chief Democratic aide on the Senate Appropriations Committee. "They do the work, 99 percent of it.

"Members of Congress are not attuned to oversight," this aide continued. "They are there to help people. They get elected because they do favors. And the way to help people is to give them money." That is really at the heart of the congressional appropriations process. Worrying over whether the money is well spent, or who ultimately benefits from it, is not of much interest to lawmakers.

A case in point is an incident that occurred during the Senate Appropriations Committee's discussion of a minor item in a foreign aid bill where $20 million had been added to a loan program, which perked the interest of Wisconsin's William Proxmire. A Senate aide described it this way: "Suddenly Proxmire asked what this outfit did. And nobody in the room knew. 'Then why are we giving them this money?' he asked. And somebody said, 'Well, that's what they asked for.' So Proxmire asked, 'What did they get last year?' And somebody said, 'About $17 million.' Proxmire replied, 'Well, do they need $20 million?' And nobody responded. Then somebody suggested cutting their request to $15 million. No one objected. So they got $15 million. But the point is that nobody in the room had any idea what the money was really going for."

"There is an appalling amount of ignorance among members of

Congress about the programs over which they are asked to conduct oversight," complained another Senate committee staffer. "We write their questions, draw up their legislation, and author their amendments. With the exception of the chairman and the ranking minority member, very few of the others [members] play much of a role in the committee's actual work."

A former Senate Judiciary Committee staff member recalled that when Senator Edward M. Kennedy of Massachusetts chaired that panel, there were "close to one hundred [professional] staff members on the committee. But I don't think that more than one or two of them had much of an idea of what goes on in the Justice Department." What were the other staffers doing? "Writing legislation for more programs, or doing investigations of the oil companies, any number of things, including a lot of work that provided Kennedy with information for his [1980] presidential campaign. But it did not include very much oversight of the Justice Department, which is the primary function of the committee.

"Meanwhile," this aide continued, "at the Justice Department, which has fifty-four thousand employees, you've got perhaps twenty divisions or agencies that are being totally neglected in terms of oversight. What Congress knows about what goes on inside the department is negligible."

The abuses that went on for many years within the Federal Bureau of Investigation illustrate dramatically Congress's continuing failure to exercise consistent and thorough oversight. "Had Congress been doing its job," a Judiciary Committee staffer argued, "instead of giving the FBI a blank check as it did for many years, those abuses would never have occurred, or they would have been stopped before they got out of control. Even today there is still relatively little ongoing oversight of the FBI's operations."

Scattered among this tarnished oversight record are some bright examples of how Congress has taken its spending responsibilities seriously. The extensive series of hearings Senator Kennedy conducted in the late 1970s, which documented the anticompetitive impact of airline regulation, paved the way for landmark deregulation legislation and a new breath of life for a stagnant industry. The House Appropriations Committee's forceful reexamination of the

Federal Trade Commission resulted in the FTC's withdrawing from several areas of needless and costly regulation. But these are the exceptions, not the rule. Frequently, in these cases, as in others, Congress was reacting, often reluctantly, to the drumbeat of criticism and the demand for reform from the private sector.

Most committee chairmen, staff directors, and chief counsels still claim they are doing a good job of monitoring government expenditures within their jurisdiction. They point proudly to volumes of testimony taken at public hearings, and to their committee reports, as proof of their thoroughness and effectiveness in fulfilling Congress's oversight duties.

Yet, as we have seen, a very different view emerges from many other committee aides and staff directors who talked candidly and critically about Congress's sorry record of oversight. And that view — expressed in not-for-attribution interviews — charges that Congress is doing an abysmal job of oversight. And the evidence, they suggest, is strewn across the bureaucratic landscape for all to see.

Take, for example, the Law Enforcement Assistance Administration. Despite the expenditure of $8 billion since 1968, LEAA failed to curb crime. Its programs, according to one Senate study, were characterized by "inefficiency, waste, maladministration, and in some cases, corruption." Yet Congress kept it going year after year because its oversight committees failed to mount the kind of tough, objective evaluation that its wasteful expenditures cried out for. Finally, after years of scandal and abuse, the program was eliminated by the Reagan administration in 1982.

Dozens of similar federal programs and agencies remain as mute monuments to congressional inattention or disinterest. The Small Business Administration has compiled a sordid history of fraud, abuse and gross mismanagement, but Congress cannot bring itself to pull the plug on SBA. Instead, its committees have either overlooked SBA's scandals and abuses, blamed its recurring problems on previous administrations and poor management, or have chosen to patch up the agency's wounds annually and reauthorize its programs while holding their noses and looking the other way.

The government's Comprehensive Employment and Training

Act (CETA) was plagued by fraud, political favoritism in the granting of jobs and other assorted scandals during the late 1970s. The
Community Services Administration, the core agency of the antipoverty programs of Lyndon Johnson's Great Society, blazed a
record of one long unbroken string of scandals throughout the
1970s. Yet both continued to receive generous annual appropriations from Congress until the Reagan administration forced a reluctant Congress to dismantle them. The Department of Energy
continues spending nearly $10 billion a year on a multitude of proj-
ects and contracts for — for what? Most members of Congress
couldn't tell you.

Perhaps no department has more skeletons in its closets than the
Labor Department. There are audits, internal reports, memoranda
and other documents locked away in its files, which deal with labor
union corruption, union pension abuses, CETA mismanagement
and much more. A lengthy 1981 investigation by the Senate Permanent Investigations Subcommittee into how the department de-
layed and then bungled its investigation into the deeply abused
Teamsters Central States Pension Fund revealed the department's
extensive mismanagement and shady dealings. In a scathing report
issued by the subcommittee, then chaired by Senator Sam Nunn of
Georgia, the panel concluded that the Labor Department's "actions
going back many years and many administrations proclaim in clear
language that it remains incapable of investigating major labor
racketeering cases."

The subcommittee report said that during the Carter administration the department's "chance to investigate and prosecute some of
the nation's most notorious criminals" in the labor movement "was
wasted." Furthermore, its probe uncovered "bureaucratic infight-
ing and naivete or incompetence" at the department's highest
levels.

The Investigations Subcommittee is one of the few really thorough oversight bodies in Congress, but unfortunately it possesses no
legislative jurisdiction. Legislative responsibility over the Labor
Department resides in the House and Senate Labor committees,
which have long been hostages to organized labor. Before the Republican takeover of the Senate in 1980, the Senate Labor Com-

mittee was chaired by Harrison Williams of New Jersey, who was convicted in the Abscam scandal in 1981. In 1970, after his re-election to a second term, Williams told a group of labor union leaders, "I owe everything to you. . . . What you want you've got. I owe that much to you." Needless to say, Williams never conducted a single inquiry into labor union corruption and abuse during his chairmanship.

Orrin Hatch of Utah, who became chairman in 1981, has conducted several inquiries into labor union abuses as well as into the Labor Department's sorry investigating record. Yet, to be fair, Hatch is hamstrung by a committee membership with little appetite for taking on the labor unions, or really ripping open the Labor Department. To this day, Congress has done little to rival the famous labor racketeering hearings of the 1950s conducted by Arkansas Senator John McClennan, who set a standard for congressional oversight that has rarely been equaled.

Even a man of Silbey's investigative talents and resourcefulness now admits that during the two years he headed Hatch's four-man investigative team on the Labor and Human Resources Committee, "Only about 10 percent of the Labor Department's programs were ever seriously examined by the committee."

There is another, even more disturbing reason behind Congress's oversight negligence. It is talked about only in whispers in Capitol corridors and committee backrooms. It is virtually ignored by the news media. It is the worst of congressional misfeasances. I refer to instances in which powerful committee and subcommittee chairmen know of abuses, mismanagement and scandals and prefer to ignore them rather than expose them through oversight hearings and legislative action.

Listen to Frank Silbey: "All too often committee and subcommittee chairmen who know of serious problems in programs they support won't do anything about them. They look the other way. It's fairly common. If you have a large program and it brings in a lot of money for the people of your district, and provides a goodly number of jobs, you're not going to look at it critically." Which ones? "All of the housing programs and a good many of the military [procurement] programs.

"It's much easier to ignore this stuff than to delve into it," Silbey continued. "It's much easier to ignore it and let it go away. Why open up that kind of can of worms? As a result they walk away from it."

Malbin, a former congressional staffer, agrees. "As long as the only person who has the power to oversee an agency is also the person who has the greatest interest in protecting that agency, then there will be no oversight."

Under the Reagan administration, he said, "Every Democratic subcommittee chairman has some interest in investigating what's going on in the agencies. But many times during the Carter administration you found subcommittees that did not have jurisdiction uncovering things that the subcommittee with jurisdiction already knew about and wasn't about to talk about."

The evidence is overwhelming that Congress is not adequately monitoring, measuring and carefully evaluating the huge bureaucracy it has constructed, much of it in just the past twenty years. Clearly, most members of Congress have little if any interest or incentive to take their oversight role seriously. And even if they did, the enormity of the federal beast they have brought forth would overwhelm them. "It is," Silbey says, "like trying to sweep back the ocean." To which Malbin adds, "Even if members tripled or quadrupled the amount of time they spent on oversight, it still wouldn't begin to do the kind of program oversight that is needed on a systematic basis."

This is the scandalous reality of Congress's failure to fulfill its constitutional role and responsibility as the funder and overseer of our national government. Over the years its members have become very good at making it appear that they are in full control of the government; that they are ceaselessly working to keep government honest, efficient and effective; that with enough hearings, testimony, audit reports and new legislation the federal Leviathan can be harnessed and made to do the will of the Congress and the people it was elected to serve. Yet the evidence reveals that this is a false picture of Congress; that our legislature does not even remotely scratch the surface of a vast federal bureaucracy; that, in truth, the congressional emperor has no clothes.

The result: abuses, mismanagement, fraud, bureaucratic negligence, excesses and waste throughout the fabric of government, on a scale no one can possibly imagine, and no one book can possibly do justice to.

What follows, then, is a broad yet highly representative sampling of what is occurring in Washington, D.C., the seat of our national government, a city of scandals.

3

Rigging Representative Democracy

O NE of the reasons Congress performs its legislative oversight role so poorly is that its members are far more concerned about surviving the next election than about the management of an efficient and frugal government. Of course, if one agrees with the anonymous nineteenth-century American critic who said "no man's life, liberty or property are safe while the legislature is in session," then perhaps the less Congress is legislating the better off we are.

However, the scandals that afflict Congress go well beyond its criminally negligent oversight performance. They also extend deeply into the political perks and benefits which Congress has lavished on itself and the alarming extent to which congressional incumbents are using tax dollars to insulate themselves from political challengers.

This is not a subject that has received much scrutiny from the national news media, which have invested most of their attention in the growing influence being exerted by the independent political action committees, or PACs, on our political process. The media seem strangely more concerned with the degree to which special interest groups are giving funds to lawmakers and political challengers who represent their social and political views, a political exercise that is certainly in keeping with the process of representative democracy. It is worth noting that the PACs spent only $95 million out of more than $1.2 billion expended in all local, state and national campaigns during 1980.

The far more important story is the disturbing extent to which Congress spends a large chunk of its $1.5 billion legislative branch budget to finance the reelection campaigns of its members. For as Congress's operating budget has mushroomed over the years, so have the office allowances, expense accounts, payrolls and myriad congressional services provided for its 100 senators and 435 House members. While many of these expenditures enable lawmakers to perform their constitutional duties and communicate with their constituents in pursuit of legitimately official business, they also generously subsidize their ongoing campaign activities.

Congress's tax-funded arsenal of campaign services has grown rapidly in recent years. It includes long-distance telephone lines; a generous travel budget; radio and television broadcast taping and distribution services; free giveaways such as flags, books, calendars, and numerous government brochures and publications; unlimited government research services; expanded year-round district and state office facilities; congressional photographers to take pictures of lawmakers with their constituents; mobile office vans; and many other types of benefits and assistance which contribute materially to the political self-preservation of our senators and representatives.

Each House member starts out with a basic "clerk hire" office allowance of $352,536 per year. Every senator is given a basic "clerk hire" office budget of nearly $1.3 million annually; almost $200,000 for "legislative assistance"; plus other expense accounts including $143,000 a year for various office expenses such as phones, telegrams and travel.

The most valuable and highly coveted campaign subsidy of all, however, is Congress's free mail, or "franking" privilege, which alone cost taxpayers more than $100 million in 1982 — $54 million more than in 1981. The evidence uncovered thus far reveals that this privilege is being shamelessly exploited by lawmakers for their political gain.

According to an unprecedented study by the Senate Rules Committee, conducted by its chairman, Senator Charles Mathias of Maryland, only a tiny 4 percent of the 269 million pieces of mail senators issued in 1982 was in response to regular correspondence. The rest was made up of mass mailings — newsletters, questionnaires, and unsolicited letters — spewed out on a scale that significantly dwarfs the campaign activities of all PACs put together.

"We are spending almost as much on mass mailings as we are on the entire Senate committee system," Mathias sternly lectured his colleagues in a speech on the Senate floor. "Just think of it, we could televise the proceedings of the U.S. Senate for the next 100 years, for a century, with the money that we spend in a single year for senators' mass mailings."

Since very few senators are present during most Senate "debates," and most sessions are held during the day when people are working, the political payoff of televised proceedings for members may be somewhat questionable. Far better, lawmakers figure, to be able to sell themselves to carefully selected constituencies through the power of direct mail, and bill the American taxpayer. To this end, lawmakers have been using their considerable office allowances to purchase state-of-the-art computerized equipment to send out thousands of personalized letters per hour to their states and districts.

Writing in the *Washington Monthly* under the pseudonym of William Haydon, a congressional aide revealed how one member of Congress plays the direct mail game:

> The key to the game is a sentence from that seemingly dull document, *House Regulations, Allowances and Expenses:* "Each member [of Congress] is authorized to acquire information and computer services and equipment consistent with the general provisions governing the allowance of official expenses." While these few words of bureaucratese may appear harmless, to Hi-Tech politicos like myself they are a golden key to a magical world. Quite simply, they grant permission to the representatives and their staffs to acquire any computer tape possible, as long as it is used for "official purposes" under the guidelines of the frank, the basic free-mailing privilege enjoyed by members of Congress. And the frank — well, as one Hill

buddy of mine put it. "The frank isn't a loophole, it's a black hole." If you can't do it under the frank, you're either dumb or hopelessly unsubtle.*

The congressional aide goes on to relate in detail how he was able to obtain computer tapes from various professional associations in his congressman's state which contained the names of every lawyer, doctor, nurse, teacher, and county and municipal official in the district. It wasn't long before he had also obtained a list, on computer tape, of all drivers' licenses in the state, cross referenced and purged the list of duplicates, and was merrily mailing letters from his boss on a broad range of issues of interest to select groups of voters.

Can such targeted, unsolicited computer-addressed letters be legitimately considered official congressional business? Says Haydon: "Per the previously quoted House regulation, computer services are absolutely kosher, as long as they are used for 'non-political' endeavors. What a joke. Nothing that comes out of a congressional office is non-political, though of course there are myriad rules prohibiting self-laudatory efforts, rules that go so far as to limit the number of personal pronouns per newsletter page and the size of a representative's photo."

The rules, however, say nothing about limiting the number of letters a House member may mail. Thus, with the help of congressional computers and computer list services, sophisticated letter campaigns are conducted to appeal to the concerns of every possible interest group that can help get that congressman elected. Individually addressed letters have much more impact than a newsletter sent to "Postal Patron," and our clever and highly industrious congressional computer whiz kid saw to it that they were churned out by the thousands each month.

When a poll of the district showed that political support for his boss was weakest among blacks and Hispanics, he pulled the names of all blacks and Hispanics from his master file and sent out a letter "detailing the congressman's support of the Martin Luther King Birthday bill and the need for bilingual teachers. . . . Sure enough, a

* "Confessions of a High-Tech Politico," *The Washington Monthly.* May 1980. Reprinted with permission from The Washington Monthly Co., 1711 Connecticut Avenue, N.W., Washington, D.C. 20009.

follow-up survey showed that the congressman's image in the minority communities had improved dramatically."

Yet the question that lies at the heart of the multimillion-dollar abuse of the franking privilege goes beyond our representatives' selfish desire to insure their own political survival with our tax dollars. Rather, says the self-styled public interest lobbying organization Common Cause, "it goes to the heart of representative democracy. At issue is the constitutionality of the extensive material assistance that the federal government gives to incumbent senators and representatives, but not to opposing candidates."

Consider the case of Senator John Heinz of Pennsylvania, the handsome and enormously wealthy heir to the H.J. Heinz catsup and pickle fortune, who flooded his state with fifteen million pieces of mail during his successful 1982 reelection campaign. Heinz's direct mail offensive amounted to three pieces of mail for every household in his state and earned him the dubious distinction of being the biggest mass mailer in Congress. Taxpayers — including those who opposed his reelection — unknowingly paid the Republican senator's stunning $2.25 million direct-mail bill. Meanwhile, his Democratic opponent was able to raise only $417,000 for his entire campaign.

Heinz has lots of company among his senatorial colleagues, who in 1982 collectively sent out nearly three pieces of mail for every household in America, 214 million pieces of which were blatantly self-promotional newsletters. During this same year, for example, Senators Alfonse D'Amato (R–N.Y.) dispatched 14.4 million pieces of mail to his constituents; Charles Percy (R–Ill.), 13.5 million; Lloyd Bentsen (D–Tex.), 11.8 million; Daniel Patrick Moynihan (D–N.Y.), 11.6 million; Donald Riegle, Jr. (D–Mich.), 10.9 million; John East (R–N.C.), 8.5 million; Carl Levin (D–Mich.), 6.9 million; Lawton Chiles (D–Fla.), 6.4 million; and Roger Jepsen (R–Iowa), 5.8 million.

The mailings for the Senate's five biggest mailers, Heinz, D'Amato, Percy, Bentsen and Moynihan, cost taxpayers more than $12.2 million. Of the big ten, only Heinz, Bentsen, Moynihan and Chiles were up for reelection. All of them won.

Many other senators took full advantage of the free-mail privilege in 1982. There are only 1.6 million mailboxes in Tennessee, but Senator James Sasser mailed six million newsletters to constituents in 1981, and another two million in 1982 when he successfully sought reelection. Iowa senators Roger Jepsen and Charles Grassley, who were not up for reelection in 1982, flooded their state with 11.3 million pieces of mail — more than ten pieces of mail for every Iowa household. Delaware's senators William Roth, Jr., who was running in 1982, and Joseph Biden, Jr., who was not, also sent the equivalent of eight pieces of mail for every household in their state. At the same time, North Carolina's Senator East, who was not seeking reelection that year, mailed 6.2 million letters at a cost of $1.4 million over less than a two-month (September 9 through October 29) period.

Meantime, in the House campaigns, where every representative was up for reelection, lawmakers sent out a staggering 509.2 million pieces of franked mail, most of it in behalf of their reelections.

Congress's entire election-year mail offensive totaled 778 million pieces of mail, dramatically leaping from 512 million in 1980 (up from 448 million in 1978 and 421 million in 1976). And the evidence is building that these mass mailings, when used in conjunction with other congressional support services and benefits, have been extremely effective in overcoming most political opposition. Out of 411 congressional incumbents seeking reelection in November 1982, only 31 lost: two senators and 29 representatives, many of whom lost due to congressional redistricting.

Most legislators rationalize their exploitation of the franking privilege with the argument that they are merely communicating with their constituents. Ellen Block, an attorney for Common Cause, sees it very differently. "The frank gives incumbents access to the federal treasury for reelection purposes," she says.

This is why her organization challenged the constitutionality of Congress's mass mailings in federal court, arguing that they violate the "constitutional rights to fair congressional elections . . . by giving large and important government assistance to incumbent candidates, but not to their challengers."

The issue raised by Common Cause is a deeply disturbing one, addressing a scandalous congressional abuse of the public purse. "It is a question of the fairness of every congressional election," the grassroots citizens' lobby declares. Indeed, it is a question of whether Congress should be allowed to shield itself from effective political competition with millions of tax dollars in campaign support services and benefits. Congress is, in a very real sense, rigging, or at least heavily tilting, the democratic elective process.

Unfortunately, Common Cause's suit, which former Watergate Special Prosecutor Archibald Cox joined as a "counsel of record," was rejected by the U.S. District Court in Washington on September 2, 1982. A three-judge panel swept aside the group's challenge on the grounds that such congressional mailings inherently served the "dual purposes" of communicating with constituents while promoting a lawmaker's image and popularity. Nevertheless, before the court made its ruling, it conducted an extensive inquiry that resulted in some startling findings of fact which seem to fly in the face of the court's final conclusions. Among them:

- "Measured in financial terms, the franking privilege confers a substantial advantage to incumbent congressional candidates over their challengers."
- The "volume and timing of franked mass mailings ... indicate widespread use to promote incumbents' re-election efforts."
- "The 'usual and customary congressional questionnaires,' frankable under [the law]," were frequently "used for purposes other than merely determining constituents' views on particular issues," such as "identifying recipients for targeted mailings, thus facilitating the member's political 'responsiveness' to various groups and interests."
- These targeted mass mailings are used in ways which "frequently have no relationship to official business and which are closely connected to re-election plans and strategy."
- "It is an undeniable conclusion that the fluctuations in the volume of franked mass mailings are caused by the electoral cycle, rather than by fluctuations in legislative activity."
- Lawmakers often receive, and implement, professional political advice from campaign consultants "to help integrate franked mailings into [their] overall campaign strategy."

However, despite these clear and undeniable findings of fact, the court was not in the end persuaded that Common Cause was right.

Indeed, the full weight of the evidence, so meticulously accumulated throughout the proceeding, apparently so confused the court's thinking that it ended up contradicting its own findings. Thus, in one breath the judges found that "Congress recognized the potential financial benefits conferred by [the law] on campaigning incumbents at the time it passed the [franking] Act" authorizing continued use of the free mailing privilege. Yet in the next breath they concluded that "Congress has recognized the basic principle that government funds should not be spent to help incumbents gain re-election. The details of the franking scheme . . . appear to be rationally designed to work for that end."

The court appeared further to side with Common Cause when in an earlier opinion it denied a motion to dismiss the suit for lack of standing, ruling that "The injury involved here occurs regardless of the outcome of any particular election. . . .

"This injury is personal to the [challenging] candidates, substantial in effect, and directly traceable to the operation of the franking statute," the court added. "In order to neutralize this advantage of incumbency, a challenger must raise substantially greater funds than he otherwise would, or, if he is able, contribute such moneys to his campaign out of his own pocket. . . . The injury is not only directly traceable to the operation of the franking statute, but as plaintiffs have framed this action, the statute itself *is* the injury because of its alleged facial invalidity."

In 1973, after growing criticism over congressional mailing abuses, Congress made some reforms in the Congressional Franking Act. But now Arizona Congressman Morris Udall, the chief sponsor of the act, and the chairman of the House Commission on Congressional Mailing Standards, admits the reforms have failed: "These mass mailings can have evil consequences. I frankly don't know how the hell we can define and control the problem," Udall told the *New York Times*. "We have virtually no limits on spending now. We thought we had these people nailed down, but they sure found a lot of loopholes. The present law hasn't worked, and we have to go back and try again."

As the rules stand now, House members may make six newsletter mailings a year to every household in their districts, and an unlimited number of letter mailings. Senators are permitted the luxury of unlimited mailings of all types to their states. But the continuing, flagrant political abuse of the mailing privilege, in addition to the many other federal services which benefit congressional incumbents beyond any justification, represents more than simply the misuse of federal tax dollars. No, this scandal really undermines our very system of representative democracy. And it calls upon us to consider whether our national legislature has so excessively granted itself campaign-related benefits and services that the people it was elected to serve are prevented from legitimately and fairly challenging an incumbent's reelection.

By the early 1970s, studies revealed the average member of Congress controlled a budget of about $500,000 a year in various services, benefits, expense accounts and office staff. Much of that money, of course, helps members conduct their official legislative duties, but much of it also helps them pursue reelection. That figure is now fast approaching $2 million a year per member. This is a formidable sum of money, one that would give any common man or woman pause to think seriously before undertaking to challenge his of her senator or representative. The chilling effect such public expenditures may have on the average American seeking change through the political process should not be underestimated.

In its appeal to the Supreme Court, Common Cause correctly noted that "Franked mail, like many other activities of a senator or representative, may serve two functions: (1) It may give constituents information about the conduct of government and the proceedings in Congress; (2) It may promote a senator's or representative's campaign for re-election. Use of government funds for the first purpose serves the public interest. No public interest is served, however, by the use of public moneys for the second function; i.e., to support the political campaign of an incumbent senator or representative while withholding support from opposing candidates."

Common Cause was not successful. On May 2, 1983, the highest court in the land summarily affirmed the lower court's judgment without an opinion. Thus, the citizens group was not even given the opportunity to present further written and oral arguments before the nine justices. "In the end," says Ellen Block, "I think [the factor that led to their defeat] was how does the court fashion a remedy for this kind of problem." Yet Common Cause was not really asking the court to interfere in the legislative branch's independence in terms of trying to eliminate the traditional franking privilege. Indeed, it left the range of remedies up to the court, suggesting that Congress could itself devise a fairer and more balanced use of the frank, one that would avoid the excesses and imbalances that the lower court had so demonstrably exposed.

In his *Washington Monthly* confessional, William Haydon told of the joys of discovering "new and wonderfully more devious ways to maximize our potential," to reach out to voters through the mails. He told of obtaining a computer tape "of all recent births in the district, along with parents' names, etc." from the State Board of Health. "They were more than happy to comply, and we now send each new parent in the district a book called 'Infant Care,' " published by the government. "When the little tyke has his first birthday, we automatically send the parents another book, this one called 'Child Care.' Rest assured that I have every intention of following up these mailings with a voter registration form 17 years later."

As Congress aggressively moves to computerize its mailing operations further, there will be increasing pressure from lawmakers to purchase still more advanced equipment, and more sophisticated mailing lists — detailing, perhaps, each voter's sex, occupation, age, membership in various trade groups or associations, and possibly even whether he or she benefits from an entitlement program, or some other government program. This is the very dangerous course upon which Congress is ambitiously and deliberately embarked. The cost, which will rise to the hundreds of millions of dollars, will continue to be footed by the American taxpayer. But the real victims of this scandal are the American voters and the future of representative democracy.

4

Pay, Perks and Privileges

In many respects, the personal profile of Congress mirrors the society it represents. Its membership is composed of high and low achievers, the industrious and the lazy, the intelligent and the mediocre, the competent and the incompetent, the creative and the unimaginative, the daring and the timid, the honest and the dishonest.

Yet whatever their personal characteristics or professional qualifications, the lives our lawmakers lead in Congress are comfortable, protected and even pampered. Despite the complaints of its members, and even considering the many alternatives, serving in Congress is not a bad job. "It beats heavy lifting," former Congressman Jimmy Burke of Massachusetts once wryly remarked to a colleague.

Economic recessions, even depressions, come and go in the unending cycles of our economy, but Congress's life-style remains remarkably unchanged. While much of America struggled with the economic problems arising from the recession years of 1979–1982, Congress never lost a single privilege, perk or payday. Indeed, throughout this difficult period Congress sought to expand them!

Even during the recession's darkest days in 1981 and 1982, as steel-workers, meatpackers, autoworkers and practitioners of countless other trades were negotiating painful wage cutbacks and freezes, the benefits, perquisites and luxuries to which our lawmakers have become accustomed continued undiminished.

Much of congressional life takes place in and around the majestic, domed Capitol which to most Americans is the preeminent symbol of the United States government. Within the vast Capitol complex lives "a city within a city" in which thirty thousand congressional employees occupy twenty-two buildings spread out over 270 acres on Capitol Hill; a lawmaking metropolis that provides legislators with every possible convenience, comfort and necessity of daily life — from beauty parlors to caterers, from doctors to ministers of God, from maids to mechanics, from cut-rate gift shops to professional masseurs. It is far from the life of deprivation and sacrifice that so many members of Congress would have us believe they lead.

Congress is first and foremost an institution concerned with money, and most especially its members'. Thus, there are banks and credit unions in the Capitol that extend a range of financial services to members of Congress and their employees. The House of Representatives bank, conveniently located one floor below the House chamber, provides members with free check cashing privileges. Should members be caught short of funds, the House Sergeant-at-Arms will loan them what they need. Representatives and their staffs are also eligible to join the chamber's Wright Patman Credit Union, and maintain their membership in it even after they have left Congress. The credit union's privileges include free checking with interest, low-cost overdraft protection, plus substantial discounts on the purchase of cars, furniture and trips through the United Buying Service that are available to government civilian and military employees. Similar credit union benefits exist in the Senate.

For those lawmakers who find it impossible to make sense out of the complex tax code they have imposed on the rest of us, there's an Internal Revenue Service office to assist them with their tax forms free of charge.

For many years the House and Senate have operated their own congressionally staffed stationery stores in which members buy their office supplies. Every congressional office pays for its supplies out of an annual allowance granted each member. Over the years, however, the inventory at these stationery stores has been expanded to the point where the facilities resemble small department stores. Now the merchandise includes silverware, cut crystal, wine and champagne goblets, books, leather attaché cases, luggage, tape recorders, clocks, jewelry, pewter beer mugs, radios, gold-embossed dinner plates, family photo albums, cigarette lighters, and other luxury gift items that have nothing to do with running an office. Senators and representatives do much of their gift buying at these stores, taking advantage of the deep discount prices available only to members and their employees. Virtually everything in these stores is sold at cost, which means discounts of 40 to 50 percent. There is a nominal 10 percent service charge applied to "nonofficial" purchases, but that is so broadly applied that only 2 percent of the stores' items are so classified, according to the GAO. The stores can get away with such incredible nonprofit discounts because the taxpayers are subsidizing them. The net "operational cost," i.e., subsidy, for the House stationery store alone was well over $500,000 in 1982, according to the GAO.

The meals members eat in the private House and Senate dining rooms are also heavily subsidized, resulting in inflation-insulated menu prices that are up to 50 percent cheaper than food served in comparable area restaurants.

Picture, if you will, wealthy senators lunching in their restricted Capitol dining rooms on tables covered in crisp linens, under crystal chandeliers, served by a well-paid staff of waitresses whose salaries (over $4.10 per hour) exceed anything their counterparts earn in privately owned restaurants, where the usual salary is not much more than the minimum wage.

The meals may include such entrées as stuffed brook trout, roast duckling à l'orange, or breast of chicken Stroganoff, along with soup, fresh vegetables, salad, rolls and butter, plus dessert, all for a mere $5.45. A bowl of soup or hot deep dish apple pie or a tossed salad are only 95 cents each, and there are unlimited coffee refills.

No comparable, medium-priced restaurants surveyed in the Washington area could afford to match Congress's inexpensive menu if they had similar overhead and labor costs.

How do they do it? The congressional restaurants operate at a substantial annual loss, which the taxpayers of course must cover. According to 1982 GAO audits, the operation of the Senate's restaurants "resulted in a net operating loss of $45,596 in 1981." The House restaurants lost $128,969 during this same period.

Not only is Congress incapable of balancing the federal budget, it cannot even run its own restaurants at a profit, despite a captive clientele. The reason: Lawmakers are unwilling to raise their prices or reduce their labor costs to cover expenses as would any private restaurateur. And congressional labor costs are considerable. The Senate restaurants' manager is paid nearly $50,000 a year, and his assistants earn up to $35,000 each. Each dining room unit manager earns up to $25,000 a year. Needless to say, management salaries in comparably priced Washington area restaurants do not even approach these sums.

For special dining occasions there is also a congressional catering service. Members of Congress or their committees often throw receptions to honor some colleague, or entertain a special interest group, or hold special affairs for themselves and the many ad hoc groups that meet regularly for lunch or breakfast in one of the many hideaway rooms in the Capitol. Here again, Congress's catering service offers its members bargain prices.

The care and feeding of our legislators also extends to their physical health. The Office of the Attending Physician in the Capitol has a staff of thirty-one full-time health-care professionals whose $816,000 annual budget includes three physicians, a pharmacist, a physiotherapist, fifteen nurses, a lab technician, and a dozen administrative personnel. Its staff provides members with free medical care which includes annual physical examinations, inoculations, X-rays, medications, electrocardiograms, lab services, physiotherapy, and emergency care. In addition, an ambulance is kept ready and waiting at the Capitol when Congress is in session.

Members of Congress also benefit from low health-care rates at Walter Reed Army Hospital or Bethesda Naval Hospital. Lawmakers are charged a flat rate of $430 a day even if they require intensive care treatment. Comparable intensive care treatment, in this case in Washington's Georgetown University Hospital, would cost $750 per day.

They also are given cheaper health insurance rates for full medical and hospitalization benefits. A high-option family health insurance plan from Blue Cross–Blue Shield would cost a private citizen in Washington $184.82 a month, but under their health insurance plan, members pay only $108.85 a month for substantially better coverage.

For nearly $72,000 in life insurance coverage, members pay only two-thirds of the premium ($37.44 per month) and taxpayers pick up one-third ($18.72). But there is a further bonus. If members die in office, taxpayers also pay the entire cost of their funeral expenses, and survivors of the deceased lawmaker receive one year's congressional salary ($72,600).

There is much more. Senators and representatives have their own private, fully equipped health spas hidden away in their respective office buildings, just minutes from their chambers via Congress's underground subway system. The Senate gym was once known as the "Senate baths" during the days when patrician senators robed in white sheets sweated off excess weight in steam rooms, emerging to cool their bodies in the nearby swimming pool. Instead of suffering through some dreary floor debate or tedious committee hearings, many members prefer to play basketball, volleyball, or, for the less active legislators, have their bodies massaged by the skillful hands of House and Senate masseurs. In the House, the popular game is paddleball, a version of handball with paddles, played aggressively on the highly polished oak courts secluded deep inside the basement of the Rayburn House Office Building. Officials in the Office of the Architect who oversee the gyms say their surveys show that 50 to 70 House members use their gym facility daily, while up to 40 or more senators use the Senate gym each day.

The gyms contain swimming pools, saunas, steam baths, bodybuilding and exercise equipment, whirlpools, a heated pool, wrestling mats, and other equipment. The gyms are open sixteen hours a day and are staffed by eleven "physical therapists," whose annual salaries total more than $250,000 a year. It is "nothing more than your typical industrial gym" an attendant says. In Washington, it costs over $700 a year just to belong to a YMCA gym, and much more to belong to a comparable commercial health spa. For lawmakers it is free and the taxpayers are sent the bill.

The Botanical Gardens regularly furnish congressional offices with potted ivies and tropical plants, and even fresh cut flowers when available. Members receive free picture-framing services for their prints, photographs, awards and other office decorations. And of course many of their offices are appointed with the finest furnishings. For example, when House Democratic Whip Thomas Foley of Washington needed a new desk, taxpayers paid $3,255 for a mahogany one. Similarly, House Republican Whip Trent Lott of Mississippi was furnished with a $2,136 desk along with a $634 armchair. Congressional offices, especially the Capitol hideaways assigned only to Congress's most senior members, are regularly recarpeted, usually with one of the most expensive grades of carpeting and padding that money can buy.

Additional perks include free parking in the Capitol's underground garages, as well as free preferential parking spaces at nearby National and Dulles airports. If a House member's car is getting a little dirty, there are congressional parking attendants to get it clean and sparkling, inside and out, before day's end for $3. Getting low on gas, Senator? No problem. During the gasoline shortages of the early 1970s, when Americans were lined up for blocks at service stations, senatorial leaders were able to avoid such discomfort by having their chauffeur-driven cars filled at pumps installed in their underground garages, and at prices less than the oil embargo highs paid by their constituents. The bitter irony, of course, was that the Congress's oil price control policies and allocation program contributed mightily to the gas shortages of the 1970s.

Other benefits to make congressional life a little easier, and cheaper, are scattered throughout the Capitol. There are cut-rate $3.50 haircuts in the House and Senate barbershops, plus a 75-cent shoeshine, suh! For the ladies of Congress there are beauty shops where a cut, wash and set, by appointment, costs only $16. Cigarettes are cheaper, and there is no sales tax charged in the Capitol.

When new members come to Congress they are given a brochure entitled "Services to Members of Congress." It describes the fabled "freebies" from Congress's Government Printing Office. Members may order any item from GPO's vast inventory of 250,000 books and publications out of their office allowance. If they wish, lawmakers can have GPO bind any and all documents in goatskin, at the taxpayer's expense, of course. Senators may have a full set of each year's *Congressional Record* bound in buckram, a handsome synthetic leather, for $4,000. To help members win points with their constituents and special interest groups back home, they are given free subscriptions to the *Congressional Record* to give away to libraries, institutions and other local organizations. Senators are each allowed fifty free subscriptions, while House members get thirty-four.

Also provided free, on request, to line their personal library are expensive hardbound sets of *Foreign Relations of the U.S., U.S. Statutes at Large, U.S. Treaties and Other International Agreements,* the entire *U.S. Code,* the complete volumes of *Presidential Papers,* among other books and documents regularly published by GPO.

Each year the Agriculture Department publishes 233,000 copies of the handsomely illustrated *Agricultural Yearbook* at a cost of $407,000 for members to give away to their constituents and thereby aid their reelection. Every senator gets 550 copies a year, and representatives each receive 400.

Each lawmaker also receives an engraved copy of the biannual *Congressional Directory,* containing all of the relevant statistics on Congress, government agencies, and key federal officials. There is also the prolific congressional calendar, which Congress prints by the thousands as one of our lawmakers' most commonly distributed constituent souvenir and gift. It costs taxpayers $689,000 to produce nearly 1.2 million calendars every year.

When members die in office, eulogies given by their colleagues are compiled and published in special memorial editions of the *Congressional Record,* 300 copies of which are published and distributed to family, friends and colleagues at a cost to taxpayers of about $15,000 and up.

Like all Americans, our lawmakers love to travel, and many get to take their vacations at the taxpayer's expense. Members have easy access to twenty-two jet planes in the Air Force's 89th Military Airlift Wing at nearby Andrews Air Force Base for their "official business" trips. Maintained and operated at a cost of $33.5 million a year, this fleet of Boeing 707s, sleek C140 Jet Stars and other aircraft is kept ready and waiting at all times to fly members of Congress wherever they may wish to go around the world. According to the Air Force, the 89th Wing, whose VIP clients include the President, vice-president, the cabinet, top military brass, and members of Congress, racked up over twelve thousand hours of flying time during 1982 for its clients.

The official charter for Congress's exclusive airline says that it "will not be used except when travel is in the national interest and commercial travel is not available or capable of meeting the movement required." Yet an examination of the 89th's travel records shows that many members frequently use the costly all-expense-paid service as their personal airline, travel agent and tourist guide. In 1982, 34 senators, 200 representatives, and 240 of their staff maintained they were unable to obtain travel by commercial means and that their trips were "in the national interest."

In addition to the convenience of having the 89th airline available whenever they choose to travel, there is the added personal luxury of having military escort officers accompanying and assisting them on their journeys. These military major domos make sure that the planes are stocked with plenty of liquor, hors d'oeuvres, and other refreshments, handle all the baggage, and pick up the incidental expenses throughout the trip. The money for tips, meals, bar bills, laundry, cabs and other expenses comes out of a $500,000-a-year air force contingency fund better known as the "black bag" account. The army and navy each maintain their own $150,000-a-year "black bag" accounts when they are in charge of squiring congressional VIPs around the world.

Of all of its scandals, Congress's abuse of the 89th Wing ranks as one of the worst. A classic example of this abuse occurred when the 89th sent an eight-passenger, four-engine C140 Jet Star to Bristol, Tennessee. Its mission: Bring Congressman James H. Quillen (R–Tenn.) back to Washington in time for him to hop aboard Air

Force One in order to fly back to Tennessee with President Reagan to attend the opening day ceremonies at the 1982 World's Fair in Knoxville. Bristol is only 120 miles from Knoxville. The basic roundtrip cost for the plush Jet Star (which costs $1,868 an hour to operate) to pick up Quillen and fly him to Andrews Air Force Base just outside of Washington was nearly $7,500. If the crew's pay is figured into the cost of Quillen's VIP flight, the per-hour cost would come to $2,800, or a grand total of $11,000. If Quillen had flown commercial to Washington, it would have cost taxpayers about $150. Quillen's aides said a regularly scheduled flight would not have brought their boss to Andrews in time to get aboard the President's flight. In that case, then, he could have easily driven the two hours to Knoxville and saved taxpayers a considerable sum of money.

Members of Congress not only exploit the 89th Airlift for their personal comfort, convenience and political gain, avoiding cheaper and more efficient commercial flights, but their costly annual junkets monotonously include the same world capitals year in and year out: Bonn, Rome, London, Lisbon, Paris, Madrid, Hong Kong. Moreover, like tourists on charter excursions, lawmakers are fond of traveling in groups, and taking their wives along for free on the "space available" military aircraft.

During Congress's 1981 Easter recess, House Speaker Thomas P. (Tip) O'Neill and twenty-one of his fellow House members traveled to Australia and New Zealand for a ten-day jaunt called "a leadership trip." The official purpose was "to discuss security and economic issues," a commonly used description for what was in reality a traditional Easter vacation junket that cost taxpayers $138,300. O'Neill and twenty-one other Republican and Democratic House lawmakers also spent seventeen days, March 25–April 10, in 1983, touring Singapore, China, Japan and Hong Kong. The cost: $108,-668.54.

Senator Paul Laxalt of Nevada and three other senators and their wives, plus seven staff members, flew to Europe during July 1982 on one of the 89th's Boeing 707s. Flight costs totaled $124,000. Living expenses for the group came to about $25,000. Their first stop: the picturesque and mountainous Basque region of France, home of

Laxalt's ancestors, where they enjoyed an activity-filled Fourth of July weekend. Their travel itinerary also included London, Rome, and Budapest where they held the usual meetings with various government officials and were given military briefings. The question is, how many times must members visit London and Rome? Each year dozens of legislators include these and other popular world capitals in their European travels.

The list of lucrative congressional perks is long, and filled with excesses and abuses. Yet in spite of the cornucopia of privileges Congress has bestowed on itself, it is never ultimately satisfied. It is always reaching out for more. It will endure ridicule, risk public contempt, and engage in the most disreputable legislative legerdemain to extract still further emoluments from the hides of the American taxpayer. Consider a few more choice examples.

In the summer of 1982, when America was in the depths of the recession, senators had the audacity to vote to outfit expensively a gymnasium in the newly built Hart Senate Office Building. Fortunately, the knowledge that our well-heeled senators were voting to spend tax dollars to equip a third gymnasium — at a time when Congress was cutting social programs and raising taxes to boot — unleashed an angry public outcry.

The Senate had wrestled with the subject of a new gym sometime earlier and rejected it. Yet just when some senators thought they had killed the proposed facility and eliminated it from the controversial and costly $140 million Hart Building, it mysteriously came to life again. The $736,400 to outfit the gym was quietly restored in March 1982 by the Senate Office Building Commission, conveniently avoiding any appropriations hearings or full Senate approval. Enraged when he heard of this back-door scheme to put the gym back into the building's final plans, Senator William Proxmire of Wisconsin surprised his colleagues on August 10, 1982, by offering an unannounced amendment to withhold any funds for the gym's furnishings and equipment. The Senate already had their fully equipped gym in the Russell Senate Office Building, and a smaller shower and exercise facility in the Dirksen Office Building. "Enough is enough," Proxmire argued. With America in the midst of a severe recession, this was hardly the time for senators to be squandering money on themselves. But Proxmire's amendment was voted down, 50–48, on a parliamentary point of order, allowing many senators to claim later that they voted against Proxmire solely to uphold the ruling of the chair. In this case, the presiding officer had ruled the amendment had no place in the pending bill because it sought to place legislation in an appropriations measure, which Senate rules forbid.

Although many senators who voted against Proxmire's amendment deceitfully hid behind the parliamentary smokescreen to explain their vote, a survey I conducted shortly thereafter showed many senators openly confessing they really wanted a new gym.

Montana's John Melcher, for example, insisted that the existing gym was too old and would be "condemned by an ordinary fire inspector." Senate officials, though, denied any fire hazard. Rhode Island's Claiborne Pell, a multimillionaire, complained the gym was "very inadequate," and besides, the vacant gym facility in the Hart complex was "unsuitable for any other purposes." In fact, the area reserved for the new gym could easily be converted to office space.

Nevada's Paul Laxalt had no apologies. He simply said he was "for it." Massachusetts' Paul Tsongas wanted it because he was "a strong believer in physical fitness," while South Carolina's Fritz Hollings, who regularly uses the gym, "felt a lot of his colleagues wanted it," an aide explained. A spokesman for California's Alan Cranston, a physical fitness buff, said Cranston believes that since businesses provide their top executives with gym facilities, "so should senators," i.e., the taxpayers.

Incredibly, of the several dozen senators I polled, not one argued, as they should have, that in light of record deficits and severe economic hardships, this was not the time to be spending money on such a frivolous luxury for one hundred well-paid senators, twenty-three of whom are millionaires who can well afford to buy their own health club.

Still, the public uproar over the vote on the Hart gym refused to subside, forcing Senate Republican leader Howard Baker one week later, on August 17, to offer an amendment to the debt ceiling bill to summarily eliminate funding for the proposed gym. The measure was unanimously approved, 98–0, but it did not fully absolve what the Senate had tried to do: sneak another unnecessary and indefensible expenditure past the American people. The Senate's rapid about-face was reported by the press. What was not reported was this: while Proxmire's original amendment would have required the Office of the Architect to return the unused $736,400 appropriation to the U.S. Treasury, Baker's amendment allowed the architect to keep the funds to spend on the Hart Building as he "deems necessary." Thus, somewhere in the darkest recesses of the Capitol Architect's office are plans to spend that money and outfit the still-empty gym as soon as senators think they can get away with it.

Meantime, one of the Senate's best-kept secrets is the tennis court on top of the Hart Building. The Senate had previously rejected the idea of putting the court facility into the Hart complex for politically obvious reasons. But when the roof was laid down, a court surface was also quietly installed. Senators are merely waiting for the appropriate time when this luxurious yet totally unnecessary senatorial facility can be outfitted and, if you will forgive the pun, put into service.

The Senate's duplicitous little gym plan was small potatoes compared to what Congress tried to pull during its now-fabled tax caper in December 1981. While millions of workers were struggling to make ends meet, or find a job, Congress voted to give itself a lucrative tax break on their Washington area living expenses. To even the most cynical of Washington observers, the spectacle of our lawmakers awarding themselves this back-door pay-hike by manipulating the Internal Revenue Code ranks as one of the greediest and most insensitive legislative acts in recent congressional history.

The loophole was greased through the legislative mill in the dead of night shortly before the Christmas holidays, appropriately enough. According to the fine print in the bill, senators and representatives would have been able to deduct almost any living expense — food, housing, servants, laundry, home maintenance, utilities, you name it.

Ingeniously designed by lawmakers who have turned the craft of writing tax loopholes into an art form, members could claim a flat $75 a day in deductible expenses except on those days when Congress was in recess five days or longer. Congress, of course, has ways of manipulating its work schedule and shrinking the number of recess periods by, for example, holding pro forma sessions where no work transpires. Thus, under one possible formulation, if Congress claimed a thirty-day August recess and was in session from January 15 to December 15, members could have written off up to $22,875 of their total income from taxation.

Moreover, this deduction could have been taken even when a lawmaker was not in Washington but was out on the speaking circuit. Also, by using the flat daily deduction, he would not have had to prove his claimed expenditures, as you or I would be required. Even in the event the congressmen were audited, their claims could not be challenged — a privilege that would have placed them, at least in the eyes of the IRS, far beyond mere mortal men.

Under this devious tax scheme, lawmakers would have also been able to reap generous tax advantages from a high mortgage and heavy property tax. By employing this option, they could deduct two-thirds of their flat deduction and add in mortgage interest and property tax payments on an expensive home. For instance, a lawmaker who paid $1,000 a month in mortgage interest and $3,000 in property taxes would automatically be eligible for a tax deduction of $30,250.

Of course, wealthier members of Congress could choose to itemize their travel and other business-related expenditures and thus devise as large a deduction as possible, though each claim would have to be proven to the IRS. By fully utilizing these changes in the tax law, which Congress greedily made retroactive to January 1981, many lawmakers with the right amount of expenses, plus the standard deductions available to everyone, could have avoided paying any federal income taxes at all.

The legislation in which this tax goody was buried was a black lung benefits revenue bill which slithered through the Senate on a 46–44 roll call vote on December 16, 1981. The sweetened bill was then immediately sent over to the House where during a late-night session the amendment was, under suspension of the rules, accepted on an unrecorded voice vote. Thus, the American people were denied the knowledge of how their representatives stood on a private tax loophole intended to enrich themselves at the public's expense.

When it became clear several days later what our lawmakers had done in the dead of night during a confused, hastily completed end-of-the-year session, few lawmakers seemed ashamed of what they had knowingly perpetrated. William Proxmire angrily branded the dirty deed "a back-door pay-raise voted by members not brave enough to raise their salaries." Sadly, his was a lonely voice in a senatorial sea of silence. Even as public outrage grew, as the sleazy legislative details began to emerge, Majority Leader Howard Baker bitterly retaliated when he snapped to reporters, "I think it's a bum rap. We're not going to repeal it. It would be a first-rate tragedy if that were to be changed."

Public anger, however, burned far too intensely on this one, surprising even Baker and his colleagues. Like the gymnasium caper, Congress was forced to repeal its little tax loophole on July 18, 1982, but not before legislators permitted themselves to take unsubstantiated tax deductions in excess of $19,000 per member for 1981.

Yet embarrassment and shame over what they had tried to pull seemed to be the least of the reasons behind their tax turnaround. There were stronger political imperatives to consider. It was, after all, an election year in which Republicans wanted to retain control of the Senate more than they wanted the tax loophole. Democrats, in turn, wanted to strengthen their hold on the House. Nevertheless, it was one of the shabbier episodes in congressional annals, certainly one that the public should not easily forget or forgive. And yet it was an all-too-frequent reminder of Congress's propensity to act in its own self-interest.

Not generally known is the fact that repeal of the tax loophole left lawmakers with a flat $3,000 tax deduction that they gave themselves in 1952, ostensibly to help them offset the costs of maintaining two homes. For more than one hundred members, however, this represents a huge tax windfall, because they do not maintain a residence in their state or district. Legislators adroitly crafted the 1952 tax law to make clear that the expense of maintaining a residence in their home state did not have to be proven. Thus, they can claim the tax deduction regardless of whether they maintain a home in the state or district they represent.

This is a substantial tax benefit for many members of Congress. A survey conducted by *U.S. News & World Report* discovered that at least forty-four lawmakers did not own or rent residences in their states. In at least fifty-one other cases, the survey showed that members owned homes in their state or district but rented them out. Yet these members, along with those who do maintain two legitimate residences, can and do benefit from this $3,000 tax windfall. Says James Davidson, chairman of the National Taxpayers Union, "an ordinary person claiming a deduction on a home he didn't have would go to the penitentiary."

It is also not widely known that senators are generally allowed to bill taxpayers up to $75 a day for lodging expenses incurred when they are visiting their home states. House members took full advantage of this perk until the House Administration Committee eliminated it on December 9, 1982. The committee concluded that it was unconscionable for Congress to let its members charge lodging and other incidental expenses to their office allowances while in their hometowns doing their job. The Senate Rules Committee, however, doesn't quite see it that way. So senators who go home to see their constituents, but who no longer maintain a dwelling there, are allowed to live off the public every day they are home.

Congress's characteristically self-centered mindset raised its ugly head again in 1982 in an even more scandalous act.

The date was December 14. Unemployment was raging at 10.8 percent. The Gross National Product had declined by 1.1 percent. Business failures for the year had leaped to 28,000, and millions of Americans had been thrown onto food stamps and other welfare rolls. Difficult though it is now to fully comprehend in light of such severe economic ill health, a lame-duck House of Representatives overwhelmingly voted 303–109 to raise its salary from $60,662.50 to $69,800, a whopping 15 percent increase. Never mind that Congress had just run up a fiscal 1982 deficit of more than $100 billion, and was facing a $200 billion deficit in fiscal 1983. Never mind that five months earlier these same legislators had approved a tax increase of nearly $100 billion to pay for their continuing spending increases. Never mind that nine days later, on December 23, they would add 5 cents per gallon in excise tax to the price of gasoline.

Never mind that throughout 1982 millions of working-class Americans were forced to accept pay cuts and multiyear wage freezes in a desperate effort to save their jobs. Never mind that the year before these same lawmakers had enacted some of the biggest budgetary cutbacks in social welfare history, cuts that were highly controversial and, some charged, impacted heavily upon the poor. Never mind that just two and a half months earlier Congress had merrily voted to allow the government's debt to rise to a mind-boggling $1.3 trillion.

No, these legislators, who had previously voted themselves a nearly $13,000 pay-raise in 1977, then another $3,162.50 raise two years later, gave little if any thought to such things. Despite record deficits, uncontrolled spending, and an economy that was dead in the water, 303 members of the House of Representatives were blissfully convinced that they deserved to reward themselves, even while millions of their fellow Americans were tightening their belts and simply "doing without."

My point is not that members of Congress do not deserve a pay-raise, because they probably do at some point. They are, after all, the board of directors of our national government, in charge of authorizing expenditures of close to a trillion dollars a year. In spite of their generally poor job performance, the argument can be made that they deserve to be paid more. The question is, when is the best time to do it? And under what criteria? The House's decision to vote itself a sizable pay-raise in the midst of the worst recession since the Great Depression was clearly not the time. Its action stands as a legislative monument to unmitigated gall and institutional selfishness.

As it turned out, the Senate refused to follow their House brethren, preferring to keep their salary at $60,662.50. However, in an equally crass and untimely act, senators chose instead to eliminate the ceiling on outside income which they had placed upon themselves in a frenzy of post-Watergate ethics reforms in the 1970s.

Congress had enacted strict limitations on its outside earned income — 15 percent of congressional salaries — when it voted itself a $12,900 raise in 1977. House members voted to raise the outside income ceiling to 30 percent in 1981, while senators kept it at 15 percent. However, the Senate's ceiling, which was to become effective in December 1982, was never realized. That December, the Senate voted 54 to 38 to erase the ceiling, allowing its members to earn as much money on the outside as they could. (No limit is placed on outside unearned income such as interest, dividends and rents.)

The decision by the Senate to forgo the House pay-raise in exchange for eliminating the ceiling on its outside earnings was a very lucrative deal for the Senate, because most of its members are in greater demand on the lecture circuit by virtue of their station as senators and the increased political visibility that comes with the job.

And, oh, how lucrative that can be. Fifteen senators earned more than $50,000 each in speaking fees from special interest groups during 1982, according to Senate records. Dozens more significantly added to their five-figure Senate salaries in various amounts. Only eight senators (and sixty-six House members) accepted no honoraria that year, while another six senators (and ten House members) contributed all of their fees to charity. Yet even after making their contributions to charity, five senators netted more from their speaking fees than they did from their Senate salaries.

Senator Ernest Hollings, for instance, added an astonishing $92,000 in speaking fees to his 1982 Senate salary, while Robert Dole of Kansas, chairman of the Finance Committee, earned more than $135,000 in honoraria, giving $51,000 of it to charity. Indiana's Richard Lugar made $63,700 speaking; David Durenberger of Minnesota, a mere freshman, pulled in $60,700 in lecture fees; New Mexico's Peter Domenici, chairman of the Budget Committee, earned $83,450 on the banquet circuit; and New York's Alfonse M. D'Amato added $56,000 to his senatorial income.

Two disturbing questions are raised by the huge incomes these and other senators earned from unlimited speaking honoraria. One is the question of conflict of interest, and the other is the responsibility senators owe to their job and to their employers, the American people.

While no conflict of interest has been proven, the appearance of such conflict between a senator's public trust and the special interests who are willing to pay $2,000 a speech is very harmful indeed. Jake Garn of Utah, chairman of the influential Senate Banking Committee, which has jurisdiction over housing programs as well, earned $76,000 in speaking fees in 1982, giving $16,000 to charity. He earned it by speaking before such groups as the National Association of Mutual Savings Banks, the Bank Administration Institute, and the Manufactured Housing Institute.

Dole, whose powerful tax-writing committee is in a position to help virtually any special interest group in America, collected $2,000 in speaking fees from such lobbying powerhouses as the American Bankers Association, the American Petroleum Institute, the National Association of Manufacturers, the Bank of America, Crocker National Bank, Mercantile Bank, and Citicorp.

Durenberger, who chairs the Senate Health Subcommittee, earned his speaking bucks by addressing groups representing doctors, dentists, chiropractors, and psychiatrists. James A. McClure of Idaho, who chairs the important Energy and National Resources Committee, collected $60,000 speaking to such groups as the American Mining Congress, the Atomic Industrial Forum and the National Forest Products Association, all organizations deeply affected by his committee.

Senators argue that the $2.4 million in speaking fees earned by their colleagues in 1982, twice what they earned in 1980, but quite a bit more than the $2.1 million earned by their colleagues in the House, is annually disclosed to the public. That is protection enough against any potential for abuse, they say. Their constituents can judge whether such outside earnings are proper or not. But would they? In the complex, often little-noticed legislative minutiae that are fed through the lawmaking process, thousands of provisions are inserted into hundreds of bills each year. Relatively few of these provisions are given any serious attention by the news media, let alone the public at large. There is, in most cases, little opportunity for constituents to judge whether any organization or special interest group has been helped by a senator for an annual $2,000 speaking fee.

Equally important, how can any legislator be conscientiously doing his legislative chores and earning his federal salary if he or she is out on the speaking circuit grossing $135,500 a year as, for example, did Dole? "It's not easy work, going out and speaking as much as he does," an aide to the Kansas senator conceded. "It's a tribute not only to his popularity but to his important responsibilities on the Hill," i.e., his responsibilities as the powerful head of one of the most influential committees of Congress. It is also a tribute to each senator's ambition and, most especially, to the talents of his personal staff and committee aides who do most of his work in his absence. Any lawmaker who is out on the mashed potatoes circuit earning $135,500 a year is not devoting anywhere near the time needed to look after the needs of his constituents and his country.

In the end, however, after a bitter debate, the Senate on June 9, 1983, reluctantly voted 51–41 to follow the House's lead to place a 30-percent-of-salary ceiling on outside income. An angry Jake Garn told his fellow senators, "I resent my colleagues trying to impose on my children what my future income will be." Then, to make that 30 percent figure larger, senators voted 49–47 on June 17 to follow the House in raising their pay to $69,800 a year. Thus, lawmakers earning the full 30 percent in outside income would be able to somehow struggle along on $90,740 a year.

The health of the economy had improved measurably when the Senate boosted its pay in the summer of 1983, but unemployment was still at double-digit levels, 10.1 percent, the budget deficit was still growing rapidly, and many businesses and key industries in America were struggling to stay alive. Yet like the House only six months before, the Senate seemed grossly insensitive to all of this. By 1984, members of Congress had further boosted their pay to $72,600.

Of all the Congress's perks, none is more highly prized than its pension system, undoubtedly the most generous legislative pension system in the Western world.

No other pension in the legislative or executive branches of government, or in the private sector, fully vests its participants after a mere five years of employment as does Congress for its members. It is the luxury liner of government pensions. Nothing in the federal bureaucracy can beat it, except pensions granted to federal judges who receive 100 percent of their salary until their death.

According to officials within the Office of Personnel Management (OPM), the agency which administers all government pensions, 368 former members of Congress were getting pensions as of the end of 1982. The average monthly annuity is $2,900 — $34,800 a year. The average age of congressional retirees is seventy-two, but the average length of service is only 20.7 years. OPM officials say the congressional pension budget now totals $12.8 million a year. According to a study by the Taxpayers for Federal Pension Reform, 87 percent, or $11.1 million, of it is paid by taxpayers.

Members of Congress contribute only 8 percent of their salary to their pension annuity, which is calculated at 2.5 percent of their average pay times the number of years they served in Congress. Average pay is figured on a member's three highest years of pay, but the basic annuity may not exceed 80 percent of a member's final salary. Years of military duty or other federal service are also figured in.

Lawmakers who serve a minimum of eighteen years may begin receiving their pension as soon as they retire. Anything less requires that they wait until age sixty, five years before most Americans are eligible for social security. After ten years, for example, a retiree would receive about $15,155 annually when he reaches sixty. A member who puts in eighteen years of congressional service would immediately retire on $23,200 a year, while thirty-two years of service would yield a $48,530-a-year pension. These sums increase rapidly, however, as a result of cost of living increases granted twice each year.

Take the case of former Congressman Hastings Keith of Massachusetts who served fourteen years in the House, retiring in January 1973 on a congressional pension of $18,720. By March 1981, Keith's pension had risen to $41,151.57 a year. By 1984, his $46,488 pension exceeded the $42,500 a year he was paid when he left the House. In less than ten years it had more than doubled.

The case of former House Speaker Carl Albert of Oklahoma is an even more egregious example of Congress's excessive pension system. Just before he retired from the House in 1977, Albert was paid $63,500, $20,000 more than other House members because of his position as Speaker. Although he retired on an annual pension of $48,200, by 1980 Albert was, at the age of seventy-one, receiving

$63,600 a year in pension payments. This was due to a 31 percent increase in cost of living raises. By 1983, according to actuaries at OPM, Albert's pension was $80,960 a year — an astounding 70 percent increase over what he had been getting seven years earlier.

For many lawmakers still in their prime and far from true retirement, the pensions mean immediate income over and above the big money they begin earning in the private sector as lobbyists, lawyers and corporate executives. Consider those, for example, who lost reelection in 1980 while still in their fifties but who were eligible for pensions on the day they left Congress.

Among them were Congressman John Brademas of Indiana who, at fifty-three, was immediately pensioned at $32,350 a year; South Dakota's George McGovern, who was fifty-eight when he left the Senate on a pension of at least $38,232; and the late Senator Frank Church of Idaho who was only fifty-six when he lost reelection and entered private life on a pension of $35,291.

Others, such as Congressman Frank Thompson of New Jersey, who was convicted in the Abscam bribery scandal, began drawing a $38,232 pension at age sixty-two. Congressman Charles C. Diggs, Jr., of Michigan was only fifty-eight when he resigned his seat after conviction in a kickback scandal. Diggs immediately began receiving a yearly pension of $38,232 even while in jail.

In the real world, of course, private pensions pay a fixed annuity throughout one's retired life. Unlike the private sector, however, members of Congress, like all other federal retirees, have had their pensions adjusted upward twice a year to keep ahead of the cost of living as measured by the Consumer Price Index. Thus, as inflation raged through much of the 1970s, no one benefited more than members of Congress, whose unbridled spending policies steadily worsened inflation.

About half of all private sector workers in America are not, outside of social security, covered by any pension whatsoever. And most of those who are must work until age sixty-five before full retirement. Members of Congress could begin receiving their pensions as early as age forty-three, presuming they won election at age twenty-five.

Moreover, congressional pension payments are voluntary. Members may join the plan at any time. Thus, a member may, if he chooses, even after twenty years of service, kick in all of his back payments — noticeably, in cheaper dollars — and be fully vested in the plan. Few private pension plans allow retroactive participation.

Albert and Keith are not unique among congressional retirees who earn more in retirement than they did in Congress. OPM will not disclose the pension figures of former members of Congress, but OPM sources say many are doing better in retirement than when they were in Congress, thanks to an excessively generous pension system.

The National Taxpayers Union did some figuring on present and former members of Congress, comparing their pensions to what they would have received if they had held a top executive post with one of the Fortune 500 companies. Former Vice-President Walter Mondale, who served as senator from Minnesota for thirteen years, will be eligible for a congressional pension when he reaches the age of sixty in 1988. NTU figures Mondale will then be getting a pension of about $28,900 a year. Had he held a top executive post in one of the Fortune 500 companies, his pension would be only $5,781.

To carry the comparison still further, by the age of sixty-five, Mondale's private pension would rise to $12,263 because he would then be receiving social security. His congressional annuity, on the other hand, would jump to a hefty $36,905. This would eventually give the Minnesotan a lifetime income of $318,841 from the taxpayers versus $144,762 from a private sector pension combined with social security.

In addition to a generous pension, there are numerous other benefits that former members of Congress continue to receive, including low-cost life insurance and health plans. They also receive free mailing privileges for three months. And, if a member has developed a sentimental attachment to his desk, he may buy it from Congress for a lot less than it would cost him in the marketplace.

For years, if members had any money left over in their stationery allowance, they could take it in cash upon leaving office. Congress has ended that practice. But if members have any funds left over in their campaign treasuries, many of them can keep it for their personal use at retirement. Retirees used to pocket their unused campaign funds automatically until Congress passed a law in 1980 that ended the practice for anyone elected to Congress after 1980.

Former senators and representatives also continue to enjoy "floor privileges" after leaving Congress. Automatic access to the House and Senate floor is a valuable perk for the many lawmakers who become lobbyists. Of course, former members are legally forbidden from engaging in any lobbying while on the floor, but the access gives them enormous clout and the ability to obtain valuable information directly from lawmakers, which can be enormously useful in their well-paid lobbying ventures.

No one begrudges the men and women who serve in Congress fair compensation and benefits for the work they do as representatives of all Americans. Yet winding its way throughout this lengthy recitation of pay, perks, pensions and privileges is a disturbing thread of institutional selfishness and greed. Congress over many years has been on a spending binge to benefit itself far beyond what is reasonably justified by the highest lawmakers in the land. The totality of costly congressional perquisites is clearly excessive and unjustified under any rational standard of need.

"We have lost our way in the continuing business of defining the role of Congress," Senate GOP leader Howard Baker lectured his colleagues in June of 1983 during an acrimonious debate over the pay-raise bill. Lawmakers, Baker said, have "become elected bureaucrats" who have wrongly turned the job of legislating into a full-time occupation. And in the process of doing that, the emoluments and benefits and perks of Congress have become grotesquely swollen and largely unaccountable to anyone. The institutional excesses of Congress have taken on a life of their own, and no matter who is elected or swept out of office, the excesses have remained and grown worse.

5

The Last Plantation

"To do good is noble," Mark Twain once wrote. "To advise others to do good is also noble, and much less trouble." Congress has too frequently chosen to do the latter. Its legislative history has been one long unbroken legislative double standard. "Practice what you preach" is not a homily that Congress can honestly defend.

For nearly half a century Congress has been redressing America's most serious social and economic ills through major legislation that has resulted in difficult and sometimes turbulent social adjustments. Its prolific legal prescriptions have dealt with racial discrimination, unfair labor practices, worker health and safety, and the public's right to know how its government spends its money.

Yet throughout this historic legislative period, Congress has seen fit to exempt itself from virtually every piece of landmark legislation it has enacted. The laws, rules, regulations, decrees and other social criteria Congress has imposed upon every American stops right at the doors of the Capitol. Inside, virtually undisturbed by these laws, there exists what has been cynically yet accurately called "the last plantation."

"The days of *Gone With the Wind* have never passed from Capitol Hill," says *The Progressive* magazine.* "While Congress for forty years has been busy enacting 'social legislation' for the rest of us, it has taken care that none touched its own tidy world. . . . For everyone who works at the Capitol, Abraham Lincoln might as well be President."

Consider just a few of the far-reaching laws that Congress has righteously — and in most cases correctly — applied to every member of our society, save itself:

- The Civil Rights Act of 1964
- The Equal Employment Opportunity Act of 1972
- The National Labor Relations Act of 1935
- The Fair Labor Standards Act of 1938
- The Equal Pay Act of 1963
- The Occupational Safety and Health Act of 1970
- The Minimum Wage Law of 1938
- The Freedom of Information Act
- The Privacy Act
- The Age Discrimination in Employment Act

In each of these and other pieces of legislation, Congress has inserted language which exempts legislators and their offices from the antidiscrimination, collective bargaining, worker safety, overtime protection, and other social safeguards it has decreed to be the law of the land.

When, for example, Congress enacted the Civil Rights Act of 1964 and the Equal Employment Opportunity Act of 1972, it outlawed discriminatory hiring practices that had relegated minorities to the bottom rung of the economic ladder. But lawmakers did not include themselves in such laws, despite the fact that at that time they belonged to one of the most lily-white institutions in America, where discrimination was practiced with virtual impunity. Indeed, black congressional aides were almost unheard of at that time, except in the rarest of instances. Even as recently as 1978, a survey by the Black Legislative Assistants Staff Group, an ad hoc congressional employee group, could find only 33 blacks holding profes-

* Jeffrey Stein, "Yesterdays," *The Progressive*, August 1980.

sional staff positions among the more than 3,200 employees who comprised the personal office staffs of senators. At the same time, in the House a mere 7 percent of all jobs were held by blacks, mostly in clerical, restaurant and custodial positions.

A House study commission had determined in 1977 that blacks were often paid less than whites who possessed the same educational qualifications. Equally disturbing, a survey by *U.S. News & World Report* in March 1978 discovered that 27 out of the Senate's 100 members had no black employees in any position on their staffs. Five of these lawmakers represented states with sizable black constituencies. Bear in mind that this was nearly fifteen years after the passage of the most sweeping civil rights legislation ever enacted in the United States.

Incredibly, by 1983 the number of blacks holding nonclerical, professional staff positions has remained largely unchanged. According to the Senate Black Professional Staffers, another ad hoc Senate employee group, there were no more than 35 blacks holding professional staff positions among the more than 4,660 persons working on the personal and committee staffs of the Senate.

Minority employment practices in the House of Representatives are equally disgraceful. A 1983 survey I conducted showed that blacks held only 90, or 7.1 percent, of the 1,266 highest professional positions on the personal office staffs of House members — i.e., administrative assistant, legislative assistant, and press secretary. But a total of 44, or nearly 50 percent, of these aides worked for black members whose staffs are virtually all black. When just the non-black members who responded to my survey were counted, only 46 blacks were found occupying these three key positions — representing a bare 3.8 percent out of the 1,209 top staff positions available among the more than four hundred non-black House members I polled.

Soon after my survey in the House, the Washington bureau of Cox newspapers conducted a similar inquiry in the Senate. Its findings were equally shameful. Out of 870 employees holding professional positions on the personal staffs of senators — i.e., those earning more than $30,000 a year — Cox reporters Andrew Alexander and Larry Checco discovered that only twenty-seven, or a mere 3 percent, were black. When they polled the Senate's committees, they found only forty-eight blacks, or a scant 6 percent, occupying committee positions and only a tiny fraction of them were holding professional jobs.

To put Congress's shocking racial record into sharper perspective, one need only understand that blacks make up 66 percent of the workforce in Washington, D.C., and more than 10 percent of the workforce nationally. While blacks are much in evidence throughout Congress as janitors, waitresses, and cleaning women, and in other blue-collar positions, they are few and far between among professional positions on committee staffs or the personal Washington staffs of lawmakers.

Job discrimination in America? Why, it has been running rampant in Congress before, during and after the enactment of the landmark antidiscrimination laws of the 1960s and early 1970s. Yet few members of Congress will admit to what is being practiced within their own institution.

During the mid-1970s, a Joint Committee on Congressional Operations examined a sampling of employment requests from legislators. Their investigation uncovered forty-eight personal requests that were blatantly discriminatory. Among other things, the job orders specified "whites only," "no blacks," "no Catholics," "attractive," and "young." The committee ordered that such personnel practices be halted, but it also made sure that the identities of the bigoted and sexist violators of Congress's antidiscrimination laws were never revealed.

Have personnel hiring preferences changed since then? Not much. Says one black House employee, "They [members] are much more subtle and careful about who they hire, but blacks are still the exception in the top jobs."

During my survey, a receptionist remarked, "I don't know why you are going to all this trouble, I can tell you that blacks in responsible positions are few and far between." Said another House staffer, "Be very careful of the titles" given to minority staffers, which often overinflate their job duties, "because many of the positions are token."

Affirmative action programs? That may be fine for the rest of the country, but not for Congress. Members of Congress sincerely believe that laws to correct decades of racial discrimination are needed in the private sector, but not for themselves. "You have to know someone to get a job here," says a black House staffer to a Northwest congressman. "Like so much discrimination elsewhere, it's historical. Congress has never abided by its own antidiscrimination laws."

Similarly, the Equal Pay Act has resulted in hundreds of court cases in which major corporations have had to pay hundreds of millions of dollars in settlements to correct years of sex discrimination against women. Congress has never been bothered by such litigation, because it exempted itself from the act's strictures. Yet women have long been discriminated against by Congress in pay, hiring and promotion practices.

Studies during the mid-1970s by the Capitol Hill Women's Political Caucus revealed that the median pay for female congressional staffers was $22,000, while the median for men was $28,000 for almost identical work. At the same time, a House study commission reported that men earning $30,500 outnumbered women 35 to 1.

A more recent study in 1982 by Congresswoman Lynn Martin of Illinois showed that pay practices have not changed very much. When Martin examined House staffers who were paid $40,000 or more a year, she found that 77 percent of them were men and 23 percent were women. Among those on the other end of the pay scale earning less than $20,000, 79 percent were women, and only 21 percent were men.

During a testy debate in early 1983 over a $43.2 million money bill to fund committee staffs, Martin complained that a vote for the bill was "a vote for perpetuating sexism in our committee structure." She told her colleagues, "It is time for members of Congress, who so frequently talk of equality and equal opportunity, to match those words with a symbol that Congress will abide by those rules that it dictates for the rest of America."

The Capitol Hill Women's Political Caucus undertook another study of pay discrimination toward women in Congress in 1980. It found that women on the average earned 71 cents for every dollar men make. In the House, women's salaries average $15,989 versus

$21,745 for men's. The pay disparity was worse in the Senate where women averaged $16,192 a year compared to $24,160 for men. The study showed that women in the House earned an average of 73 cents for every dollar earned by men. In the Senate, women earned 67 cents for every dollar earned by males. By 1983, those pay discrepancies had not changed significantly.

Elsewhere, the Fair Labor Standards Act and the National Labor Relations Act require that businesses must pay their employees the minimum wage and overtime. It also gives them the right to organize labor unions and bargain collectively. But no such privileges exist within Congress for its workers. Cooks, waitresses, doorkeepers, elevator operators, policemen, press gallery attendants and other congressional staffers are required to work overtime without pay whenever Congress decides to work late.

Lawmakers often use their employees for a variety of personal chores outside their congressional responsibilities. House and Senate staffers are frequently asked to do everything from ghostwriting books as well as speeches for use on the lecture circuit; chauffeur the congressman to work, the airport, or about town; babysit, run errands and mow lawns; and even assist lawmakers with their private parties at home. For many employees, said one House staffer, "it is just part of the job," but with no additional pay.

There is no recourse to a higher power for those who feel they are due additional compensation for extra hours worked. There is no fair labor standard practiced here. Congress is the sole authority over its personnel.

How about the right to bargain collectively? The mostly black and Hispanic restaurant workers in the Capitol complex have long sought the right to unionize but powerful congressional leaders have denied them that freedom as effectively as Poland's communist leaders have denied recognition to Solidarity. Under the National Labor Relations Act, any employer who dared deny the right of workers to unionize would be held in contempt of court, fined, or perhaps even imprisoned, but not members of Congress.

Since its passage in 1970, the Occupational Safety and Health Act (OSHA) has certainly been one of Congress's most hated programs. Businesses have had to submit to unexpected inspections of their premises by OSHA agents, who have fined them for even the most minimal of safety infractions — from faulty electrical outlets to shaky stairway banisters to dirty restrooms. On the other hand, few lawmakers are willing to admit it, but many congressional offices could never pass an OSHA inspection. In many offices, employees are crammed in desk-to-desk, sometimes in offices with no windows. There are poorly lit hallways, in some cases dangerously torn carpeting on building stairways, and other infractions that pose serious dangers to worker safety. Once again, lawmakers need never worry about being punished for such infractions of the nation's occupational safety laws.

The list of exemptions is as long as it is scandalous. The Freedom of Information Act gives the public the right to examine most government records, documents and other data, except in specific areas dealing, for instance, with national security and personal privacy matters. Congress also passed the Privacy Act to insure that there are safeguards on the files government maintains on its citizens, even to the point of allowing individuals the right to examine their files and correct false information. Again, Congress has exempted itself from these laws, refusing public access to its files on people, businesses and organizations. It has also very often denied access to basic information about its most private practices as well as to the way it spends public funds in its own behalf. For example, reporters are forbidden from examining the congressional gymnasiums, or reviewing the substantive textual changes members make in their recorded remarks for the *Congressional Record.*

Social security was certainly one of the worst of Congress's double standards. When Congress voted in 1977 to impose $227 billion over the next ten years in new social security taxes on 110 million American workers and their employers, legislators took some comfort in the fact that they would not have to pay one dime of that tax. From the day the program was created in 1933, members of Congress and their employees were fully exempt from contributing to its support, but not from sharing in its benefits.

Widely condemned for this highly visible legislative exemption,

Congress stubbornly resisted demands that it integrate itself into social security until 1983 when new tax increases were enacted to save the system from impending bankruptcy. After years of ridicule and contempt for its two-faced position on social security, Congress finally agreed that lawmakers should also pay into the system, just as they compelled their constituents to do. On January 1, 1984, members began for the first time to contribute to the system — paying the maximum tax of $2,400 per member. However, if the truth be told, Congress didn't fully eliminate its exemptions. It was decided that all other congressional employees who were part of the congressional pension system as of December 31, 1983, would remain exempt from paying social security taxes — though they, too, will one day receive at least the minimum retirement benefit in addition to their lucrative congressional pensions. Thus, future increases in social security benefits and taxes, which congressional aides will help their legislators to write, understand and enact, will not affect most of the 30,000 congressional workers who are now grandfathered into this continuing exemption from the nation's second largest federal tax.

Congressional exemptions also extend to a broad range of other programs, regulations and regulatory agencies. For example, when Amtrak, the government rail passenger corporation, was established in 1970, Congress made sure the federally subsidized enterprise was exempt from the regulatory nightmare that lawmakers forced on private sector railroads. Congress allowed Amtrak to raise or lower its fares at will and change its routes without going before the ICC to plead its case in long-drawn-out proceedings. Fully aware of the costs of such regulation, lawmakers did not want the ICC impeding the operation of its experiment in nationalized rail service. In other words, what was good for the private sector's rail lines was not good for Congress's railroad. This regulatory double standard persists to this day.

Surely no better example of congressional prejudice exists than in the Federal Election Commission which Congress established in 1975 to regulate and monitor presidential and congressional campaigns. However, Congress made sure that when it comes to its own campaigns, the FEC was to stay out of its hair. FEC's history reveals that it has largely obeyed its narrowly drawn legislative mandate — generally avoiding any serious investigations into the campaign finances of congressional incumbents.

Congress's hypocrisy even extends to God.

In the early 1960s the Supreme Court banned organized prayer from our public schools. Many members of Congress defend the ruling and argue that prayer has no place in the schools because it violates the Constitution's separation of church and state. There have been proposals before Congress for a constitutional amendment to restore voluntary prayer to our schools, but for years they remained bottled up in the House and Senate Judiciary committees. Then in February and March of 1984 the Senate took up several school prayer amendments, none of which received the necessary two-thirds vote approval to be submitted to the states for consideration. In the House the bills remained unconsidered, never emerging from committee.

Nonetheless, at the beginning of each daily session of the House and the Senate, a prayer still is given by an official chaplain, as it has for nearly two hundred years. Somehow, the separation of church and state argument applies to our school kids but not to legislators. They are not at all bothered by the double standard of using taxpayers' money to hire full-time ministers of God to prepare and deliver a daily prayer for their souls. As each house opens for business, members dutifully stand beside their desks and chairs, much like schoolchildren once did, their heads devoutly bowed, their eyes closed, participating in Congress's daily ritual of prayer. "Lord God of Heaven and Earth, all powerful, all wise, knowing all things past, present, and future, we pray for Thy guidance in all Senate deliberations," Senate Chaplain Richard C. Halverson intoned before the Senate in a typical daily prayer. To prepare a prayer each day, the Senate pays Reverend Halverson $59,507 a year. His counterpart in the House, Reverend James David Ford, is paid $59,756.68. Both have secretarial support.

The words "Let us pray," which begin each day in Congress, would probably be enough to get a public school teacher fired.

Prayer in Congress, on the other hand, is not only practiced religiously (as it should be), but is fully and generously subsidized by the U.S. Treasury to the tune of over $142,700 a year.

Congress, in yet another double standard, prohibits federal officials who leave the executive branch from engaging in certain representational contacts with their former departments or agencies for a specific period of time. No such prohibition, however, is placed on former members of Congress. Many retirees become bigtime, well-paid lobbyists who are frequently seen buttonholing lawmakers in Capitol corridors, attending committee hearings, and fully exploiting their continued access to the House and Senate floor.

"It is hypocrisy at its very worst," says Senator Dennis DeConcini of Arizona, "when we in the Congress stand on the floor and orate about civil rights and equal opportunity employment at the same time we are not required to practice it ourselves. The double standard that runs through our government is deplorable. The time is long overdue that we put an end to this disparity and apply to ourselves the same laws we passed for the rest of the nation."

Since 1978, Senator Patrick J. Leahy has been pushing a bill, cosponsored by DeConcini, which would eliminate congressional exemptions from the government's major antidiscrimination and labor laws listed earlier in this chapter. Predictably, from the moment Leahy introduced his proposal, he encountered stiff, occasionally bitter opposition from his colleagues. Shortly after the then-freshman Vermonter had delivered a speech on the Senate floor which sharply criticized such congressional hypocrisy, he felt the sting of his colleagues' rebuke. In the Senate cloakroom, a southern senator asked Leahy, "Going home this weekend?" When Leahy indicated that he was, the senator acidly remarked, "Why don't you stay there?"

Yet Leahy's observations about Congress's disingenuous legislative deeds are deadly accurate in every respect. "This place is the last plantation in America," he told a near-empty chamber. "It is time that we in Congress begin to live by the same rules we have set for others. We should no longer allow such a double standard."

Unfortunately, the vast majority of Leahy's colleagues see no double standard at all. Many legislators insist that they cannot submit themselves to the same laws they enact for the rest of us because that would place their employment, pay and labor practices under the regulatory powers of the executive branch, thus endangering the constitutional separation of powers doctrine. Members of Congress insist that they must also remain flexible to operate and pay their personnel and hire their staffs as they deem best for their constituents and the orderly operation of Congress. There is a grain of merit to that argument. "But those special needs in no way justify congressional exemption from principles of fairness and equal opportunity," declared *The New Republic*.* "A Representative should not be able to claim *ex officio* immunity from charges of racism and sexism."

Sadly, the prospects of ending this congressional elitism do not appear bright. In 1976, Senators Lee Metcalf of Montana, Abraham Ribicoff of Connecticut and John Glenn of Ohio tried to implement some voluntary guidelines to remove the stain of hypocrisy from the Senate's legislating, only to run into unyielding opposition from Democratic leaders. Even when Massachusetts Senator Edward Brooke, then the Senate's only black member, tried again with a similar proposal in 1978, he was forced to withdraw the measure when faced with a threatened filibuster.

"America may have witnessed the demise of the Great Southern Plantation System, a social, political and economic way of life whose last vestiges disappeared with the Civil War," says Leahy. "But there is one last plantation that exists and flourishes today. This last plantation, sitting on the Hill in Washington, is the Congress which has shielded itself from the ravages of time and the effect of the laws it passes."

* "Unequal Opportunities," *The New Republic*, May 30, 1983.

6

Stop the Presses

WHAT Danford Sawyer uncovered inside the Government Printing Office, Congress's $633 million printing enterprise, came as a complete shock to the highly successful Florida businessman. After brushing away the agency's bureaucratic cobwebs and thumbing through its dusty ledgers, GPO's eighteenth Public Printer soon realized that he had inherited "one of the government's worst scandals."

Sawyer, a feisty entrepreneur with a background in cost accounting, had built a successful advertising and publishing business in Sarasota, Florida, before Ronald Reagan appointed him in the spring of 1981 to run GPO. After he had installed his own team of top managers and had scrutinized the agency's accounts, Sawyer quickly determined that taxpayers were being victimized by featherbedding, severe overtime abuses, unbelievable inefficiency, and what he called "unconscionable pay scales."

GPO has been around since 1860 when Congress established the agency to print its daily debates, hearings, reports, bills, and other documents. It also serves as the printer for most executive branch agencies, though 71 percent of GPO's work is contracted out to private printing firms.

Headquartered in an ugly nineteenth-century red brick building at the foot of Capitol Hill, GPO is one of those faceless, little-known agencies of Congress that you are not likely to hear much about, unless it is hit by scandal. Yet in this case, even the hot breath of scandal did not bring it much attention from the media.

An intense, dapper man with a flair for making waves and challenging prevailing orthodoxies, the forty-two-year-old Sawyer had no sooner arrived at his new job than he began a top-to-bottom reappraisal of GPO's seven printing plants, thirteen regional procurement offices, twenty-seven bookstores, and extensive warehouse facilities. What he uncovered shocked the socks off his private-sector beliefs. "GPO is overstaffed, overpriced, overpaid and terribly inefficient," he told his subordinates.

Sawyer discovered that GPO's bookstores, which sell a representative selection of the government's vast inventory of 250,000 different books and publications, were losing money, and receiving little if any supervision from the agency, and even less attention from Congress. Twenty of GPO's bookstores are scattered around the country and seventeen of them had already experienced a total loss of over a half-million dollars for fiscal year 1981. Overall, the twenty-seven bookstores showed a loss for the year of over $100,-000. When Sawyer examined their books, they revealed that most of the revenue came from the seven bookstores packed into the Washington, D.C. area and only 9 percent of GPO's total receipts of over $50 million for the entire publication sales program came from the bookstores.

Surveys further revealed that over 80 percent of the stores' customers were government agencies — federal, state and local. "The American public is not breaking down the door to get these publications," Sawyer said. "It is irrational and almost insane to believe that these stores are serving the general public." Earl Clements, deputy superintendent of documents and formerly director of the stores, bluntly says they were set up by Congress because "some senators thought it would be a feather in their cap" back home.

"We would be 50 percent better off without them." Despite all the evidence to the contrary, however, Congress has ordered Sawyer to keep the stores open.

Yet Sawyer discovered something much worse about the agency: its pay-scales. He found that GPO's journeymen printing and lithographic employees — whose average annual income was $27,-000 — were earning substantially more than their counterparts working elsewhere in the government, or in the private sector. GPO compositors, for instance, earned $14.35 an hour compared to $11.22 paid to compositors in commercial printing plants in the Washington, D.C. area. Offset pressmen earned $14.84 per hour versus $12.12 paid in the private sector; offset strippers, $14.84 versus $11.17. Overall, GPO printers earned an averge of $14.67 an hour compared to an average of $11.50 for the private printing industry nationwide.

Sawyer's figures were largely confirmed by a 1982 General Accounting Office audit that matched GPO wages in six occupations with comparable jobs elsewhere in the government. Comptroller General Charles Bowsher's report to Congress concluded, "GPO employees in all six occupational comparisons were paid more than their . . . counterparts."

The agency's printers unions, which represent about 3,400 workers out of GPO's 6,350 employees, do not of course think they are paid excessively more than their colleagues in the industry. Even in cases where they concede their pay levels are substantially higher, their argument is that they are worth it. "Would you pay the printers of a small-town paper the same as the printers at the *New York Times?*" Bill Boarman, president of the Columbia Typographical Union, GPO's biggest union, asked a reporter.

To finance its fat $163 million annual payroll, GPO has had to bill Congress and other executive branch agencies, i.e., the taxpayers, significantly higher printing rates than competitive commercial companies would charge. Sawyer found that GPO's printing prices were "up to twice what the private sector would charge."

If, as surveys showed, "there is always somebody out there willing to do the job" for substantially less than it costs the government, "why do we do anything in-house?" an incredulous Sawyer asked.

"Why do we burden ourselves with an operation that has a payroll of $160 million a year? Why do we pay the highest wages in the Western world for the classes of work done here?"

By law, GPO is the government's printer. But it processes — prints in-house or purchases commercially — only about a third of the $2 billion-plus in total annual government printing. As government grew over the years, the big departments and agencies demanded their own printing facilities, and Congress willingly granted them waivers to establish them independent to GPO.

There are about one thousand separate federal printing facilities scattered across the country. Collectively, they are costing taxpayers over $400 million a year.

A preliminary GAO examination of some of these facilities found that they are highly inefficient and that their unit printing costs were up to eight times those of GPO. Since GPO's in-house printing costs were up to twice what commercial printing shops charged, these plants were churning out printing that cost up to sixteen times that of commercial rates. An internal GPO memorandum said taxpayers were losing a minimum of $71 million a year on these facilities.

Sawyer's subsequent proposal for a fifty-state audit of these independent printing shops was summarily rejected by the Congress's Joint Committee on Printing (JCP), which wanted no part in opening this can of worms. When he continued to press for such a review the committee reluctantly agreed to allow only a pilot study of facilities within the New York City area. The report that followed this 1982 review did not surprise Sawyer. It recommended point blank that virtually all of the independent facilities be closed, suggesting that their work could be handled far more economically by the private sector through regional GPO offices. In spite of this, Congress has made no moves to eliminate or seriously curb these federal printing facilities around the country.

"What you've got here is one gigantic, reeking mess," said a high GPO official. "The JCP doesn't want to answer questions about why these plants are allowed to continue without rejustifying themselves."

Why such resistance from Congress? Many lawmakers benefit politically from the jobs these extra facilities bring to their states and districts, not to mention the subsequent political support they receive from the printers unions.

As he probed deeper into the agency, Sawyer also discovered a bureaucracy that was moving slowly, almost reluctantly, into the modern age. He had built his cost-efficient publishing business upon the latest in electronic photo composition technology. But as he roamed through GPO's thirty-six acres of printing plants, he discovered it was still using linotype machines and "still training people as monotype operators and castermen," which preserved outdated jobs and perpetuated featherbedding practices. He quickly moved to get rid of the last of GPO's linotype machines and other vestiges of a bygone era, completing a modernization process that had already begun. Yet featherbedding remains entrenched in the agency. GPO work rules, for example, still require that all printing be proofed by two proofreaders, even though the standard in the industry is single proofreading.

Wherever he looked, Sawyer and his team found inefficiency and waste — from dusty warehouses bulging with tons of unneeded and forgotten publications to the requirement that he print thousands of nebulous brochures, periodicals and other government literature on everything from bathrooms to flower gardens. "I don't want to sound like a revolutionary," Sawyer told a reporter in the spring of 1982, "but if the American taxpayers knew the kind of screwing they were getting in this operation, they'd all pick up a rifle and march on this place."

The blame for this mess rests with Congress's Joint Committee on Printing, GPO's legislative lord and master, and the twenty-two union bargaining units which represent the agency's employees. After reviewing the history of GPO's wage demands and the files of correspondence from the committee, it did not take Sawyer long to understand that GPO's typographical unions have pretty much gotten what they wanted over the years from JCP members who deeply meddled in the agency's labor affairs, almost always siding with the AFL-CIO unions. The unions, in turn, provided their allies on the committee with campaign worker support and financing.

In response to GPO's problems, Sawyer swiftly moved to curb

overtime, instituted a hiring freeze, cut the agency's printing rates, called for a series of furloughs to curb an excessive payroll — which accounts for over 75 percent of GPO's budget for work done in-house — and had the audacity to suggest that 800 to 2,000 employees could be dismissed without diminishing the agency's capabilities.

However, Sawyer's most controversial proposal was a three-year, 22 percent wage rollback that would save taxpayers $18 million a year. It would, he argued persuasively, bring GPO workers in line with their counterparts elsewhere in the bureaucracy. The unions, on the other hand, were demanding a preposterous 20.6 percent wage hike over two years in the midst of the 1981–82 recession. After months of wrangling between management, labor and Congress, the JCP ended up rejecting the unions' demands as well as Sawyer's counterproposal. Instead, the committee agreed in the fall of 1982 to a three-year contract for the unions which essentially amounted to cost-of-living increases that could not exceed 5 percent a year — a raise far more generous than most other trades were getting in the recession-racked economy. It was not, however, a total defeat for the GPO administrator. Had Sawyer not made the public stink that he did on wages, it is very likely that the committee would have given GPO workers much more of what they demanded.

In the end, despite GPO's revealing pay comparisons and GAO's wage audits, the JCP stubbornly refused to accept Sawyer's claims of excessive pay at GPO. It took six House and Senate lawmakers, only two of whom were members of the JCP, to request independently that the GAO thoroughly evaluate GPO's pay-scales and report back to Congress.

When the watchdog agency came forth with its report in the summer of 1983, even Sawyer was stunned by its contents. Incredibly, the GAO found that the wage levels at the agency were even worse than Sawyer had charged.

The carefully prepared 58-page audit submitted to the Joint Committee on Printing was not the sort of document that produces banner newspaper headlines, or that makes the evening TV news, though it should be. It conclusively showed that wages for GPO workers were sharply higher than those of their professional counterparts in other federal agencies and within the commercial sector. In short, GAO found that "The average wage difference between GPO employees and their federal counterparts for calendar year 1982 came to 42 percent, or $8,410."

When GAO auditors compared twenty-one different job classifications, they found that GPO workers were being paid from $3,222 to a staggering $17,879 a year more — representing from 18 percent to 143 percent more — than workers doing similar jobs in other government agencies. In hourly wages, this means GPO printers overall were paid between $1.55 to $8.59 an hour more than their federal counterparts doing virtually identical work.

The most alarming salary difference existed among compositors, or typesetters, which is GPO's largest craft. GAO auditors said they were "one of the most highly paid groups" they found, "receiving 58 percent more than their federal counterparts."

When GAO compared what GPO printers were paid to their private-sector counterparts, the study showed the printers earned up to $5.15 an hour more "than private sector employees doing similar work."

This scandalous pay disparity has come about as a result of years of congressional submission to GPO's labor union demands. The agency is the only one in the legislative branch that allows blue-collar-worker pay to be set through the collective bargaining process. Elsewhere throughout the government, the pay-setting process is geared to making federal salaries comparable with prevailing private-sector wages. But at GPO there is a huge loophole in the Keiss Act, which gives the agency's unions their bargaining authority. It neglects to say a word about salary levels being comparable to anything. Its vague criterion for setting GPO pay-scales is that wages must be "in the interest of government and just to the persons employed."

Thus, over the years Congress's Joint Committee on Printing, whose members have betrayed a conspicuous bias toward organized labor, has been notoriously generous in handing out tax dollars in wage settlements. When, for example, GPO managers flatly offered a 5.5 percent pay-hike in 1979, the JCP merrily substituted a 7 percent across-the-board pay increase. Between 1973 and 1982, in fact, GPO's cumulative pay-increases have ranged from 112 to 131 percent. Pay-raises for all other government blue-collar workers during this time ranged from 93 to 120 percent. Pay-raises for federal white-collar workers increased by only 75 percent.

All of this has produced a bloated payroll for GPO workers, a payroll that bears no relation to wages in the real world and one that Congress shows no intention of cutting.

While Sawyer made significant reforms at GPO, dragging a reluctant Congress kicking and screaming all the way, substantial institutional problems and spending excesses remain. Thus far, unfortunately, lawmakers have stubbornly resisted the best solution to GPO's problems: give the Public Printer the authority to manage GPO on a businesslike, cost-benefit basis, including responsibility for all labor contract negotiations. This would mean eliminating the JCP as well. Further reforms must also include curbing the government's vast printing empire by allowing private printers, through competitive bidding, to provide the bulk of the government's printing needs. Greater contracting out, say GPO officials, could save taxpayers an estimated $100 million a year in lower printing costs.

"What we have here is a blank check on the U.S. Treasury," Sawyer said in 1982 in the midst of his battle with Congress to control GPO's spending excesses. Many of these excesses continue at GPO and a nationwide housecleaning of Congress's costly printing empire is long overdue. But thus far lawmakers have shown no signs that they intend significantly to reform this antiquated, costly and largely unnecessary legislative branch agency.

7

Controlling Congress

Name any government scandal, any bureaucratic outrage or excess, and its origins can with unerring accuracy and predictable consistency be traced to the doorstep of Congress.

Each wasted dollar, each nebulous or questionable program, each excessive expenditure, each needless regulation, each fraud or abuse, each counterproductive law is the result of the acts or negligence of Congress. Though its members may indignantly criticize government officials and bureaucrats for every scandal that seeps to the surface, it is Congress, in one way or another, that has allowed each scandal to germinate, grow, and bear its bitter fruit. Its members may hurl accusations and charges at everyone but themselves, but Congress must ultimately bear the blame.

The statistics tell part of the story of this flabby institution's enormous size and rapid growth: its yearly administrative budget took ten years, from 1968 to 1978, to climb from $282 million to $1 billion. It took only half that time for the legislative branch budget to leapfrog to $1.5 billion by 1983.

Now, $1.5 billion may not seem like much money when you consider that it must finance an institution entrusted with the oversight of a budget of nearly $1 trillion a year. Still, Congress's growth has been remarkable. "In the years between 1946 and 1981, legislative branch appropriations increased 2,279 percent," according to *Vital Statistics on Congress*, 1982, published by the American Enterprise Institute (AEI), a Washington think tank. Yet, "Over the same period, the Consumer Price Index went up 'only' 366 percent. As recently as the mid-1960s, the cost of operating Congress was less than one-fifth what it is today."

In staff size alone, Congress is the biggest legislative branch in the world. A payroll of nearly thirty-one thousand employees makes it bigger than the Departments of Housing and Urban Development, State, and Labor combined. The personal staffs of senators have grown sixfold during the last four decades, while personal House staffs have grown fivefold. There are over eleven thousand men and women on the personal staffs of our senators and representatives, and over three thousand employees staffing the House and Senate committees. In comparison, Canada's parliament is the world's second largest legislative body, with a total staff of only thirty-five hundred.

Significantly, the sharpest growth among congressional staffs has been at the state and district level, where lawmakers have deliberately invested an increasing share of their resources in order to maintain the daily constituent contact and service that translates into political support on election day. "More than one-third of the personal staffs of representatives and one-quarter of those of the senators now work in district or state offices," AEI's congressional analysis finds.

Yet such numbers, remarkable as they are, reveal only a part of what has happened to Congress. They tell us something about Congress's excesses, but not about what Congress has become in an institutional sense — how its members have wandered far from what they were meant to be as representatives of the people.

During a long and at times acrimonious debate over senatorial pay in June of 1983, Senate Majority Leader Howard H. Baker, Jr., got up to make some off-the-cuff remarks. It was a speech born of some frustration, one he had given before, usually when the bickering among colleagues over one issue or another got too much for him to take any longer. Yet this time Baker's remarks carried an eloquence and an inner conviction that gave renewed strength and deeper meaning to his thoughts. And though he spoke to his colleagues in the Senate, he was really speaking to all of Congress, and to the people, about institutional excesses, how Congress had lost its moorings, its constitutional focus, and its sense of purpose; about how the public's servants had lost touch with their employers; how Congress had been turned into something America's founders had never envisioned.

"I wonder sometimes how we lost our way in the continuing business of defining the role of Congress," the Tennessee Republican said. "For I am sure that the Founding Fathers never intended us to be what we are today — an aggregation of senators elected by popular vote, committed full-time to the legislative undertaking in the federal city, returning to our homes for periodic visits on weekends. . . . We have become elected bureaucrats."

The Founding Fathers gave us a government in which Congress was to be, in a sense, the nation's board of directors, charting overall programs and policies, he said. Congress would "set the general policies of the government in the name of the people . . . to [transmit] those policies to the executive department; with all of these activities to be monitored by the court. . . .

"But for the life of me," Baker continued in his extemporaneous remarks, "I cannot see any place in the Constitution or the early documents of the republic where it says Congress was supposed to compete with the bureaucracy in the detailed daily nitty-gritty of governing this country."

Congress has become so preoccupied with the bureaucratic minutiae of government, so involved in a continuing attempt to micro-manage each and every activity, Baker said, that lawmakers have "lost our self-image of the policy-setting people's branch of government." In most cases, of course, such congressional meddling has nothing to do with improving efficiency or saving tax dollars, but instead usually seeks to protect special interests, pay off special constituencies and to spend more money.

There was a time when Congress was not a body of full-time bureaucrats but an "aggregation of lawyers and doctors and farmers and architects," Baker told the few senators present in the near-empty chamber. He would like to see that system restored, he said. "I would like to see us once again immersed in the business of our country so that we understand what it is about and what we are legislating about."

When he walked onto the Senate floor, he happened to pick up one of the pending bills on his desk, a supplemental appropriations measure. It was 125 pages long and half an inch thick. He was sure, he said, that there were "not more than ten members of the Senate who have read it all the way through, and I do not blame them.

"I saw one once that was 1,200 pages," Baker continued. "It appears like the product of a bunch of anonymous bureaucrats instead of elected senators. It sounds like we do not know what we are supposed to be doing, and we do not."

He remembered the days when his father, Howard H. Baker, first went to Congress as a representative, taking the overnight train from Tennessee and staying in Washington until late in the spring when he would return home to learn what was on the people's minds, lugging two trunks full of files to work on while he attended to other business. "He never thought about moving his family permanently to Washington or giving up his home in Tennessee," said Baker. "For that matter, he never thought about giving up his profession or his business or his civic enterprises and interests. He was a Tennessean, temporarily in Washington to speak for the people of his congressional district."

Times have changed, it is said, and so have Congress and the way its members go about the business of lawmaking, which has needlessly been turned into a well-paid, full-time occupation. After Baker was elected to the Senate in 1966 he flew to Washington in a jet and took his family with him to set up a permanent residence in the nation's capital. He flew home the following weekend, and continued to go home almost every weekend, to keep in touch with constituents. Yet by his own admission such weekends were nothing more than "a hurried grazing pass at the people of my state, masquerading in the guise of a man trying to find out what is going on.

And who in the world can find out what is going on in the people's minds on a Saturday or Sunday when people would rather not be talking to politicians to begin with?"

The problems of Congress represent something much larger than the sum of its bloated and disorganized parts. It is an institution that is as out of control as the bureaucracy over which it pretends to exercise oversight and fiscal authority. And at the very core of Congress's problems, as Baker so intuitively and accurately points out, are its members who have become "permanent full-time employes of the federal government" — seeking always to feed and fatten a bureaucracy that has outgrown the capacity of Congress to control it.

How do we pull ourselves out of this legislative morass into which Congress has become almost hopelessly mired? One way, says Baker, "is to redefine our role. And our role is to represent the people on major policy decisions and to transmit those judgments on policy to the executive department to execute.

"This is why," he thinks, "the answer is not more money but less money. That is why I think we ought to be in session not twelve months out of the year but six or seven months. . . . That is why I think there ought to be a positive disincentive for the Senate to stay around instead of an incentive for us to do so."

This is a part of the commonsense answer to restoring Congress to its rightful, limited role as chief architect and overseer of the government. But it does not begin to reexert legislative control over an undisciplined government that clearly remains out of control.

While the problems I have recounted in these preceding chapters expose some monumental failures on the part of Congress to fulfill its constitutional and political responsibilities, they also pose an extraordinary opportunity for change. Congress has the means to tame and harness the Leviathan it has created, to restore fiscal order to government, and to implement a new set of federal spending priorities. But to achieve this, Congress must undergo some radical alterations of its own.

Not long before she left Congress to pursue a career in higher education, the articulate and always thought-provoking Barbara Jordan of Texas told me she did not believe the country needed "any more new programs or new laws. The challenge before the Congress is to make the programs we already have work." That is a very large order but not an impossible one. There are a number of reforms that can be instituted to achieve it.

First, Congress should formally declare a four-year moratorium on any new legislation, except in cases of national emergency.

Such a declaration, set forth in a joint resolution of Congress, would be accompanied by a clear directive for both houses to begin a thorough reassessment and evaluation of the entire federal budget — from the Interstate Commerce Commission to the Department of Education, from National Public Radio to the Bureau of Indian Affairs. During this reevaluation period, every federal agency and program would either have to be reauthorized or go out of business.

Second, in order to be able to undertake this unprecedented inventory and review, Congress's committee system must be completely revamped. Such restructuring would require consolidating the present tangled mess of committees and subcommittees into an orderly and limited number of authorization panels that would be able to deal with each department and agency of government efficiently and effectively.

Third, selected auditors within the executive branch departments and agencies would be detailed during this period to their respective oversight committees. Moreover, each committee would be given complete access to all internal agency audits and reports within their jurisdiction.

Fourth, key General Accounting Office auditors assigned to each department and agency would be temporarily reassigned to work with their respective committees.

Fifth, each legislative review would include a thorough reconsideration of every neglected management reform and money-saving recommendation made by GAO and internal auditors over the past ten years, and require that each legitimate recommendation be specifically mandated by law.

Sixth, each budget-savings recommendation made by the President's Private Sector Survey on Cost Control would also be considered in each reauthorization and appropriation measure approved during this housecleaning period, and each proposal would be voted up or down by recorded vote.

Seventh, House and Senate authorization committees would be required to conduct joint hearings and investigations, and to report jointly their findings and legislative recommendations to their respective houses of Congress for action.

Finally, each authorization bill and accompanying appropriations measure would be promptly reported to both houses of Congress for floor action and disposed of by recorded roll call vote.

This, admittedly, is a large order, and obviously a revolutionary one for a Congress satisfied with the status quo, content simply to change expiration dates and add several new zeros to a program's budget authorization. Yet it is one that would win the overwhelming endorsement of the American people. For Congress would be putting the people's house in order. As things stand now, it is very much in disarray.

Before Ronald Reagan took office he assembled an army of transition teams to examine every major department, agency and program of government and recommend policy reforms to his incoming administration. In most instances, perhaps because their reports were to be kept private, these study teams produced some surprisingly thorough and refreshingly uncompromising recommendations for budget savings, management reforms and other procedural overhauls. Many who worked on or headed these teams ended up being appointed to run the programs they had studied. Unfortunately, many, upon appointment, promptly proceeded to ignore some of their own recommendations.

Nevertheless, a number of transition team leaders today wonder why Congress cannot do exactly what they had done in so short a period — but do it more thoroughly; that is, take a fresh look at each program, evaluate its performance, its management, its accounts, its personnel structure, and its efficiencies and deficiencies, and then determine whether or not that program should be restructured, reduced, consolidated or simply abolished.

"When you think of the resources that Congress has, the thousands of staff people, they could do what we did," one former transition team leader said. "But Congress could do it much more effectively and thoroughly, because they've got the subpoena power, the authority to have hearings under oath, and, of course, all of its manpower resources, which we did not have."

The Fortune 500 corporate executives who served on President Reagan's Private Sector Survey on Cost Control in 1983 did much the same thing — only more thoroughly in many respects — and came up with a staggering $424 billion in potential budget cuts and savings that could be achieved over three years. Working under the direction of businessman J. Peter Grace, more than two thousand corporate executive officers and assorted experts fanned out across the government and produced a monumental study that put Congress to shame. The ambitious management-spending survey, bankrolled by $75 million in materials, equipment and personnel from major corporations, produced forty-seven thick, richly detailed reports, backed up by dozens of appendixes, which in turn were supported by over one million pages in raw "work papers" compiled by Grace's investigators. Yet Grace's private-sector strike force, which included some of the sharpest business minds in America, only scratched the surface of government. "We only uncovered the tip of the iceberg," confessed Grace's task force director and right-hand man, J. P. Bolduc. Even so, they left behind a massive documentation of stunning disclosures and mind-boggling spending scandals and a lucrative blueprint for reform.

In the final analysis, however, Congress must decide whether it wants to spend the time doing something "which isn't very glamorous, and which involves a lot of hard, tedious, detailed work," as one House Appropriations Committee aide put it. Contrary to the conventional wisdom, the political rewards for such an undertaking could be very great indeed. For the party that seriously takes up the banner of congressional oversight and effectively leads a crusade for change and spending reform is the party that will dominate Congress and our government for many years to come.

BOOK II

*T*HE *BUREAUCRACY*

8

The Persecution of George Spanton

GEORGE Spanton, a wiry, white-haired, sixty-two-year-old accountant with a whiz-kid knack for figures, blew the whistle on a multibillion-dollar Pentagon scandal, and soon found himself running a gauntlet of bureaucratic harassment, threats and intimidation. His story is both a profile in unyielding integrity and an anatomy of the way the defense system can punish those who dare to challenge it. It is a story virtually ignored by the major news media.

Spanton was nearing retirement in 1983, after thirty years as an auditor with the Defense Department, sixteen of them in the Defense Contract Audit Agency (DCAA). During those years he had seen many of his colleagues either leave public service as a result of pressure from superiors or simply remain silent about what they had seen. "There's a certain amount of risk a manager has to take in this kind of job to do it right," he says with characteristic daring.

His last assignment was as DCAA branch chief at West Palm Beach, Florida where he was the resident auditor at the Government Products Division of Pratt & Whitney Aircraft, the nation's major producer of military aircraft engines. Yet unlike many of his

Pentagon colleagues, Spanton was not looking for a fat job with a big defense contractor. An avid fisherman, the soft-spoken, self-effacing auditor was simply looking forward to spending a quiet pensioned life of leisure in sunny Florida.

But his plans were suddenly placed in jeopardy in March 1981 as a result of a routine wage-rate audit he conducted at the huge aircraft engine division of United Technologies Corporation. What he discovered made his blood boil. The company had built huge pay increases into its defense contract costs for its workers, increases that exceeded wages paid for comparable work performed anywhere in the economy.

Over a three-year period, he found, the company's raises would boost wages 178 percent higher than estimated increases planned for federal workers and 108 percent higher than estimated pay-raise levels for private industry.

In a confidential, hard-hitting, fifteen-page audit stamped "For Official Use Only," the result of an investigation he had begun in October 1981, Spanton laid out his findings. He did not try to soften his conclusions with the cold, clinical language usually used by government auditors. On the contrary, he flatly pointed out that Pratt & Whitney had "proposed over $150 million of excess labor costs" in wage contracts running from 1981 through 1984. He charged that these pay increases were "extreme, damaging to the economy and ureasonable.

"This unwarranted waste of public funds . . . which fuels inflation and contributes to government deficits, must be challenged now by the government acquisition community," he told his superiors.

Spanton recommended that the pay-raises — from 15 to 20 percent — "be scaled down to insure that [the contractor] becomes fully responsive to both government and public expectations rather than a driver of inflation in our economy."

Moreover, he believed, but could not prove, that the scandal he had uncovered went far beyond this single defense contractor.

He urged that a national wage-rate audit be conducted of all defense contracts. "I felt that what I had seen at Pratt was probably the tip of the proverbial iceberg," he later said. "Nationwide, we are talking about billions of dollars in waste that nobody is really cracking down on."

"Based on the statistics that we see," Spanton told a reporter, "the average machinists, draftsmen, engineers and other defense contract employees are being paid far in excess of what they would earn for doing the same work elsewhere in government or private industry."

Spanton, however, was not the only one outraged by his findings. In a personally written internal memorandum, Air Force Secretary Verne Orr also complained that it was "absolutely ludicrous to expect" federal employees and retirees to submit to pay and pension curbs "while at the same time, through our contracts, we pay substantially larger increases to labor forces building our weapon systems."

Spanton's charges of excessive pay-scales were eventually proven true. A separate Defense Department study reported to Secretary Orr that Pratt & Whitney had proposed wage increases of more than 25 percent for 1983 alone. In comparison, President Reagan's fiscal 1983 budget requests sought to hold federal civil service employees to a modest 4 percent pay increase.

Spanton's March 1982 audit was preceded one month earlier by another report. This time, he alleged that Pratt & Whitney had possibly violated DOD's standards of conduct by running up more than $150,000 in improper travel and entertainment expenses, including a series of parties and dinners attended by some of the Pentagon's top brass. Company officials resisted Spanton's requests for access to some of their accounts during his investigation. However, he managed to obtain a list of people who were entertained by the company, including trips to the Paris Air Show, and even to a massage parlor. And he produced vouchers that indicated Pratt & Whitney had apparently charged these and other entertainment expenses to the taxpayers. The Pentagon never made Spanton's findings public, but his audit resulted in an FBI investigation that in turn led to a federal grand jury inquiry.

Now, any reasonable person would expect Pentagon officials to follow up immediately on Spanton's findings. On the contrary, the

99

career bureaucrat's discoveries triggered a furious campaign by his superiors to discredit and harass him and nearly cost him his job.

Spanton had pierced the veil surrounding the cozy relationships between defense contractors and military procurement officials. He had disturbed the business-as-usual atmosphere between the government and the defense industry — somewhat akin to threatening a nine-hundred-pound gorilla — and it was not long before the military-industrial complex became very angry and began to retaliate in all its fury.

For one thing, Spanton's wage audit was clearly unpopular with his superiors in the DCAA's Atlanta regional office and at headquarters in Washington. Charles O. Starrett, Jr., director of the DCAA's staff of three thousand auditors, did not exactly leap into action when he saw Spanton's report. In fact, DCAA did not begin a major investigation into defense labor pay-scales until actually ordered to do so in August 1982 by Secretary Orr. Nor did DCAA shift into high gear immediately after Spanton's report on Pratt & Whitney's entertainment expenses. DCAA waited until seven months after he made his accusations.

Spanton had submitted his report alleging improper travel and entertainment of government officials, on February 11, 1982. But instead of investigating the charges, the Defense Criminal Investigative Service (DCIS), now the department's Office of Inspector General, began investigating Spanton! Vague allegations were raised against him, one of which suggested that he was getting "too close" to Pratt & Whitney, but no evidence was found to substantiate any of them. It was during the course of this inquiry that the DCIS investigator asked Spanton what he thought should be looked into. Spanton obligingly produced his February 11 report, pointing out that his allegations against Pratt & Whitney were being ignored. The DCIS looked into the audit's findings, and ended up turning its evidence over to the Federal Bureau of Investigation on October 13 for further investigation, which led to a grand jury inquiry.

Actually, since 1980 Spanton had been subjected to persistent pressures from superiors to retire, having on more than one occasion angered Pratt & Whitney and DCAA officials with his aggressive auditing. Indeed, regional DCAA officials at one point "threatened that if Spanton did not retire he would find himself in difficulty with headquarters," according to a Merit Systems Protection Board memorandum. At one point, in August 1980, Spanton submitted a request for retirement, but later, on further reflection, withdrew it.

The harassment of George Spanton also extended to his official performance rating. Though he was graded satisfactory and higher on all DCAA performance standards, in the summer of 1981 his superiors unexpectedly ranked him near the bottom of the list. In previous ratings, Spanton had always been ranked among the southern region's top auditors. By early September 1982, however, more than five months after his wage-rate audit of Pratt & Whitney, superiors again ranked him among the bottom three of DCAA's twenty-one auditors in the region.

Moreover, on May 11, 1982, two months after he had submitted his controversial pay-scale audit, Spanton was suddenly told by James R. Brown, Starrett's chief deputy, that he was to be transferred to the Los Angeles region. Spanton immediately asked that his five-year tour of duty be extended at West Palm Beach, which the department's rules allow in cases of employees nearing retirement or engaged in an investigation. But Brown denied the request even though Spanton was due to retire the following December and the regulations specify that auditors be reassigned every five to seven years. Through it all, his superiors made no attempt to hide their displeasure over Spanton's attempts to challenge his managers over his unfair performance ratings, among other complaints.

Nor were they happy when the startling findings of Spanton's audits, along with the news of his abrupt transfer order to the West Coast, resulted in a string of blistering articles by veteran investigative reporter Clark Mollenhoff in the *Washington Times* — though the story was virtually ignored by the major national news media.

Why the unexpected transfer? Starrett admitted to Spanton that the main reason behind his reassignment was Pratt & Whitney. "The contractor has voiced an intention not to provide certain data to you, although it will provide the data to your superiors," he wrote to Spanton. "This would impede your effectiveness as a resident auditor since you are responsible for all the audits performed at that office. . . .

"In order for this agency to perform its mission in the most efficient manner, it is essential that all our FOA [field audit office] chiefs maintain a professional rapport with contractors," Starrett's justification concluded. What the Pentagon's chief auditor seemed to be saying was that the Pentagon does not want auditors to make defense contractors angry by uncovering unpleasant things they are doing with the taxpayers' money, by holding them rigidly accountable for their contract performance and practices. It is much more important, apparently, to "maintain a professional," i.e., agreeable, "rapport with contractors," according to this way of thinking.

On March 10, 1983, after efforts to negotiate Spanton's complaints failed, Starrett flatly rejected his renewed request that the mandatory five-year rotation be waived because his retirement was coming up within a matter of months.

As events turned out, Spanton's job was saved mainly by one K. William O'Connor, special counsel to the U.S. Merit Systems Protection Board, a federal agency not previously known for its aggressive defense of whistle-blowers. In this case, O'Connor and his team of investigators, spearheaded by Delbert R. Terrill, Jr., and Richard Gordon, did a superlative job — digging into Spanton's accusations soon after the beleaguered auditor had filed a complaint charging that he was being punished merely for doing his job.

After a thorough investigation, O'Connor concluded that Starrett and other top DCAA officials had engaged in a "pattern of discrimination and harassment" against Spanton.

In a bluntly worded sixteen-page letter to Defense Secretary Caspar Weinberger, O'Connor said the Pentagon's chief auditor had relied upon "half-truths," assertions that were contradicted by the evidence, and had violated federal employee discrimination statutes by demonstrating "a pattern of harassment against Spanton."

The justifications used by Starrett and his subordinates to support his harsh reprisals against Spanton, O'Connor found, "either seriously misstate the facts or rely on questionable or biased reports."

For example, when he demanded Spanton's transfer, Starrett had argued that the move would not interfere in any way with the grand jury and FBI probe into Pratt & Whitney. He further insisted that the move had been cleared with government investigators in charge of the grand jury inquiry. "In fact," said O'Connor, "the FBI agent involved [in the investigation] told DCAA that he personally preferred that Spanton not be moved."

Moreover, O'Connor reported, a top Defense investigator warned "his superiors that removal or reassignment of Spanton at this time would have a chilling effect on the cooperation of other DCAA audit staff and therefore on the investigation as a whole."

Since it is DCAA's policy to move its auditors around every five to seven years, Starrett turned down Spanton's request for a waiver of rotation, insisting that this was standard operating procedure. However, O'Connor argued that Spanton's reassignment would involve a "permanent change of station." A survey of DCAA regional offices, he said, "shows that DCAA generally grants waivers from such rotation, particularly when the auditor plans to retire within one year of his rotation date."

O'Connor concluded that Spanton had been the victim of "bias and harassment," and he recommended that Weinberger "direct DCAA officials to cease their pattern of discrimination and harassment of Spanton."

He further urged the secretary to "inform Starrett, in writing, that it is a prohibited personnel practice to take a personnel action in reprisal for an employee's protected activity, and direct Starrett to so advise other DCAA managers."

Were Defense officials embarrassed by O'Connor's harsh reprimand over what they had attempted to do to an honest and conscientious public servant? Not in the least. In fact, a top aide to Weinberger generously praised Starrett's handling of the Spanton affair. Nevertheless, Assistant Defense Secretary Vincent Puritano, the Pentagon's comptroller, conceded in a letter to Starrett on April 29, 1983, that "continuation of the controversy surrounding the rotational reassignment of Mr. Spanton is not in the best interest of the Department of Defense."

With Spanton expected to retire from the agency in a matter of months, Puritano said in a classic bit of understatement, the proposed reassignment was "becoming increasingly less cost-effective."

While avoiding any reference to O'Connor's findings that Spanton had been the victim of an internal campaign of persecution, Puritano blandly asked Starrett merely to "remind your managers that it is a prohibited personnel practice to take a personnel action in reprisal for an employee's protected activity," thus passing on O'Connor's directive word for word, without further embellishment.

As for the shameful way Starrett had treated one of his agency's best auditors, Puritano gently assured Starrett that he had "the highest regard for the quality of work performed by the Defense Contract Audit Agency and am confident that, under your leadership, the auditors will continue as they have in the past to look carefully at all claims and question any they feel should be questioned."

Yet one wonders to what lengths will other DCAA auditors challenge sensitive and potentially controversial defense practices after what had happened to one of their own colleagues? Puritano's "confidence" to the contrary, how aggressively will defense auditors question the questionable after witnessing George Spanton's harrowing escape from exile?

Spanton's audit, as it turned out, eventually forced negotiations between the air force and Pratt & Whitney on its proposed payscales, and a partial settlement was achieved that reduced hourly wage increases for production workers. Similar negotiated reductions were achieved among at least two other defense aircraft contractors.

Charles Starrett did eventually initiate a survey of air force contractors. One survey found the average wages at seventeen major aerospace companies were "greater than the average wage paid the same area for similar services" — nearly $2 per hour greater. The average aerospace worker was earning over $11 an hour. Still, there was no department-wide examination to find out the degree to which the abuses Spanton uncovered existed throughout the Pentagon's nearly $90-billion-a-year procurement business.

Little has changed for the better in the way defense programs and services are audited. Despite an army of three thousand auditors, the DCAA has not been terribly effective in slashing wasteful military spending. Its visceral weaknesses were perhaps most vividly revealed by the Better Government Association (BGA), a private, public-interest organization set up to examine and expose wasteful government spending, during its investigation into defense contracts in the Pascagoula, Mississippi, naval shipyards. A BGA report noted that "Although $46 billion in naval contracts are budgeted each year, and DCAA annually conducts about 60,000 pre- and-post award audits, between 1978 and 1982 an average of only 36 cases per year were referred to investigative agencies."

George Spanton's story is in many ways a metaphor for what is wrong with the way the Pentagon spends our money and what happens to those who sharply challenge contract practices which continue to waste billions of tax dollars.

Spanton was not only scrupulously correct in his findings. He exposed a deeply ingrained complacency within the Pentagon, showing that program-wide practices, when uncovered, get swallowed up by a bureaucracy that resists change and will go to great lengths to protect itself and the special interests it serves.

Curiously, Spanton's name did get some attention at the highest level of government and it helped him at a time he needed it most. Senator Charles Grassley of Iowa, a member of the Senate Budget Committee, raised Spanton's case during a White House meeting on April 5, 1983, with President Reagan, Secretary Weinberger, and members of the committee. The senators were trying desperately to reach a consensus with the administration on the fiscal 1984 defense budget. It was during this two-hour meeting that Grassley unexpectedly brought up the case of George Spanton.

"If you are really going after defense waste," an irritated and unconvinced Grassley blurted out, "why are you treating George Spanton this way?" Reagan, who undoubtedly did not have even an inkling of what the Spanton case was all about, said nothing. But according to Grassley, "Weinberger replied, 'Well, if that's all it will take to make you happy, I'm sure we can make arrangements to leave him where he is.'"

Later that month the order sped through the Pentagon's chain of command, from Weinberger to Puritano to Starrett: Keep Spanton where he is.

A still-angry O'Connor, however, wasn't through with the Spanton case. In late August of 1983 he issued a second report that demanded disciplinary action against those who had mistreated Spanton, including Starrett, Deputy DCAA Director James Brown, Regional Director Paul Evans, and Regional Audit Manager Arlin R. Tueller. Said O'Connor in an eleven-page complaint, "I have determined that [these men] violated civil service laws in their treatment of Mr. Spanton.

"The job of an auditor is to root out problems within government," O'Connor said, adding that "Mr. Spanton did his job and for that he was punished."

As for the way in which the auditing agency's top officials appear to go out of their way to please and protect defense contractors, O'Connor bluntly concluded: "Evidence indicates a pervasive attitude at DCAA that reflects undue regard and solicitude for the concerns of contractors and procurement officials in the audit process."

The lesson to be learned from the Spanton affair is that a system that attempts to expel people like George Spanton, that resists uncovering, punishing and eventually correcting wrongdoing, is a system desperately in need of reform.

Were it not for a few dogged reporters, primarily Pulitzer Prize–winner Mollenhoff, who tenaciously pursued the Spanton story, special counsel O'Connor, who fought for Spanton's rights, and Grassley's intervention at the highest council of government, Spanton would have been shipped far from the abuses he had exposed. Such is the way the Pentagon can treat those who make waves, who cause trouble, and who care more about the integrity of their work than the toes they may step on.

Yet even though the Spanton case was eventually brought to the attention of officials at the highest levels of government, it led to no ceremonies honoring him as an uncommon and praiseworthy public servant. His face did not appear on the cover of *Time* or *Newsweek*. His story was not headlined on the front page of the *New York*

Times or the *Washington Post.* This lack of interest, too, shows the benign neglect the national news media often apply to those who dare to challenge the status quo. Pentagon whistle-blower A. Ernest Fitzgerald is the rare exception, though even in the beginning of his thirteen-year struggle to win his job back — for exposing the cost overruns on the Lockheed C-5A air transport — the media largely ignored him.

It is a rare bureaucrat who is willing to put himself through the kind of persecution that Spanton was forced to undergo. It is a rarer bureaucrat who will do so now. "There's a lot of competent people hesitant to speak out because of what happened to me," Spanton told a reporter when his long battle was over. Nonetheless, he said, "I would like to encourage others to come forward. It's in the public interest."

Still, this fear of getting one's head chopped off if one challenges the system permeates government, particularly the Pentagon. It was forcefully illustrated when Washington writer Greg Rushford asked a GAO auditor assigned to the Pentagon why the congressional watchdog agency had been so quiet during the Spanton controversy. The auditor's reply: "Look, you're talking about billions of dollars here. There are pressures from big labor on wages, and from big businesses like Pratt & Whitney. Why should I stick my neck out?"

George Spanton stuck his neck way out and came perilously close to the executioner's blade. But he was persistent, brave, and perhaps just a little lucky. Yet as long as Pentagon officials continue to show hostility toward the George Spantons of the Defense Department, wasteful military spending practices, contract abuses and mismanagement will continue to prevail, be covered up and ignored, for many years to come.

9

Waste and Wantonness in the Pentagon

W~HEN~ Ronald Reagan named Caspar "Cap the Knife" Weinberger to head the Defense Department, the appointment was widely perceived as a clear signal that Reagan wanted a stronger as well as a more efficiently run military machine.

Weinberger earned a reputation as a tough budget-cutter when he served as budget director and then as secretary of the Department of Health, Education and Welfare in the Nixon and Ford administrations. As Reagan's secretary of defense he promised to cut, squeeze and trim fat and waste from the Pentagon budget, even while presiding over the biggest peacetime military buildup in American history.

However, an examination of recent Pentagon budgets reveals a mountain of wasteful and low-priority military spending that has hardly been scratched. Consider these all-too-typical examples:

— The Defense Department spends more than $2 billion a year on consultants who provide program and systems evaluation, advice, in some cases management services. Auditors, and even a few consultants, say a large number of consultants and the costly reports they submit are worthless. They further argue that many consultant services can and should be performed within the department by military or civilian personnel.

GAO auditors believe that up to 50 percent of these contracts — most of which are awarded without competitive bidding — could be cut from the Pentagon budget.

— Operating with an unfunded liability of nearly $500 billion, the military's twenty-year-and-out retirement system is needlessly squandering billions of dollars on "retired" employees who are not truly retired. Nearly 90 percent of all retired military personnel are of working age. In 1982, 31 percent were in their forties, and over 40 percent were in their fifties. The most common "retirement" age in the military: forty-three years of age for officers, and thirty-nine for enlistees.

As for the cost to the taxpayer, the average "normal cost" of a pension plan in the private sector ranges between 5 and 6 percent of pay, while the cost of the average military pension plan is 50.7 percent of base pay. By 1985 the Pentagon projects the cost for "retirement" pay to hit $17.6 billion a year, rising to $25.2 billion by 1990 and to $44.7 billion by the year 2000.

"Unless changes are made," warns defense personnel expert Kenneth Coffrey, "there is doubt we will be able to afford a continuation of the present system without sacrifice in other areas" of needed military spending. Reforming the pension system to keep military personnel in service to their country longer, and paying pensions only to retirees who are truly retired, would save billions.

— GAO auditors have long recommended that military base support services, costing more than $12 billion a year, be consolidated. There are, for example, seven military bases surrounding Sacramento, California, which require nearly ten thousand service personnel for maintenance, accounting, repairs, etc. "By combining base support systems for all seven military bases, scale economies saving millions of dollars are realized at no loss of military effectiveness," according to a study of military costs by The Heritage Foundation, a Washington-based think tank.

If a national consolidation plan achieved only a 5 percent reduction in support personnel costs, taxpayers could save $370 million.

— Government auditors say that more than $100 million could

be saved if the military services would consolidate their purchase, storage and distribution of common supplies in a single agency. Audits reveal that parts and supply inventories among the various military branches are wastefully overstocked and inefficiently used.

— A study by the Congressional Budget Office found the Pentagon can save more than $2 billion by eliminating over thirty thousand pages of excessive procurement regulations, which add from 20 to 100 percent to the cost of everything the military buys.

— Nearly half of the Pentagon's $231 billion in annual outlays is consumed by manpower costs. The military pay system, a major part of these costs, is an antiquated, overly complex contraption in need of a complete overhaul. It is so complex and misunderstood, says GAO, that "few members who are paid under it know accurately how much of what they earn is equivalent to a civilian salary. They usually underestimate their equivalent salaries, which clearly does not help recruit and retain personnel."

The Pentagon's tangle of pay, bonuses and other tax-free, in-kind benefits should be replaced by a straight salary system geared to comparable work in the private sector.

But this is only a relatively small portion of the degree of waste that still exists within the Defense Department, totaling nearly $20 billion a year according to the President's Private Sector Survey on Cost Control.

It took a team of forty-five private-sector experts six months of exploring the Pentagon's bureaucratic labyrinths to come up with its findings. But for freshman congressman John R. Kasich of Ohio, who did not have the luxury of time or a big staff, a visit to the air force's Aerospace Guidance and Metrology Center in Newark, Ohio was a crash course in the realities of defense spending — where cost control frequently is an irrelevant factor in the procurement process. The thirty-one-year-old Kasich was astonished to discover millions of dollars being wasted on wildly excessive prices for replacement missile and aircraft parts. When he delivered his report in April 1983 to the House Armed Services Committee, it stunned even those who thought they had heard every Pentagon horror story imaginable.

Among Kasich's findings: A Minuteman II machine screw, used in the missile's guidance system, which cost $1.08 in fiscal 1982, had jumped to $36.77 one year later, an increase of 3,400 percent. The Center said it had used two hundred of these screws over a twelve-month period. Under the original price, the total cost would have been $237.60. Under the inflated price, the two hundred screws cost taxpayers $8,089.40.

Similarly, a Minuteman circuit card assembly, which is used in the missile's guidance system, cost $234.05 each in 1982, but went up one year later to $1,111.75, an increase of 475 percent. A simple connector-plug, which is used in the electronic housing of the FB-111 aircraft, had cost $7.99. By 1983 the price tag was an incredible $726.86 apiece.

Following up on Kasich's findings, Pentagon auditors reported in June 1983 that he had only scratched the surface of the scandal that lay buried deep within the military's $8.6 billion spare parts contracting business. Digging into years of overcharges that had become almost routine on many military contracts, auditors uncovered many more prices that had increased by 500 percent and up over a twenty-four-month period.

In one instance, they found the navy paying $110 for an electronic diode that had cost four cents just two years earlier. A bulb used in an instrument panel zoomed from seventeen cents to $44. A $2.37 microcircuit shot up to $112. One-inch plastic knobs, used on the navy's A-7 fighter planes' canopy releases, were purchased for $37.25 each in 1979. By January 1983 the Pentagon's Defense Industry Supply Center was paying $400 apiece for the knobs which a Texas small businessman said could be produced for less than $20 each.

The most outrageous case of spare parts overpricing concerned a tiny white plastic stool cap made from 26 cents' worth of nylon, for which the Pentagon was shelling out $1,118.26 apiece. Manufactured by the Boeing Corporation under a sole-source contract, the plastic component is used on the leg of a folding stool aboard the air force's sophisticated AWACS radar plane. In 1979 Boeing set the price of the cap at $219.19, raising it to $916.55 in 1981 — including a "profit fee" of $119.55 per cap — without so much as a peep from Pentagon contracting officers. Boeing said the increase was due to "cost growth." The Pentagon added its own surcharge of $169.22 to the cap's price for handling, packaging and other over-head costs, boosting the delivery price to $1,118.26 for a lump of plastic that Defense officials later admitted should cost no more than ten dollars.

Out of fifteen thousand spare parts examined, auditors found prices on two-thirds of them had shot up 50 percent or more within a two-year period, and more than half of them had doubled in price. Making matters worse, auditors also discovered that in many cases the spare parts being purchased were already overstocked on military supply shelves. In a monumental understatement, the auditors said it was clear that Pentagon contracting officers "were not buying engine spare parts in a cost-effective manner."

The reasons for these incredible price hikes? Wanton greed among some defense manufacturers is one reason. Huge pay increases built into defense contracts, which George Spanton exposed in his 1982 audit, is another. In many cases, contracting officers were also using "fixed price redeterminable" ordering agreements, which allow prices to be easily escalated by contractors. And finally, there is the egregious failure among defense contracting officers to seek competitive bidding. Defense auditors found that spare parts were being procured under sole-source agreements more than 60 percent of the time — meaning the contracts were awarded without competitive bidding. Even when contract officers insisted they had opened a contract up to "adequate competition," auditors found that this occasionally meant only two bids were received, one from the contractor and the other from the subcontractor.

Sadly, the spare parts scandal is not an isolated case in defense mismanagement and extravagance. Generously scattered throughout the Pentagon's budget are hundreds of similarly wasteful and excessive expenditures that in no way contribute to America's military readiness and strength.

This was dramatically illustrated when Oklahoma Congressman Mickey Edwards, a staunch defense spending supporter, examined the Pentagon's $100 billion military construction budget in the spring of 1983. The sums he questioned were small, but he knew the Defense Department was filled with thousands of similar expenditures that unnecessarily balloon its budget. Among them:

- $1.5 million for an arts and crafts shop at Anderson Air Force Base in Guam.
- $525,000 for covered walkways at the Alimanu Military Reservation's recreation center in Hawaii.
- $525,000 to remodel bathrooms in the homes of fifteen generals at Fort Myer, Virginia, among other refurbishing.
- $3.7 million for a gymnasium at Maryland's Bolling Air Force Base near Washington, D.C.
- $354,000 to build homes for two generals stationed in Vicenza, Italy, at a cost of $177,000 per house.
- $450,000 to relocate the golf course at Minot Air Force Base in North Dakota.
- $1.7 million to build recreational facilities at Fort Irwin, California, a community of three thousand servicemen and their families, which was to include: four basketball courts for $18,900 apiece; three handball courts at $42,000 apiece; six tennis courts at $30,500 apiece; twelve volleyball courts at $12,600 apiece; one football field at $97,200; four softball-football fields at $139,000 apiece; two softball fields at $97,200 apiece; and one track at $143,000. In addition, $5.8 million was requested for a physical fitness center, including indoor swimming, exercise rooms, squash, handball and basketball courts; plus two little league baseball fields at $106,000 each.
- $65,000 to make improvements at the general's home at the U.S. Air Force Academy.
- $380,000 to build two additional racquetball courts for $190,000 each at California's Vandenberg Air Force Base. (There are already seven courts on the base.)
- And $890,000 to fence 240,000 acres at Fort Carson, Colorado, even though the land has been used for open cattle grazing for over a hundred years.

At the time he released his findings, Edwards said that it would be "unfortunate and very dangerous, if the administration is unable to proceed with a very necessary buildup because of the Defense Department's inability to lay out a credible list of priorities." As it turned out, Edwards succeeded in having these spending requests rejected in the House Appropriations Committee, but he also knew that the military budget has many nooks and crannies in which to hide similar low-priority expenditures. The spending items he had killed in 1983 would most likely spring to life again in some other area of the Pentagon's complex budget.

Such frills and fluff are ingrained in Pentagon spending habits, as they are in almost every agency of government. By its very nature the military must be a lean and tough arm of government, perhaps leaner and tougher than any other area of government. This, unfortunately, is not always the case.

Consider what the navy spent making "habitability improvements" for its top brass in some of its newer warships. Some of the refurbishing would rival anything on "The Love Boat." In one case, the navy outfitted the USS *Kidd*, a guided missile destroyer, with a custom-made leather sectional sofa, a custom-made Chippendale-style sofa and wingback chair — at a total cost of $18,000. The *Kidd*'s interior decorating also included five custom-made brass end tables, for which the navy shelled out $6,500, along with plush wool carpeting at a luxurious $57 a yard, which cost a total of $41,071. Such is the lean and frugal life for the top brass aboard our warships.

Examples such as these are not untypical, and they have enraged some of Congress's staunchest defense spenders. Iowa Senator Charles Grassley, a conservative Republican with a fairly strong defense voting record, says he was "shocked" by what he learned of military spending practices and abuses. Grassley declared in early 1983 that the Pentagon has its own "welfare queens." To this, Mickey Edwards complains that the Pentagon's chiefs seem unable or unwilling "to economize, to trim out the fat, to separate the essential from the trivial."

But as we shall see this is only a part of the Pentagon's continuing spending scandals.

10

Gold-Plating the Defense Department

In the last decade no other component in the Pentagon's budget has risen faster than procurement. Between fiscal years 1974 and 1983 personnel costs increased by 111 percent. Operations and maintenance surged up by 175 percent. Research and development budgets jumped by 202 percent. But military procurement costs have skyrocketed by 369 percent!

Out of a fiscal 1974 defense budget of $81.1 billion, procurement totaled $17.1 billion. But by fiscal year 1983, procurement was consuming $80.2 billion out of a total budget authorization of $239.4 billion. The grim reality of this increased defense spending is that it is taking far more bucks to buy much less bang.

Much has been written about the sharply escalating costs of major weapons systems. And, indeed, there is much to be critical about, though it is rarely pointed out that some degree of cost overruns are inevitable and necessary when developing a defense technology that has never been built before.

Still, a great deal of the military's overrun problems lie within the Pentagon's propensity to underestimate substantially the projected costs of new weapons systems, as well as its seeming inability to resist gold-plating virtually every weapon with complex, costly and often unnecessary and counterproductive technology.

The habit of "suping up" weapons systems with state-of-the-art technology has in many ways weakened America's ability on the battlefield and sent defense budgets soaring into the stratosphere. "Our strategy of pursuing ever-increasing technical complexity and sophistication has made high-technology solutions and combat readiness mutually exclusive," says Franklin "Chuck" Spinney, the brilliant Pentagon analyst, who leaped from obscurity to America's front pages as a result of his extraordinarily candid public briefing on military costs before a packed Senate Armed Services Committee hearing in March 1983.

Another major factor in cost overruns, Spinney points out, "is a systematic tendency [on the part of Pentagon procurement specialists] to underestimate future costs," perhaps by as much as 30 percent. "Deep-seated structural problems need to be addressed."

All too often the military's "tactics have been driven by technology," adds George Kuhn, a former army cost analyst, in a study for The Heritage Foundation. "Unfortunately, the evidence suggests that complex technology is usually relatively ineffective. Its poor performance stems from three causes . . . : complex systems are too expensive to be built in adequate numbers, and system complexity makes readiness problems more likely and less manageable. The third problem is that the very performance goals of complex systems are often only marginally useful in combat," Kuhn says.

In recent years the Pentagon has been on a technology binge that increasingly has led to outrageously expensive weapons that sometimes do not fulfill their mission and whose enormous costs have resulted in reduced defense procurement elsewhere. Consider these examples of gold-plated super-weapons and their often doubtful, sometimes scandalous results:

— The Viper Antitank Weapon: Designed to give infantrymen a cheap, light bazooka to knock out enemy tanks, the Viper's costs skyrocketed over ten years of development and design changes from $75 apiece to nearly $800.

Sadly, the weapon would give our troops little security in battle. The army announced that the Viper could not even penetrate the front armor of a Soviet tank. Congress has ordered that the Viper weapons program be killed, but Pentagon sources say that further funding for the weapon remains hidden in the defense budget.

— The army's Air-Defense Gun: It looks like a tank and is called the Sergeant York, after the famous World War I sharpshooter. Unlike its namesake, however, the DIVAD (for "Division Air Defense") is so inaccurate that the army has changed its purpose from shooting down maneuvering aircraft, which it cannot do, to knocking out helicopters, which it cannot do very well, either. To make the DIVAD's tests look successful, the army disingenuously reduced performance criteria by having it knock out stationary helicopters rather than attacking difficult, and more realistic, maneuvering attack aircraft.

In the end, this $5 billion air-defense weapons program produced a computerized, radar-equipped, highly sophisticated and costly piece of equipment that costs at least $6.8 million apiece, or three times the cost of M-1 tanks it was designed to defend. The DIVAD's ammunition will cost $275 per round compared to the 30mm cannon which shoots $20 shells and in sixty seconds can fire seven times as many rounds as the DIVAD.

— The M-1 Abrams Tank: When they field tested the M-1, called the "Cadillac of tanks," at Fort Hood, Texas, only twenty-one out of forty-one were still running after five days of mock warfare, according to declassified army documents. The twenty inoperable tanks had not been gunned down by the mock enemy. They had just broken down.

Breaking some kind of record for cost overruns, this sixty-ton, turbine-powered tank was to cost $1.5 million in January 1980, but that figure zoomed to about $2.6 million each just one year later. It is estimated that eventually the M-1 tank will end up costing the army $3 million apiece or $21 billion by 1988 to produce over seven thousand of them. By comparison, the M-60, the army's veteran warhorse tank, costs no more than $1 million.

Dina Rasor, director of the Project on Military Procurement, a highly regarded public-interest watchdog group, says of the M-1's many test failures: "One could hardly find a more revealing case study of the way operational testing has been so deformed by the

Pentagon bureaucracy and porkbarrel pressures that soldiers continue to end up with weapons that will fail them on the battlefield."

In 1982 a General Accounting Office report criticized army audits on the tank's cost performance, noting that its "statistics mask the fact that the M-1 sustained many component and part failures that did not figure in the Army's scoring."

Pointing out that the Soviet Union vastly outnumbers the United States in the number of tanks, Rasor says, "We're not saying that the M-60 is marvelous or can't be improved. We're saying, 'Is one M1 worth three M-60s?' "

— The navy's Aegis System: This is a highly complex system of radars, computers and missiles which costs $1 billion to install on a naval cruiser. The navy wants seventeen of them, arguing they would protect the U.S. fleet from attack in a Falkland Islands–type naval encounter. Navy researchers support the Aegis, saying it would improve naval readiness and technology. But for all its super technology and huge costs the navy acknowledges they are not sure if it will work effectively in combat. "The Aegis has never been tested against sea-skimming missiles of the Exocet type that sank the British *Sheffield* in the Falklands conflict," defense analyst Kuhn points out.

Seemingly endless examples such as these threaten to price the minimum level of defense readiness America needs far beyond her ability to pay. Little wonder, then, that despite substantially larger defense budgets, in constant dollar terms, we are buying less and less military hardware to replace an aging arsenal of weaponry.

For example, the army's budget for new tanks is about what it was in the early 1950s, roughly $2 billion in 1983 dollars. Yet the number of new tanks being purchased today has declined significantly — from 6,700 to a mere 700. Toward the end of the Korean war, it took $7 billion in 1983 dollars to purchase 6,300 fighter aircraft. By 1983, the expenditure of $11 billion bought only 322 fighter planes.

Similarly, the navy in 1983 was forced to mothball twenty-two of its older, though newly overhauled vessels in order to be able to afford to buy six new ships at a cost of $4.2 billion: including three CG-47 guided missile cruisers, which cost over $1 billion apiece;

two FFG-7 guided missile frigates, which cost $400 million each; and a $400 million marine landing dock and cargo ship. The price for these six ships not only resulted in cutting some of the most reliable and better-equipped war ships in the fleet, but the navy was also forced to pay for it by cutting sailing time and other readiness requirements for naval operations and maintenance.

The compelling need for simpler, less costly weapons systems, ones that will not only reduce procurement and maintenance costs, but will give taxpayers "more bang for the buck," has still not been heeded by either the Pentagon or Congress. Thus, the Pentagon's gold-plating scandal continues.

At the same time, while the national news media uniformly tend to criticize only the Pentagon for excessive and wasteful military spending, the real culprit more often than not is Congress. Members of Congress to a large degree treat the Pentagon's appropriations as they do all other pork barrel budgets. Even the most dedicated military-spending critics in Congress will fight tooth and nail to keep nonessential local military bases open and low-priority or unwanted military procurement projects alive and well at home, all in the name of protecting jobs.

Even when making the case for specific weapons systems, military contractors play up to Congress's political appetites in this regard, sometimes dropping any pretense over military or national security arguments. In 1982, for example, when Rockwell International lobbied members of Congress heavily for the B-1 bomber, it did so largely on the aircraft's potential for job creation.

The A-10 aircraft, or Thunderbolt, is a classic example of how members of Congress base major military spending decisions largely on their own parochial interests. The air force has repeatedly chopped this Fairchild Corporation aircraft from its budget, but Congress always restores its funds.

Navy Secretary John Lehman, who is an open and frequent critic of the way Congress abuses the defense budget, complains that "Congress should not approve programs that nobody wants, like the A-10. Pork barrel. That's where [Pentagon spending] reform ought to take place."

But the A-10 has a powerful friend in Congress. New York

Congressman Joseph Addabbo, chairman of the House Defense Appropriations Subcommittee, likes the aircraft. As head of the subcommittee that funds military programs, Addabbo has the power to keep its defense contract alive and thriving — whether the air force wants it or not. Why is the Queens Democrat so interested in the Thunderbolt? The A-10 aircraft is manufactured in his congressional district at the Fairchild Republic plant in Farmingdale, New York.

11

The $30 Billion Swamp

"Hell, I think there's a kind of swamp of $10 to $20 to $30 billion worth of [Pentagon] waste that can be ferreted out if you really push hard."

— Budget Director David Stockman

DURING the 1950s the General Accounting Office, Congress's investigating arm, often audited individual military procurement contracts until Defense Secretary Robert McNamara initiated a department-wide auditing reform in the 1960s that resulted in GAO eventually getting out of the defense contracts business. Many believe the move has had costly repercussions ever since.

In the name of military efficiency McNamara created the Defense Contract Audit Agency (DCAA) by merging the four military auditing services into a single agency. He then proceeded to argue that the GAO no longer needed to audit Pentagon contracts since it would be merely duplicating the DCAA's work. Some in Congress began making this argument, too, especially when GAO audits into big defense contracts would anger defense contractors who would then complain to their allies on Capitol Hill. Indeed, a series of hearings in the late 1960s by Congressman Chet Hollifield of California, chairman of the House Government Operations Committee, sharply criticized the GAO for its relentless audits on Pentagon procurement. The intensity of that criticism eventually led to a significant modification of the GAO's policy toward procurement audits. The legislative agency decided it could better apply its resources by concentrating on "the big picture" in Defense Department expenditures and management and leave the contract audits to the DCAA.

What McNamara wanted all along, of course, was for the Defense Department's top brass to monitor and control all contract audits, not an independent outside agency that worked for the Congress. The result over the years has been relatively little aggressive auditing by the DCAA or the program contract officers they report to as procurement scandal after procurement scandal has been swept under the rug. The spare-parts procurement fiasco recounted earlier may appear to be the exception to this, but it was initially brought to light and exposed by lower level officers, not by the DCAA.

Still, even though the GAO no longer audits major military procurement contracts to any real degree, the auditing mandate of this congressional agency does extend to just about every other aspect of Pentagon operations and expenditures. Unfortunately, what the GAO often uncovers rarely gets reported by the Washington news media, and usually elicits no more than a yawn from lawmakers.

Each year General Accounting Office auditors heave a collective sigh of frustration and send Congress a summary of all Defense Department audits and investigations they have undertaken during the previous year. The reports always contain shocking new disclosures about how the Pentagon's military and civilian managers have wasted our tax dollars. And the 200-page document which GAO quietly submitted to the House and Senate Armed Services committees and Defense Appropriations subcommittees in March 1983 was no exception. It displayed an awesome array of military waste and mismanagement, much of which continues to this day.

Few if any members of Congress, even those who serve on Congress's defense subcommittees, bothered to read the original 165 audit reports this document summarized, just as they did not bother to read the summary. This is a tragedy because a careful review of GAO's comprehensive year-end report reveals vividly the depth of wasteful and excessive spending that exists throughout the Pentagon.

Consider these highly representative samples:

— According to the GAO, "The military services, for the most part, do not account for the estimated billions of dollars in government-furnished material provided to Department of Defense production contractors."

Good accounting practices require that government property "be under accounting control from the time it is acquired until it is disposed of or consumed." Instead, GAO found that the Pentagon was irresponsibly giving defense contractors access to military supply systems "without [Defense Department] accounting control over materials obtained."

Moreover, GAO found the military operating under a "policy of almost total reliance on contractor's property control records," which auditors called "unreliable." Reviewing only four of the Pentagon's many defense contractors, GAO auditors uncovered $1.3 million in excess government materials that had been shipped to these companies.

— Upon examining two shipyard and support facilities under the direction of the Naval Sea Systems Command (NAVSEA), GAO discovered inadequate spending controls over NAVSEA's multimillion-dollar payroll and invoice accounts. Such "weak internal controls make some Navy activities vulnerable to fraud, waste and abuse," the auditors said.

Over a seven-month period GAO found invoices totaling $8 million were paid without being "reconciled to supporting documents to determine if only legitimate invoices were paid." In many cases they were not. In another case, $5.8 million in accounts receivable at the navy's Charleston, South Carolina, shipyard was written off the books over a two-year period "without adequate justification."

— After investigating military loans between fiscal 1977 and 1979, auditors found $67 million owed by former military personnel had been written off as uncollectable. Auditors found that only 13 percent of the total owed was collected, and that this sum "barely" covered "the costs incurred for processing and collecting the debts." The army said it was attempting to correct its loan account deficiencies, but by the end of 1982 GAO found that "significant problems" continued to exist.

— GAO also found that the Defense Personnel Support Center's control systems to be in "chaotic condition" and that the material supply center had mismanaged millions of dollars in stock funds.

The Center, located in Philadelphia, is the second biggest among the Defense Logistics Agency's six supply facilities, and it is responsible for purchasing and supplying more than forty-two thousand items, from blankets to medicines, for use by the military. The GAO said the Center was incapable of controlling "hundreds of millions of stock fund dollars because of its ineffective accounting systems." In fact, the Center "could not accurately determine" how much it had paid out or how much it owed. It tried some creative bookkeeping to correct its accounts, but auditors said the validity of its financial adjustments "could not be determined" due to lack of "adequate documentation." Even after making some suspect accounting adjustments, which totaled $566 million, GAO said "many of the records were still inaccurate."

One of the Center's creative account adjustments, for example, involved a little strategic mathematical maneuvering to the tune of $68.8 million "to force agreement between the fund control accounts and subsidiary accounts."

The scandal worsened after the Center's erroneous accounts balances were certified to be accurate by the facility's overseer. GAO officials found that the Center's lord and master, the Defense Logistics Agency, was fully "aware of the Center's problems," including its "unsupported adjustments," yet it still "certified the Center's accounts as correct."

Worse, GAO auditors said the "chaotic conditions" surrounding the Center's accounts "prevented it from systematically detecting fraudulent contract payments" which have occurred. In one instance a fraudulent contract payment for $306,749 was caught only as a result of a clerical error.

— Out of $231 billion in yearly budget outlays, you would think the Pentagon's mobilization program would be in tip-top shape. On the contrary, GAO found that "DOD planners still do not have adequate information to plan for wartime needs" in order to airlift equipment and soldiers to combat areas.

Auditors concluded that the World-Wide Military Command and Control Information System, which the U.S. must rely on for adequate warning and response to an enemy attack, "has a limited capability to provide timely, accurate, and complete information to commanders, particularly during times of crisis." Pentagon planners have acknowledged this problem for years, but GAO finds that efforts to modernize and improve the system "are slow, do not address the fundamental issues, and will not lead to a timely responsive solution."

— Meanwhile, "the Army continues to spend millions of dollars annually on unneeded materiel." The GAO estimated that "65,000 invalid orders were on hand at Army wholesale supply sources, and that the Army will spend $100 million over a three-year period to fill invalid orders to fund inflated forecasted requirements for the related items."

In a random survey, auditors found "validation checks included orders for parts to repair inoperable equipment which did not exist or had already been repaired, orders for the wrong item, duplicate orders, and orders for materiel for special projects that had been terminated."

Said the auditing agency: "Significant imbalances of as much as 53 percent exist between the records of Army wholesalers and their customers relative to either the number of outstanding orders or the quantities on order."

— When GAO investigated military supply depots, auditors found that lax procedures often make it questionable at some supply facilities whether military equipment that has been bought and paid for is ever delivered and used.

Auditors discovered cases where Pentagon "customers were being charged for material they did not receive." It found that "overdue material shipments costing millions of dollars were either written off as inventory losses or remained on the books as items due in for a considerable period of time" but have never been found.

— The auditing agency also disclosed that the air force has wasted "significant" sums of money by not charging foreign governments for the costs of labor, "transportation, packing, crating, and the use of government-owned facilities" in its sales of military equipment to foreign countries. In one instance at the San Antonio Air Logistics Center, the GAO said the military failed to "charge hundreds of thousands of dollars to foreign governments even when clear and concise pricing procedures were provided."

These pricing procedures were specifically developed "to eliminate subsidies in the foreign military sales program," GAO says. But they found that the air force had not implemented them and that the subsidies were continuing.

— Similarly, when GAO reviewed defense-related costs between the U.S. and Egypt, it "uncovered apparent inconsistencies in the tolls U.S. warships are being assessed by the Egyptian government for transiting to the Suez Canal." In short, the U.S. was getting gypped by those it was helping to defend.

Auditors said that "Since the U.S. Embassy in Cairo began retaining records of Canal transits in 1979, overcharges have amounted to over 18 percent of the total payments. These overcharges primarily stem from inaccurate computations by the Suez Canal Authority and the absence of any verification of bills received by the U.S. Embassy."

— After examining the figures on the McDonnell-Douglas Corporation's F-15 jet fighter contract, GAO found taxpayers were paying more than necessary. GAO concluded that "the target cost for the F-15 contract was overstated by about $2.4 million because the contractor did not use current, accurate and complete cost or pricing data for negotiated production material cost."

— GAO discovered in 1982 that Boeing Computer Services "submitted an unbalanced proposal to the Pentagon in which commercial rates were charged for teleprocessing services" far beyond what had been projected. This resulted in enormous cost overruns on army and navy contracts for teleprocessing computers to support recruitment processing. "The Army's initial cost projection of $8.5 million for the life of the contract currently projects a cost of about $120 million," the GAO said, "and the Navy's initial cost projection of $524,000 now projects a cost of about $13 million."

The GAO blamed the excessive costs on "lack of appropriate management controls."

GAO also questioned the cost hikes in light of present recruitment levels. While army enlistments decreased by 18 percent, "the cost for teleprocessing services almost tripled," GAO says. Similarly, though navy enlistments rose only 3 percent, its teleprocessing services nearly tripled.

— When GAO performed a sample survey of eight out of forty-eight defense programs, which handled 250,000 contracts valued at $73 billion, it revealed widespread duplication, clerical errors, needless personnel, and other serious accounting problems.

GAO says Defense Department officials have resisted implementation of standard accounting management procedures, which were to have been operational by 1970. If these procedures had been implemented, they would have eliminated duplicate operations at eight locations, which alone could cut defense costs by up to $2.7 million a year.

Auditors identified over $90 million in errors, "on 286 out of the 856 transactions they reviewed."

— GAO also discovered that over the past twelve years the navy has spent more than $150 million to develop and operate a central automated military pay system that is largely unreliable and inefficient. One audit showed that 42 percent of 291 selected pay accounts reviewed "were inaccurate and 52,200 accounts remained in an overpaid status for more than 90 days."

Another random audit found that thirty-four accounts "were in error in amounts ranging from $5 to over $1,800." The GAO says that "Despite costly efforts to overcome system inefficiencies, the system continues to operate inadequately."

— After GAO examined the navy and marine corps' Aviation Bonus Program, it found that nearly "80 percent of their total payments during fiscal year 1981 were spent unnecessarily." In many cases auditors discovered that the two services were paying bonuses "to officers who are not in specialties where there are critical shortages or who are past the point in their careers where retention is a problem."

They charged that neither service had "judiciously managed the bonus program," finding that all the navy bonuses for naval flight officers "was unnecessarily spent" and that the marines' "approach to retaining officers is not an economical way to solve its shortages."

Tragically, these examples represent only a tiny portion of the Defense Department's continuing waste and mismangement. There is within the Pentagon's multitude of programs, as David Stockman says, a "swamp of waste" that is needlessly costing taxpayers up to $30 billion a year, and perhaps much more.

The Pentagon employs a total of eighteen thousand auditors and investigators in nineteen different agencies, at a cost of about half a billion dollars a year. Nevertheless, an unacceptable level of military waste and wantonness within the Defense Department's $231 billion budget continues. Why?

Though the problem is complex, the answer is relatively simple and known to most defense experts in Washington. The iron triangle of the defense establishment — the Pentagon, Congress, and the defense industries — all benefit from the status quo.

The military bureaucracy prefers sole source contracting, which continues to dominate defense procurement, because of the control it gives them over major weapons systems. But the failure to broaden competitive bidding in the procurement process is needlessly costing taxpayers billions of dollars. According to the Project on Military Procurement, "only 6 percent of the Pentagon's purchases are truly competitive," and most of this "is for minor items."

The insidious and costly impact this has on military spending was intelligently explained in the Project's 1983 book, *More Bucks, Less Bang:*

> The growth of the bureaucracy and the strangulation of competition bring enormous problems in their wake. Each development and production program automatically grows bigger in dollars and longer in duration because the corporate and government bureaucracies involved, quite naturally, wish to inflate their programs to assure their future security and influence. Since successive major programs are increasing in cost much faster than the total defense budget, there are fewer and fewer technical choices, less and less innovation, and longer and longer development cycles. As a result,

more money is equipping our troops with increasingly obsolete, ineffective, and unnecessarily complex weapons.*

Moreover, as previously pointed out, many members of Congress, including the most rabid defense critics, often profit politically from defense contracts, bases and other military facilities in their states and districts. For example, Senator Alan Cranston of California, one of the most outspoken defense spending critics in the Senate, is nevertheless a strong supporter of the controversial B-1 bomber program because it is built in his state. Thus, the Pentagon has become quite adept at spreading its procurement contracts and subcontracts among the fifty states, thereby making virtually all of Congress in one degree or another dependent upon the maintenance, and the growth, of military spending.

The big military defense contractors also maintain expensive lobbying operations in Washington. And they know how to wine and dine lawmakers and Pentagon bigwigs, make political contributions to congressional campaigns, and otherwise influence members of Congress in whose state or district their corporate headquarters or defense plants are located. Much of their lobbying is also aimed at top Pentagon officials who, upon retirement, can be hired on in a consultant capacity by big defense contractors who can afford to pay lucrative fees.

All — the Pentagon, the defense contractors, and members of Congress — would lose something from the kind of fundamental reforms that must be made. But nonetheless change must come and any set of reforms must include:

— A complete overhaul of the procurement process, including consolidating weapons acquisition; elimination of most sole-source contracting; reducing the number of new weapons starts each year; simplifying overly complex weapon systems design; establishment of an independent weapons testing facility; and introducing greater stability into the weapons acquisition process. Savings: $10 billion a year.

— A total reform of the military retirement system: Taxpayers

* *More Bucks Less Bang: How the Pentagon Buys Ineffective Weapons,* Editor, Dina Rasor, published by Fund for Constitutional Government, Project on Military Procurement, Washington, D.C.

can no longer afford to retire their trained military personnel as early as age thirty-seven. The President's Private Sector Survey on Cost Control estimated that under current average life spans for a thirty-seven-year-old, "it is probable that the total amount he or she received in retirement pay will exceed the total received for active duty compensation, even before allowances for inflation." Requiring thirty years of service, instead of the current twenty, among other reforms, would generate billions of dollars in defense savings.

— Revamp all personnel benefits and programs, including the elimination of all military commissaries within the continental United States. Providing cut-rate, subsidized groceries is totally unnecessary. Indeed, nearly 60 percent of those using these supermarkets are retired military personnel. Its annual support costs are rapidly approaching $1 billion a year.

— Close unneeded bases and facilities in the U.S. which have been kept in existence solely because of congressional and political considerations. According to the Private Sector Survey's study, it is costing taxpayers between $2 billion and $5 billion annually to keep these unnecessary bases open.

— Restore the General Accounting Office's full authority to audit procurement contracts on a regular basis, and assign GAO auditors to major defense plants and facilities.

Putting GAO back in the business of defense contract audits would provide Congress with the independent evaluation and investigation it needs to deal effectively with wasteful procurement practices.

Not long after Ronald Reagan named David Stockman in 1981 to direct the White House Office of Management and Budget, Stockman vowed in an interview with *Washington Post* reporter William Greider that he was going to apply his budgetary scalpel to the defense budget. "The defense budgets in the out-years won't be nearly as high as we are showing now, in my judgment," he said. "Hell, I think there's a kind of swamp of $10 to $20 to $30 billion worth of waste that can be ferreted out if you really push hard."

Nearly four years after the Reagan administration came to power, the swamp has yet to be drained.

12

The Selling of the C-5B

T HE Defense Department, like almost every other federal agency, spends a lot of its money and time aggressively promoting its programs and selling its budget requests on Capitol Hill. The defense establishment just does it bigger and better than anyone else. "When the Pentagon boys come up here to sell us on some plane or tank," says Congressman Les Aspin of Wisconsin, "believe me, they give you the full treatment."

Officially, the Pentagon says it spends no more than $10 million a year on what it euphemistically calls "legislative liaison activities," which is in fact lobbying. But the true cost of its Madison Avenue sales program on Capitol Hill is hidden in a multitude of budget accounts and big defense contracts. There are laws, of course, against using federal funds to influence the votes of members of Congress. But Defense Department lobbyists who mastermind, coordinate, and carry out the Pentagon's hard-sell promotional campaigns know how to skirt the laws without getting caught.

However, in the summer of 1982 they did get caught in perhaps the most brazenly orchestrated Pentagon pitch ever waged on Capitol Hill. A General Accounting Office investigation concluded that this illegal lobbying drive "was initiated and directed" by high-level Defense Department officials who knowingly spent appropriated funds "for the purpose of influencing" Congress's decision on a major defense procurement. Yet to this day no one has been punished in this little-noticed military scandal, and the matter has been virtually swept under the rug by both Congress and the Pentagon.

The sales campaign was aggressively waged on behalf of buying fifty of the Lockheed Corporation's C-5B aircraft, after the Senate on May 13, 1982, turned thumbs down on the huge air cargo transport, voting to purchase wide-body Boeing 747s instead of spending billions more for a new aircraft.

Mounting a virulent lobbying drive that was fully coordinated between Lockheed, the air force and top officials in the Office of the Secretary of Defense, the Pentagon turned its full fury on the House of Representatives in a last-ditch effort to save the C-5B. The intimate details of this tenacious selling campaign are known as a result of its coordinators' extraordinary decision to maintain computerized records of each sales pitch, lawmaker by lawmaker. After a printout of the computer's lobbying data was leaked to an outsider, Lockheed president Larry Kitchen ordered that the master records be destroyed.

According to these records and the findings of a thorough GAO investigation, this high-powered military-industrial lobbying blitz — known secretly in the Pentagon as the "C-5B Group" — engaged in the following practices:

- Nearly daily strategy sessions were held between air force and Lockheed officials, as well as some subcontractors, to plot and coordinate their lobbying activities.
- The air force drafted "Dear Colleague" letters for friendly House members to send to their colleagues in support of the C-5B.
- Lockheed encouraged subcontractors in various states to lobby their local congressmen in behalf of the C-5B.
- Lockheed contacted all the major commercial airlines and asked them to stay neutral in the controversy between the Boeing 747 and Lockheed's C-5B.

- Lockheed submitted a draft for a Defense Department position letter on the aircraft, and offered comments and advice on other air force–Defense Department lobbying plans.
- Lockheed officials coached congressmen friendly to their position on how to answer "dirty questions" about the C-5B's controversial performance.
- The Defense Department even considered, but eventually rejected, a proposal to "energize" various military associations to organize "back-home support" for approval of the C-5B.
- Air force and Lockheed officials both promoted a demonstration of the C-5B at nearby Andrews Air Force Base.
- The air force and Lockheed jointly targeted House members for lobbying pressure. And Lockheed developed and maintained detailed computerized records of each lobbying contact, the status of each lawmaker's position on the controversy and whether "further action," i.e. lobbying pressure, was necessary.
- Lockheed officials paid numerous visits to the offices of wavering House members to talk with their staffs or the members themselves. GAO said that according to the company's computer printouts, "more than 500 visits were to be made by employees of Lockheed and other companies" serving as subcontractors.

If what the Pentagon and Lockheed were engaged in was not exactly breaking the antilobbying law (18 U.S. Code 1913), and the GAO believes that it was, then they came perilously close to it. While the law permits "communication" with Congress at the request of a member or "through proper official channels," it specifically prohibits indirect lobbying such as urging grass roots lobbying by the public or private organizations, such as contractors.

And it clearly states that appropriated funds cannot be used "to influence in any matter a member of Congress, to favor or oppose, by vote or otherwise, any legislation or appropriation by Congress."

Further lobbying restrictions are contained in Section 607(a) of Congress's Treasury, Postal Service and General Government Appropriation Act, which states: "No part of any appropriation contained in this or any other Act, or of the funds available for expenditure by any corporation or agency, shall be used for publicity or propaganda purposes designed to support or defeat legislation pending before Congress."

Yet despite these clear lobbying prohibitions, the Pentagon mounted a full-court press on the House, soon after Senate rejection of the C-5B, with the apparent approval of Defense officials at the highest levels of the department.

According to a bluntly worded, twenty-three-page GAO audit, the lobbying drive was "initiated and directed" by high-level Defense Department officials who knowingly spent tax dollars "for the purpose of influencing" Congress's decision on the aircraft. It found that the director of the air force's Office of Legislative Liaison "held almost daily" meetings in his office with Lockheed officials and several C-5B subcontractors. Moreover, auditors discovered that these meetings occurred "with the knowlege and consent" of Air Force Secretary Verne Orr and then–Deputy Defense Secretary Frank Carlucci.

One air force official candidly told GAO, "Lockheed did things that the air force couldn't. It was a great advantage cooperating with them because they could work the Hill every day."

Lockheed kept a meticulous, daily record of each congressional lobbying contact. For example, an entry in the computer log for June 14 revealed the status of a key vote in the House, that of Congressman Joseph P. Addabbo (D–N.Y.), who chaired the all-important Defense Appropriations Subcommittee. The entry by Addabbo's name noted the urgent need for "Further Actions: Carlucci one on one. Orr one on one." Addabbo, in other words, was getting what Congressman Les Aspin calls "the full treatment."

A typical entry in the air force–Lockheed computerized record-keeping system looked like this:

ACTION: 05/27 DoD
     AF/LK

Develop list of members that Sec Def, Dep Sec Def, Sec AF, Chief of Staff AF, Lloyd and Hecker should see or call.

STATUS: Continuing

"Hecker" is Major General Guy L. Hecker, Jr., who was director of legislative liaison for the air force, and who ran the C-5B Group.

"Lloyd" is Lloyd K. Mosemann II, a Defense Department deputy assistant secretary in charge of logistics and communications for the air force.

In the computer's "Congressional Contact Tally" a list of House members slated for further lobbying was entered, along with key members who were assigned to contact them in behalf of the C-5B. For example, under "Further Actions," alongside the name of House Republican leader Robert H. Michel of Illinois, was the notation, "Call again after visiting floor leaders. AF/DoD should visit. President call & Sen. [Republican leader Howard] Baker call."

Without mincing words, the GAO flatly charged that the air force had "initiated, organized and directed an intense legislative liaison and lobbying effort to promote the C-5B in the House."

"We found that an extensive and cooperative effort was made by officials of the Air Force, the Office of the Secretary of Defense (OSD), the Lockheed Corporation, and several other Defense contractors and subcontractors during the period May 14, 1982, through July 22, 1982, to influence members of the House of Representatives, and later the House and Senate conferees, on the proposed $10 billion procurement of the C-5B aircraft," GAO's auditors reported.

The Pentagon heatedly denied it had done anything illegal, but the GAO took the unusual step of turning over its findings to the Justice Department for possible criminal violations. This was a rare action for the auditing agency because in the first place, such lobbying activities are routinely ignored, and in the second place, Justice officials say they have never found a violation.

To no one's surprise, the Justice Department did not break its longstanding record. Assistant Attorney General D. Lowell Jensen, in a May 24, 1983 letter to the GAO Comptroller General Charles A. Bowsher, said his department's investigation concluded that no violations had occurred.

Jensen's incredible opinion said, in part, that the

lobbying law does not restrict the ability of the Executive Branch to implement the national policies of the incumbent administration through proposing legislation directly to the Congress, or through communicating directly with the Legislative Branch concerning matters of official concern that are pending there. As such, the use of appropriated funds by Lockheed and by Defense Department personnel to communicate directly with the Congress does not violate this statute. This statute is also not violated by small and incidental disbursements made in connection with legislative strategy sessions of the type described in your report which do not entail aggressive and clandestine stimulation of grass roots lobbying by the public-at-large.

In other words, the clear and convincing evidence amassed by the GAO was blithely swept aside as if it did not exist. The Justice Department was saying, essentially, that "this sort of thing goes on all the time, boys. So a few Pentagon officials were pushing one of their programs in Congress? What's the big deal?"

Unfortunately, this was essentially the same attitude of indifference taken by the House Armed Services Investigations Subcommittee, chaired by Representative Richard C. White (D–Tex.) during five days of hearings held late in 1982. Instead of conducting an objective investigation into GAO's clear findings of fact, the subcommittee leaped to the Pentagon's defense. In fact, it ended up putting the GAO on trial instead of the officials who had engaged in this extraordinary, and questionable, lobbying campaign.

A careful reading of the hearing transcript shows White benignly questioning witnesses for the Defense Department, the air force and Lockheed the way a lawyer would speak to his client on the witness stand. Other subcommittee members defended the Pentagon and Lockheed's action in almost knee-jerk fashion, while frequently denigrating GAO's methods and findings.

Especially disturbing was the fact that three members of the panel who were entrusted with the responsibility for independently investigating the lobbying charges were in fact listed on Lockheed's "Congressional Contact Tally" as key contacts to help win House support for the C-5B: Congressmen Robin Beard (R–Tenn.), Jack Brinkley (D–Ga.), and Dan Daniel (D–Va.). Notably, Lockheed's main assembly plant is in Marietta, Georgia, Brinkley's home state. The C-5B's wings are made by a subcontractor, AVCO Corporation, near Beard's district.

Was Beard outraged by the evidence that the Pentagon and a huge defense contractor had worked hand in glove to influence a major congressional vote? Not in the least. Everybody does it, he said.

At the end of the hearing Beard said, "I would just like to say that it is somewhat ridiculous to think that the Air Force would have to direct a company such as Lockheed or any corporate structure to do what common sense tells you to do. And whether it be a group that supports a social program or whatever, the list of things that were done is done in almost every government program that comes before Congress."

Some subcommittee members even praised Defense Department officials for their vigorous denials of the GAO's charges. Congressman Samuel Stratton (D–N.Y.) told Deputy Defense Secretary Carlucci, "This whole thing struck me as a tempest in a teapot and I'm glad that you nailed it as you did, Mr. Secretary."

But when the subcommittee began questioning the GAO auditors, who in fact work for Congress, the interrogation suddenly became exact, demanding and at times even hostile and mean. The members demanded that the auditors produce concrete evidence or testimony that proved that any individual had broken the law. They told surprised GAO officials that by "proof" they meant sworn statements, not "assumptions or conclusions."

The GAO countered that they considered the computer printout sufficient evidence of collusion between Lockheed and the Pentagon. But the subcommittee rejected the computerized lobbying scorecard as hard evidence. Instead, they chose to believe the testimony of Pentagon and Lockheed witnesses who said the printout was only a record of independent lobbying actions conducted separately by Lockheed and Pentagon officials.

GAO pointed out specific instances of collusion on the printout, but in each case the subcommittee dismissed the auditors' findings. "What I see here," White lectured the frustrated GAO officials, "is an innuendo, a conclusion based on innuendo or suspicion and nothing else."

At one point in the hearings, GAO chief Bowsher was forced to defend his auditors simply for doing their job, as they had been requested to do by two members of Congress: Senator William Proxmire (D–Wis.) and Representative Norman Dicks (D–Wash.), who, admittedly, was a Boeing supporter. Yet incredibly, Congressman Stratton blurted out, "Just because they asked you to do a review does not mean you have to come up and find their charge has any basis in fact or find the defendant guilty." In other words, just because you are the auditing agency for Congress, that doesn't mean you have to tell us the truth!

The subcommittee's deep hostility to the GAO report was revealed by this exchange between Milton Socolar, GAO general counsel, and Chairman White:

> WHITE: Show me where the statement was made by any witness that they had broken or violated the law.
>
> SOCOLAR: I don't know that we can show it to you in the terms that you are asking for it.
>
> WHITE: You are doing it by suspicion?
>
> SOCOLAR: No. I guess what I am saying is that, in terms of the evidence we examined, we have reached the conclusion that the purpose of the meetings could not have been otherwise. . . . I think it is backed by the evidence.
>
> WHITE: Give it to me then, please.
>
> SOCOLAR: The action item on the printout.
>
> WHITE: I read it to you. Where does it show it?

Not surprisingly, the subcommittee's final report concluded that no violations of the lobbying laws had occurred, and criticized GAO for failing to adhere to "the rules of evidence." However, the panel did grudgingly support GAO's recommendation that legislative lobbying procedures should be reviewed by all agencies to "avoid even the appearance of involvement in improper lobbying activities." The panel further agreed with GAO's findings that laws prohibiting lobbying by federal agencies should also be reviewed by Congress because they are "imprecise, vague, and largely unenforceable." But the subcommittee never formally pressed for such a review.

Stratton, in separate views in the report, blustered that the investigation was a waste of money, "a mere will o' the wisp," adding that the hearings "In my judgement . . . constitute a misuse of the vital oversight responsibilities of Congress."

In the end, the subcommittee swallowed the Pentagon line that it never used the printout in question, and rejected GAO's finding that air force officials had in fact accepted copies of the computer printout at each strategy meeting of the C-5B Group and at least once even called Lockheed to relate new information for the printout.

For GAO auditors the subcommittee's hostile reponse was a bitter experience that could only have a chilling effect upon future investigations into government abuses and mismangement. "Why put your head on the block when you see Congress treating its own auditors this way," a GAO auditor said later. "The subcommittee's response [to GAO's investigation] was outrageous."

A key government official who closely followed the C-5B lobbying investigation acidly remarked: "Congress should have rotating tours on the various committees so they don't get into bed with the agencies they're supposed to oversee." Clearly, he complained, "there was a parochial interest" among the subcommittee's members who were only concerned with protecting Lockheed's interests and that of its subcontractors who do business in their states or districts. "The decision gets political . . . and there's no oversight."

"Even if whatever [Pentagon and Lockheed officials] did wasn't illegal, it was immoral," this official said.

Government auditors may never again get their hands on a case as flagrant as the C-5B episode. "There has never been another case as well documented," said Dina Rasor, director of the Project on Military Procurement, who first made the printout public after it had been leaked to her by an inside source. "If you don't enforce the law, you make a mockery of it," she adds. "One look at the printout makes it clear that [Lockheed and the Pentagon] were directing each other."

The tragedy in the C-5B lobbying scandal is that similar lobbying abuses are occurring in one form or another throughout the government, with apparent impunity from prosecution or even administrative discipline. And the scandal will continue until Congress adopts tougher and unequivocal prohibitions, and stiffer penalites against violators, to end the bureaucracy's heavy-handed lobbying in behalf of itself and the special interests it serves.

13

Billions for Boeing

EARLY in 1981 when Budget Director David Stockman was trying to forge a consensus within Ronald Reagan's cabinet for the administration's forthcoming budget cuts, he tried to slash $752 million from the Export-Import Bank's $5.4 billion in lending authority. "I've got to take something out of Boeing's hide to make this look right," Reagan's youthful budget chief remarked at the time, meaning that if the budget was to be perceived as fair, the administration had to show that it was cutting corporate welfare as well as social welfare.

Surely, Stockman believed, this costly and dubious program of subsidized, cut-rate loans and loan guarantees to some of America's richest corporations — including Boeing, Lockheed and McDonnell-Douglas — was ripe for the budget-cutter's ax. But Stockman encountered fierce resistance around the massive oval table in the White House cabinet room, particularly from Commerce Secretary Malcolm Baldrige and U.S. Trade Representative William Brock. Neither man apparently understood that when Reagan talked about the need to control federal spending, he also meant government subsidies to big business.

The two cabinet officials launched a major counteroffensive against Stockman's proposed cut. According to the story Stockman told to journalist William Greider in a now-famous *Atlantic Monthly* confessional, Baldrige and Brock "fought, argued, pounded the table" and refused to yield in their opposition to touching this sacrosanct altar of corporate America.

As Greider relates the story, the resourceful Stockman tried a little political psychology on the stubborn cabinet officials. "I sort of innocently asked, well, isn't there a terribly political spin on this? It's my impression that most of the money goes to a handful of big corporations, and if we are ever caught not cutting this while we're biting deeply into the social programs, we're going to have big problems."

Then Stockman inquired "if anyone at the table had any relevant data. Deputy Secretary of the Treasury Tim McNamar thereupon produced a list of Ex-Im's major beneficiaries [a list that Stockman had given him before the meeting]. 'So then I went into this demogogic tirade about how in the world can I cut food stamps and social services and CETA jobs and EDA jobs and you're going to tell me you can't give up one penny for Boeing?' "

That was too much even for Baldrige and Brock to resist and Stockman won the first round by skillfully employing an old populist debating tactic. Yet while he won the battle in the cabinet council, he soon lost the war. For later that year as Congress worked its will on Reagan's budget proposals, a coalition of Republicans and Democrats teamed up in the Senate to restore the proposed Ex-Im Bank cut. Republican Senator Nancy Kassebaum of Kansas, where Boeing is a big employer, led the effort to give Ex-Im $250 million more than Stockman's budget asked for. The House soon followed suit, raising this figure even further.

Briefly, the Ex-Im Bank provides cheap credit to countries and overseas corporations who buy U.S. exports. Under the terms of its direct-loan program, the bank provides up to 65 percent of the export value of each purchase, with the buyer required to pay 15 percent of the export price in cash to the U.S. supplier and the balance coming from private lenders. Repayment can take from five to ten years, but these terms can be extended.

Interest rates for Third World nations were reduced in January 1983, from 11 percent to 10 percent. Industrial nations pay between 12.1 percent and 12.4 percent, depending on the repayment terms, while countries in between the poorest and the wealthiest are charged between 10.8 percent and 11.3 percent.

The bank also extends loan guarantees for up to 85 percent of a loan made by a U.S. bank, and offers insurance to protect the exporter "against the failure of the buyer to pay his dollar obligation for commercial or political reasons."

For years the bank, its powerful congressional patrons, and the corporate special interests who reap its rewards have insisted that the agency does not cost taxpayers a cent. In fact, they boasted that it actually made money for the government.

Yet not only do economic studies reveal that the bank has been enormously costly for the American taxpayer, but government audits have more recently shown that the bank itself is sustaining some huge losses.

According to a little-noticed 1982 study by John Boyd, senior economist for the Federal Reserve Bank in Minneapolis, Ex-Im's lending is "indeed subsidized and much more heavily than previous studies have suggested."

Exploding the myth that Ex-Im's corporate loans have cost taxpayers nothing, Boyd says that a detailed anlaysis of the agency's lending between 1976 and 1980 shows that "this program's annual costs exceeded its benefits by an average of about $200 million." Moreover, he found that "the subsidy increased substantially over the sample period and by 1980 may have reached as high as $650 million."

"Recent data show clearly that, in order to offer loans at below-market rates, Eximbank has been giving taxpayers a below-market return on their investment," says Boyd. "The difference between the return they could have been making and Eximbank's return has thus been the agency's hidden cost to taxpayers."

Boyd's conclusions were soundly supported in a study issued the previous year by the Congressional Budget Office which said in part:

> U.S. citizens who are not beneficiaries of the program pay additional interest costs of between $200 million and $900 million annually (at current program levels and interest rates). The report is unable to document any offsetting gains in economic efficiency or in achieving foreign policy objectives from the program as it currently operates; it finds that payments by non-beneficiaries are largely redistributed to U.S. exporters, foreign importers, and banks, with the remainder absorbed in efficiency losses from misdirection of resources.

"The Eximbank has shown a profit on its books," the CBO observed, but "it cannot be shown to run a profit when the costs of all citizens are taken into account."

Not long after CBO issued its conclusion in March 1981, however, Ex-Im confessed that it could no longer even boast that it was making a "profit" for the government. In 1982 the president of Ex-Im Bank, William S. Draper III, admitted before a Senate Appropriations subcommittee that his agency was suffering its first loss, estimating that it may be as high as $120 million. The bank ended up losing almost $160 million that year.

When General Accounting Office auditors examined Ex-Im's loan portfolio in 1982, they said they could not predict whether any of its delinquent and relatively risky loans would ever be paid off or become losses. Yet they cautioned Congress that if the bank's losses "continue to increase at a faster pace than Ex-Imbank's net income, Ex-Imbank's reserve will soon be inadequate to cover these prospective losses."

Repeating what they had told Congress the previous year, GAO auditors warned of the possibility of "exhaustion of Eximbank's reserves as early as fiscal year 1986."

As the months passed Ex-Im's position steadily worsened. On March 9, 1983, Draper was saying that the bank had written off $240 million in bad loans to Mexico, and that by the end of the 1983 fiscal year, losses from bad loans could amount to as much as $500 million.

By the end of fiscal 1983, which ended September 30, the Ex-Im Bank expected to lose a staggering $700 million.

Yet while taxpayers were losing their shirts from these losses, a handful of America's richest and most powerful companies were reaping its benefits.

Out of the more than $3.1 billion in loans the bank authorized in fiscal 1982, 43.7 percent of the money boosted the sales of ten major corporations — seven of which are Fortune 500 companies or their subsidiaries.

Here are the top ten corporations that profited from nearly half of Ex-Im's loans in 1982:

1. General Electric: Rated eleventh on the Fortune 500 list, with gross revenues of $26.5 billion in 1982, GE benefited from Ex-Im loans totaling $275 million.
2. Allis-Chalmers: Though rated 217th on the *Fortune* list, it increased its sales by approximately $252 million thanks to Ex-Im loans, despite gross revenues of $1.6 billion.
3. Fluor Corporation: It enjoyed $7.3 billion in gross revenues in 1982 when Ex-Im loans added at least $150 million to its sales.
4. Morrison-Knudson: Raked in $2.3 billion in revenues yet received a total of $146 million in sales through Ex-Im loans.
5. Boeing: Earning $9 billion in gross revenues, this huge aircraft corporation was ranked thirty-fourth in size and nineteenth among America's fastest-growing companies by *Fortune*. Boeing's hefty sales were helped by $117 million in Ex-Im loans in 1982.
6. General Motors: The number two company among the famous 500, with gross revenues of $60 billion a year, GM was helped by $100 million in Ex-Im loans.
7. Babcock & Wilcox: This is a subsidiary of McDermott, Inc., which is ranked seventy-second by *Fortune* and enjoyed 1982 gross revenues of $4.8 billion. Yet Babcock & Wilcox was aided by $99 million in low-cost bank loans.

8. WABCO: A subsidiary of American Standard, Inc., it is 178th on the *Fortune* list, having posted revenues of $2.1 billion in 1982. Nonetheless, WABCO's sales were boosted by $83 million in Ex-Im loans.
9. Westinghouse: Ranked thirty-first by *Fortune*, with gross revenues of $9.7 billion, this giant corporation was helped by $74 million in bank loans.
10. Wean United: It profited from $60 million in loans despite gross revenues of $179 million in 1982.

Even more staggering are the huge sums of Ex-Im money which have been cumulatively poured into these and other major corporations over many years. While the actual totals per exporter were not available, a computer scan conducted of all outstanding Ex-Im Bank loans as of June 30, 1983, ranked by exporter, reveals some of the awesome breadth of Ex-Im's corporate welfare.

For example, the outstanding loans that benefited Boeing alone totaled over $3.1 billion, more than any other U.S. corporation. McDonnell-Douglas was a close second, with a portfolio of $3 billion in outstanding loans; Westinghouse was third with $1.5 billion in loans; General Electric was fourth with $797 million in loans; and Western Electric was fifth with $358 million in loans.

The handful of other multinational corporate giants that have been helped by this multibillion-dollar program include the Bechtel Corporation, which has profited from $325 million in outstanding Ex-Im loans to its foreign customers; Lockheed Corporation, whose sales grossed $5.6 billion in 1982, and which is ranked fifty-sixth on the *Fortune* list, has benefited from a total of $272 million in loans; and GTE International Systems, whose parent company, GTE, racked up $7.8 billion in sales in 1982, profited from $69 million in loans.

In all, Ex-Im's records showed that eighteen major U.S. corporations had benefited from 65 percent, or $11 billion, of the total outstanding loans that remained in Ex-Im's portfolio.

Ex-Im's defenders have always managed to obscure the scandalous nature of its huge corporate subsidies by arguing that it helps provide jobs for Americans. In truth, however, it has in many cases helped to boost the industries of foreign competitors, which has cost jobs here at home. When Pan American World Airways hit the skids several years ago, Pam Am pilots purchased full-page newspaper ads that bitterly criticized the bank's cheap loans to its foreign airline rivals. Similarly, Japanese and other overseas textile manufacturers who bought raw materials here with below-market Ex-Im loans were given a major advantage over domestic manufacturers.

If the goal is to produce more jobs among U.S exporting firms, a 1981 analysis by the Congressional Budget Office insists that there are other economic policies which would "have more neutral expansionary effects. While some loans might reduce unemployment, others are made at times when they will probably aggravate inflation."

Moreover, the CBO argues that any U.S. economic gain does not necessarily "follow directly from the subsidized rise in exports," pointing out that "a subsidized increase in exports will not itself raise productivity."

More important, perhaps, is the CBO conclusion that any subsidized increase in net exports "will typically not produce an increase in savings, but rather will channel savings into foreign investment at the expense of domestic investment."

This is in part why John Boyd believes that "half a billion dollars or more is quite a sum for taxpayers to pay each year for such tenuous indirect benefits," and why he has concluded that Ex-Im's lending program "appears to be a program which society would be better off without."

14

The Million-Dollar Stallion

IN the summer of 1982 — when Congress was saddling a $100 billion tax bill on the American people and Ronald Reagan was hanging tough on trade with the Russians — the administration waived a major import tax for a U.S. business tycoon who had bought an Arabian stallion from the Soviet Union.

When the special tax break was formally approved by the government, the billionaire had saved a tidy $200,000 and the partnership that owned the stallion was well on is way toward making millions of dollars in profitable stud fees.

Pesniar, a purebred, seven-year-old Arabian stallion, was bought by oil billionaire Armand Hammer, chairman of Occidental Petroleum. Using his substantial connections with the Russians, Hammer purchased Pesniar for $1 million — the highest price ever paid for a horse in the USSR — through OPL Associates, a financial partnership between Occidental, financier David H. Murdock, and the Lasma Corporation, a string of horse breeding ranches.

Hammer, of course, expected the Agricultural Department to waive the 20 percent U.S. duty that is required under the 1930 Tariff Act except in cases in which recognized purebred horses may be imported into the United States duty-free for the purposes of breeding.

However, shortly after Pesniar was imported into the U.S. in December 1981, customs officials objected to waiving the $200,000 duty when they discovered that the Soviet Union's stud book, which would verify Pesniar's pedigree, was not recognized by the Agriculture Department's list of "recognized breeds and books of record." They told Hammer that since USDA did not recognize the stallion's pedigree, they could not exempt the horse from the duty.

One might think, perhaps, that someone of Hammer's considerable means, knowing of the debt into which the U.S. Treasury was sinking at the time, and knowing that his partnership expected to recoup millions of dollars on their investment, would happily pay the tax to his government. Indeed, Lasma's chairman, Alec Courtelis, revealed in an interview that he had sold $3 million in breeding bookings within a week of Pesniar's purchase. He estimated the horse's future income from syndication would be between $10 million and $15 million.

Yet despite the hefty profits the partnership would make on Pesniar, they had no intention of shelling out an import duty like some common tourist bringing back goods from a vacation abroad. Instead, Hammer petitioned the Department of Agriculture to add the Russian book to its list of recognized breeding books, and waive the duty fee retroactively.

This set off a minor flap within the government, particularly among a few members of Congress who got wind of what Hammer and his friends wanted Uncle Sam to grant them. Several House members, including Republican leader Robert Michel of Illinois, bitterly condemned the request. Pointing out that the United States has never granted the Russians "most favored nation" trading status, Michel wrote to Agriculture Secretary John R. Block that it "would represent a unilateral preferential trade concession to the Soviet Union."

"This not only seems to be a most inopportune time for such an action," Michel told Block, "but it seems to me that any such trade liberalization should be part of an overall foreign policy scenario with the Russians." Michel also noted that with the federal debt reaching record levels, this was not the time for the government to be merrily waiving import duty fees for wealthy Americans. "At a time of triple-digit federal deficits, I do not believe our government should be casually forgoing needed revenue, especially from a class of citizens who seem well able to afford to meet the existing tariff schedule."

Congressman Sam Hall, Jr., of Texas was even more indignant: "Let Mr. Hammer pay his import duties like everyone else," he complained to Block. "There is no valid reason to grant Mr. Hammer and the Soviet Union this preferential treatment."

In all, USDA said it received twenty-six letters on the duty waiver issue, seven in favor of granting the waiver, and nineteen — including five congressmen — opposed to recognizing the breed book "on grounds of economic or political policy." But the overwhelming opposition to Hammer's request did not sway the government's decision. On August 31, 1982, the department decided to recognize the Russian breed book and retroactively waive the import duty for Hammer and his wealthy partners. Breed recognition is decided "only on the basis of standards for recording and maintaining breed registry," explained John K. Atwell, deputy administrator of USDA's Animal and Plant Health Inspection Service (APHIS). "The requirements have been fulfilled."

As it turned out, Hammer's OPL Associates quietly imported three more Russian horses, for $242,000, a few weeks after Pesniar was brought into the U.S., and the USDA made them duty free as well.

There was "nothing unusual about this request except that it came from Armand Hammer," an internal USDA memorandum said of Hammer's demand for the import duty waiver. But Mark Dulin, staff veterinarian for imports and exports at APHIS, while duly noting Hammer's vast wealth and influence, bluntly told a reporter, "I know I couldn't get that done."

From the beginning of this controversy over a sleek Arabian stallion, Hammer's enormous wealth and power hung over the government's ultimate decision. In the end, it was hard to escape the public perception, held by many within the government as well, that this $200,000 import duty waiver represented another special tax break for the rich and influential.

15

Synfuels: The $88 Billion Mistake

AGAINST a backdrop of fear and political hysteria, Congress created the multibillion-dollar Synthetic Fuels Corporation in July 1980. The U.S. Embassy in Tehran had been seized by Iranian terrorists. The Middle East was a cauldron of crises. The Organization of Petroleum Exporting Countries was blackmailing the United States with oil prices that had reached $41 per barrel. Americans feared a cutoff of foreign crude would cripple our economy and threaten national security.

Motivated by insecurities, both real and imagined, Congress established a new federally financed Synthetic Fuels Corporation, and bullishly gave it an $88 billion mandate to achieve a synfuels production goal of two million barrels a day by 1992.

Four years later, the Synthetic Fuels Corporation (SFC) had squandered over $70 million — mostly for administrative expenses — hired nearly two hundred employes at big salaries, and ensconced itself in lavishly furnished offices. Yet it has not produced a thimbleful of synthetic fuel. Moreover, it now admits that the production goals Congress has set were unrealistic and impossible to achieve.

SFC was established by the Energy Security Act of 1980 which envisioned a two-stage synthetic fuels program. The first phase called for funding of up to $20 billion, followed by a second phase in which authorized funding could reach an additional $68 billion. Congress began its synfuels drive by establishing the Energy Security Reserve, a special $17.5 billion Treasury account from which SFC was authorized to make direct loans, price and loan guarantees, and purchase commitments as part of the program's first stage.

By 1983 Congress had actually appropriated nearly $15 billion for SFC's use, while $1.61 billion in synfuels funds had been separately committed by the Department of Energy before SFC became operational.

Before its enactment, critics warned that SFC would turn out to be another pipeline to the U.S. Treasury for energy corporations already rich enough to bankroll their own synfuels investments. They were right. The federally financed corporation proceeded to enter into big money commitments with some of America's wealthiest energy giants, who were delighted to let taxpayers subsidize their riskier corporate research and development projects.

Internally, the corporation was beset by a rash of scandals: its officers were raking in unprecedented salaries; the wife of SFC's first president was paid $32,000 a year to be the chairman of the board's secretary — despite a corporate policy that secretaries could earn no more than $23,819 annually. There were allegations of cozy deals among corporate cronies, and repeated squabbles among its seven-member board of directors.

A Senate subcommittee discovered in 1983 that then–SFC president Victor A. Schroeder had issued fifty-one consulting contracts without competitive bidding between 1981 and 1983 — some of which went to former business associates. An internal audit also charged that Schroeder had improperly billed SFC over $25,000 for a real estate broker's fee and interest payments on his Alexandria home.

There were also allegations that the SFC president had offered to help another board member do some business with the Mobil Land Development Corporation in exchange for the member's support for Schroeder's plan to reorganize the SFC. A report by SFC's inspector general, S. Kenric Lessey, Jr., said, "The most troubling aspect of the conversation . . . is the juxtaposition of a request for a personal favor with a discussion of corporation policy decision-making." This, said Lessey, "raised questions which might have involved violations of federal criminal law. . . . It was certainly an indiscretion and may well have given rise to an appearance of wrongdoing." The Justice Department declined to pursue the case due to "insufficient evidence."

Schroeder resigned his post in August 1983, denying all charges of mismanagement and impropriety, though he did repay $20,000 of the real estate payments.

Senator William Cohen of Maine, chairman of the Government Management Oversight Subcommittee which investigated the allegations, said SFC's history has been "marked by management failures, an absence of planning, and missed opportunities. The evidence suggests that the SFC has operated more like a family-run corporation than a public entity charged with the responsibility of wisely investing billions of tax dollars."

Two years after SFC's creation, members of Congress, including Senators Bill Armstrong of Colorado and William Proxmire of Wisconsin, were calling on Congress to abolish the corporation, which they labeled "an $88 billion mistake"; an advisory study panel created by the corporation, made up of business, government and academic leaders, issued a report that questioned whether the corporation should even exist; and most of the corporation's projects were either going down the drain or were in deep financial trouble.

"It is time to end our experiment with inflated synthetic fuels projects which disrupt our credit markets but don't deliver on their promise of achieving energy independence," Proxmire said in April 1982. "The Synthetic Fuels Corporation is an idea whose time has passed."

Simple economics proved Proxmire's observation. The OPEC-induced price incentives that gave synfuels its investment potential had vanished. In 1980 the price of oil had reached $41 per barrel and the U.S. was importing 5.3 million barrels a day. But by 1983 the price had plummeted by 30 percent to $28 a barrel and U.S. oil imports had decreased by 51 percent to 2.6 million barrels per day.

Since its inception, the Synfuels Corporation has been a perfect example of what happens when government goes into business, and when business people go into government. When businessman Edward Noble headed the Reagan administration's transition team, which studied the federally financed corporation, Noble favored abolishing it. But the worm turned when Reagan named Noble to be Synfuels' chairman. Soon after taking over the corporation, he was calling for committing all of the $15 billion that Congress had authorized to underwrite synthetic fuels projects.

Meantime, for a corporation that had not earned a dollar, its salaries and benefits, at least by government standards, were exceedingly generous: SFC's president was paid $135,000 a year, while its vice-presidents earned between $108,000 and $69,630. Sixty-one percent of the corporation's 105 middle- to upper-level management staff were earning yearly salaries in excess of $50,000.

Despite a rash of unfavorable publicity over its inflated salaries, SFC shelled out $44,226 to a consultant for a study of what its federally funded salaries should be. The report did not disappoint corporate bigwigs: it proposed that the chairman of the board should earn between $152,000 and $228,000 a year; the president, $132,000 to $198,000, and the senior vice-president, $91,000 to $136,000 a year.

As for benefits, the corporation will put up to 6 percent of each employee's salary, plus an additional 50 percent contribution, into a savings plan. It pays the full cost of all medical and dental insurance premiums, plus life insurance for each employee at premiums based on individual salaries. It also picks up the parking bills for its 102 top employees.

By 1983 Synfuels had about 190 employees, whose annual payroll totaled $8.2 million. By fiscal 1984 its staff was projected to rise to 238, though it has a congressionally set limit of 300.

SFC did not skimp on its offices either, locating in Washington's high-rent K Street corridor in a new office building whose $30-per-square-foot rent included saunas, and racquetball and squash court facilities for SFC officers. The corporation signed a noncancellable, five-year lease for $1.9 million a year.

While SFC was spending $2.8 million a year for rent, utilities and communications, it was squandering another $626,000 to furnish the offices lavishly, including $103,000 for an interior decorator, $375,000 on furniture and $83,000 for wall-to-wall carpeting in executive offices.

The Congressional Budget Office (CBO) calculated that at its present rate of expenditures the corporation would spend a total of $234 million in administrative expenses alone between fiscal 1982 and 1987.

CBO also estimated the corporation's total outlays could reach $4.6 billion between 1982 and 2001 for price guarantee commitments. Moveover, CBO said loan guarantees "may create a contingent liability of $7.2 billion by 1991, and may result in outlays" of $800 million if only one project defaults.

Yet for all of Congress's free-spending bravado over synfuels production, there is serious doubt that the corporation has anywhere near the funding to achieve the goals Congress set for it. Jimmie Bowden, then SFC executive vice-president, confessed before the House Interior Appropriations Subcommittee on April 11, 1983, "It is quite clear we don't have enough money to sponsor two million barrels of production. . . . At the present level, [the cost to achieve this] would look like it would exceed $150 billion."

Lured by the government's tempting handouts, the synfuels business may have looked like a lucrative idea at the time. But the growing costs of producing synthetic fuels, plus the world oil glut, has forced one big energy company after another to abandon their projects. Consider these examples:

- Exxon: Number one on the Fortune 500 list, with $97.2 billion in revenues, Exxon pulled out of the Colony Oil Shale Project in 1982. Rather than apply for government subsidies, it chose to absorb its $920 million investment in synfuels and get out — though they are holding on to their shale rock, clearly with the intention of developing synfuels when it becomes economically feasible.
- Atlantic Richfield: Ranked twelfth on the Fortune 500, with $26.5 billion in gross sales in 1982, Atlantic ended up selling out its 60 percent share in Colony to Exxon in 1980.
- Tosco Corporation: Listed 112th among the Fortune 500, it became Exxon's partner in the Colony project, but chose to exercise

its option to sell out to Exxon rather than go it alone. After paying off what it owed on a $1.1 billion Energy Department loan guarantee, Tosco will have made a $220 million profit, "nearly ten times its 1981 earnings," according to *Fortune*. Tosco had gross sales of $3.5 billion in 1982.

- Gulf and Shell: Ranked ninth and thirteenth respectively on the *Fortune* list, both of these multibillion-dollar oil corporations pulled out of the Alberta (Canada) Tar-Sands project, shortly after Exxon's decision to withdraw from the Colony project. It was supposed to produce bitumen, a tarlike substance that can be refined into oil products.
- Ashland Oil Company: After pulling out of the Breckinridge project in 1982, SFC dropped the project from consideration. SFC's 1982 annual report said the "project's economics no longer supported [Ashland's] continued involvement."
- Standard Oil Company of Ohio: SOHIO, which was twenty-first on the Fortune 500 list, participated in the Hampshire Energy Project on its own, though other Hampshire sponsors were asking for SFC assistance. In late 1982, when SOHIO withdrew from the project, it cited "the project's uncertain economics." By December 1982, the project's other backers put the $2 billion project on indefinite hold.
- Panhandle Eastern Corporation: Not long after Panhandle dropped out of the WyCoal Gasification project, the Pacific Gas & Electric Co. and Ruhrgas Carbon Conversion, Inc. also abandoned the project.
- New England Energy Park Project: Though a candidate for Synfuels support, design work on the project was suspended when its sponsors were unable to find customers for the electricity their coal gasification plant would generate. The sponsors canceled the project in May 1983.

An examination of SFC's project solicitation process since 1980 also reveals the precipitous decline in new synfuels proposals for government support:

There were sixty-eight proposals submitted to SFC by the end of 1980, though forty of them did not respond to requests in 1981 to submit additional information by January 1982. Of the twenty-eight applicants who did respond, four withdrew their applications, seventeen subsequently failed SFC's review, and seven were bumped to the second solicitation phase. In truth, the review postponement was merely a delaying tactic to make SFC look busy without really doing anything. At the time there weren't any projects remaining in the first review stage that would have been held up if the seven postponed projects had been given additional consideration. So at the end of the first solicitation, SFC had no active projects under consideration for federal support.

SFC's second project solicitation, in June 1982, yielded thirty-seven proposals: twenty-three were resubmissions of earlier proposals and fourteen were new. But eleven of them failed the review test and one lost its equity sponsor. Out of two new proposals and three resubmissions still in the running, only one resubmission was awarded. Thus, at the end of its second solicitation, only four new projects were under consideration.

By January 1983 the third solicitation elicited forty-six proposals, though twenty-nine of them were resubmissions and only seventeen were new proposals. By late 1983, only eighteen of these projects were being seriously considered for review, yet only seven of them were actually new synfuels proposals.

The point is that there were not a lot of new synfuels applicants beating down SFC's door with viable projects. Despite SFC's propensity to point out the number of responses it has had, the figures show there was hardly a landslide of interest in synfuels from the private sector.

By mid-1983 a survey of the top candidates for SFC backing revealed the little-noticed extent to which SFC's pending portfolio represented the private sector's richest and most powerful energy corporations:

1. The Cool Water Coal Gasification Project: SFC's first award recipient, the corporation granted its sponsors $120 million in price guarantees, i.e., for a maximum of five years SFC would guarantee a price of $9.75 to $12.50 per mmBTU (million British Thermal Units) of natural gas. The 1982 average sales price was $4.55 per mmBTU.

Who were among this project's corporate sponsors? General Electric Corporation, ranked eleventh on the Fortune 500 list, with $26.5 billion in gross sales (all corporate revenue numbers given here are gross annual receipts); Texaco, ranked fourth by *Fortune*, with $47 billion in annual sales; Southern California Edison Co., with $4.3 billion in sales; Bechtel Power Corporation, whose multinational parent company did over $11 billion in business in 1981; and JCWP, a Japanese consortium.

2. Calsyn Heavy Oil Conversion: SFC signaled its intention to back this West Pittsburgh, California, project, which was requesting a $51 million loan guarantee.

The project's financial backers included Tenneco, ranked nineteenth among the Fortune 500, with gross sales of $15.2 billion; Dynalectron Corporation, with $458 million in sales; and Ralph M. Parsons Company, $1.2 billion in sales.

3. Hop Kern Tar Sands: This project, whose sponsors were seeking $76.7 million in loan and price guarantees, was backed by the Holly Corporation, ranked 432nd on the Fortune list, with $540 million in gross sales, and SEDCO, Inc., with $523 million in gross sales, among a handful of other energy companies.

4. Santa Rosa Tar Sands: Sponsors of this project, which in 1983 was seeking $20 million in loan guarantees and $21 million in price guarantees, included: Foster Wheeler Energy Corporation, a subsidiary of the Foster-Wheeler Corporation, ranked 215th on the *Fortune* list, with $1.6 billion in gross revenues.

5. First Colony Peat to Methanol: After failing SFC's first review, this Creswell, North Carolina, project was awarded $820,750 to improve its project cost estimates. It leaped to notoriety in 1982 when it was reported that CIA director William Casey was an investor in the Energy Transition Corporation, one of First Colony's sponsors.

Other sponsors of First Colony were Koppers Co., Inc., the diversified $1.7 billion Pittsburgh-based corporation which was listed 208th on the *Fortune* ranking; and Transco Companies, Inc., which had gross sales of $3.9 billion.

According to the Environmental Policy Institute (EPI), one of First Colony's critics, four Koppers subsidiaries were lined up to do contractual work on the project. EPI charged that ETCO Methanol, a subsidiary of the company in which Casey was an investor, would invest nothing in the venture, yet would "retain a 5 percent interest in the project as well as a contract for project management."

6. North Alabama Coal Liquefaction: Like the other projects, this was seeking both loan and price guarantees and had some enormously wealthy backers.

They included Kidder Peabody and Peabody Coal Co., both subsidiaries of Peabody International, which racked up $484 million in gross sales in 1982 and was ranked 460th on the *Fortune* list; Air Products & Chemicals Co., ranked 223rd, with $1.6 billion in revenues; Raymond International, $1.1 billion in 1981 revenues; Houston Natural Gas Co., with $3.2 billion in gross sales; and Santa Fe International, which is owned by the Kuwait Petroleum Co., i.e., the government of Kuwait.

As with so many other project sponsors, all of the companies sponsoring the North Alabama project were providing contractual services to the project either directly or through their subsidiaries. Raymond International had a $46 million engineering contract through a subsidiary. A Santa Fe subsidiary was to receive a contract to furnish overall design and procurement services for the project.

Yet if Congress needed any warning of the folly of its corporate enterprise, it could be found in the Great Plains coal gasification project in Beulah, North Dakota. Once considered a synfuels industry showpiece, Great Plains has become an ominous symbol of the problems that afflict the government's synfuels program.

Backed by a commitment of up to $2 billion in Department of Energy loan guarantees, before SFC's creation, the project was pushed by a consortium of five major energy corporations, including Tenneco, Inc. and American Natural Resources Co. By the spring of 1983 the companies had invested only $300 million of their own money, while the government had committeed $622 million to the project. When completed — it was scheduled to go into production by December 1984 — Great Plains would be America's first commercial-size plant for converting coal into a natural gas substitute.

At first, the consortium was optimistic it could show a net profit of $1.2 billion in its first ten years of operation. However, by April of 1983 its backers were gloomily predicting that they could face "losses in excess of $770 million." They blamed the government's pricing formula, arguing that it unfairly tied the price of the plant's synthetic gas to the price of heating oil and the producer price index, both of which had not been rising as fast as originally expected. There were hints that the firms would pull out of the synfuels project if they did not receive further federal subsidies.

But the Great Plains project was not as financially disastrous as its corporate sponsors, who came to Washington with their tin cups, made it appear.

According to a General Accounting Office study issued in August 1983, the enterprise could just possibly "realize an average annual 20 percent return on their investment over the first 20 years the plant operates." The reason for GAO's rosier view: the investing companies did not factor in tax writeoffs and benefits for their parent companies in their profit and loss projections to the government.

"Although Great Plains estimates significant losses during the first eight years the plant operates, we found that there could be a positive cash flow to the partners throughout the life of the project if taxes are considered," the GAO said. The auditors found that as a result of investment and energy tax credits, and interest deductions, the investors' parent companies would benefit from tax savings of $400 million during the facility's construction. Further tax savings down the road were also substantial. "For example," the GAO continued, Great Plains' March 1983 report, which predicted heavy future losses, "shows that the partners would have to put $841 million into the project during the first eight years it operates. During this same time period, however, the parent companies' tax liability could be reduced by $922 million."

Watching the huge multinational conglomerates lining up for the government's subsidies, and then witnessing failure after failure in a declining synfuels market, two senators declared that they had had enough. Backed by a coalition of environmental, taxpayer and small business groups, Proxmire and Armstrong submitted legislation in the spring of 1982 to abolish the entire misguided enterprise.

"Times have changed since the Synthetic Fuels Corporation was first proposed," Proxmire said. "Oil imports have dropped substantially and even the price of oil is starting to decline. Conventional fuel exploration has increased while conservation has taken hold. ... Creating the Corporation was unwise in 1979. It's an even worse idea today."

Their bill was greeted with stony silence by most of Congress. But they received some unexpected support in the summer of 1982 when four members of the twelve-member Synthetic Fuels Study Panel, an advisory group set up by the SFC to study issues facing the fledgling corporation, strongly questioned whether SFC should continue to exist.

Despite the fact that industry was deserting the synthetic fuels field in droves, the majority of business executives, government officials and academics represented on the panel backed continued government support for synfuels, largely on national security grounds. But in a minority report the four dissenters suggested that it would be far better if natural gas prices were fully deregulated or the so-called windfall profits tax on crude oil was repealed: "By making the production of fossil fuels more profitable, these steps would increase conventional fuel supplies and, in the case of gas-price deregulation, reduce demand."

They conceded "that the private market will not generate synthetic fuels on its own, given today's economic environment." However, they believed "that a private synthetic fuels industry will develop on its own as soon as the correct price signals occur in the market. After all, firms do seek profits by trying to anticipate price changes," they said.

The four dissenters rejected the argument that the cost of developing synthetic fuels is so enormous that only the government can handle it.

Although the capital outlays associated with a synfuels project may be very large, the sums involved represent only a tiny fraction of the assets currently employed in the energy industries. This fact and the drive for profits will bring about the creation of a private synfuels industry as soon as the most optimistic small fraction of all investors inside or outside the energy industry expect crude-oil prices to move to levels at which synthetic fuel becomes competitive.

If investments are not made in the synfuels industry without government support, [they added] this is a sure sign that the resources are more efficiently used in other industries. Diverting resources into the synfuels industry is inefficient and costly to the nation's economic growth when private investors cannot make sufficiently profitable investments to be enticed into the industry without government inducement.

Further support for this position came from the Energy Information Administration, the Department of Energy's statistical gathering arm, which said in its *1982 Annual Energy Outlook* report: "In the current environment, even with government assistance, the private sector cannot justify major investments in synthetic fuels facilities."

Though the Proxmire-Armstrong bill to abolish SFC died in committee in 1982 without receiving serious consideration, Proxmire and Senator Gary Hart of Colorado offered a new repeal measure in 1983, while similar legislation was introduced in the House. Its prospects remain bleak.

The energy industry, comprised of over ten thousand oil companies, is the wealthiest business sector in the United States. In 1982 America's twenty-two largest oil companies alone had gross revenues of more than $467 billion. Clearly, the energy industry is more than capable, technologically and financially, of researching and developing the alternative fuels that America will need in the decades to come. Once again, Congress has created another corporate sugardaddy for America's biggest and richest industrial giants. Only in this case the corporation has been a conspicuous failure that could end up costing the American people billions of dollars.

16

The Gravy in the Deal

O<small>NE</small> brisk winter day, Rich DeVos was aboard his princely 162-foot yacht, the *Enterprise*, enjoying an elegant lunch with a group of journalists, when the subject of his company's ritzy new hotel came up. The hotel, DeVos said, had been built with the help of a $3 million Urban Development Action Grant from the federal government. When asked why a company as enormously wealthy as the Amway Corporation, which is so demonstrably opposed to Big Government, would look to Uncle Sam for assistance, the deeply conservative DeVos replied, "We've been sending our money to Washington for years, and this is a chance to get a little of it back."

This, of course, is the rationale that people of all political persuasions have used again and again for dipping into a bankrupt U.S. Treasury for all their material needs. It is an especially popular excuse among those in the corporate world who love to rail against "uncontrolled federal spending" and "unacceptable deficits" at chamber of commerce meetings, yet have no trouble justifying their own needs for a seemingly endless array of federal grants, loans, bailouts, subsidies, tax loopholes and payoffs of one sort or another.

In the continuing war being waged against rising government

spending, an accusing finger is frequently pointed at something called the "special interests," a disembodied group that is always up to its waist in the public trough. The problem with this convenient but vaguely identified scapegoat is that all of us are these special interests. With few exceptions, most of us receive or defend some government expenditure or benefit from which we profit.

Which brings us back to the Amway Corporation. Built from the ground up — in this case the Michigan company started in a garage — by its two brilliant and innovative chief executives, Rich DeVos and Jay Van Andel, their business enterprise has become one of the truly great American success stories. The company has had annual revenues of more than $1.4 billion, maintains a huge international sales force, and manufactures a highly regarded and diversified line of products, from cleaning liquids to food bars.

At the same time, both men have become articulate and untiring apostles against excessive government spending and in support of a stronger private sector. Their corporation has run newspaper advertisements saying that "The success of Amway Corporation is proof that free enterprise can and will flourish in any free society." Other Amway messages declare: "Inflation — The Price We Pay When Government Won't Say No!"; "The Federal Nanny — Domestic Help We Can't Afford"; and "Why There's No Such Thing as a Free Lunch."

DeVos, who has served as finance chairman of the Republican National Committee, has given speeches throughout the country, vigorously denouncing federal giveaway programs. In one speech DeVos said, "Democracy will collapse when the government takes too much control of the treasury, or when the public votes themselves largesse from the treasury. The result of such actions leads to dictatorship."

Van Andel, who was a former chairman of the U.S. Chamber of Commerce, has said that "everything that government gives to the people, it first takes away from them. . . . For forty years we have turned increasingly away from our inner resources and toward the central government for the solution of all our problems. And we have reached the point where the cost of additional government service surpasses the benefit to be gained from it."

Yet both men make no secret of the fact that the $38 million hotel and office complex that Amway built in downtown Grand Rapids, Michigan, was helped along in part by a $3 million-plus Urban Development Action Grant from the U.S. Department of Housing and Urban Development.

The $440-million-a-year UDAG program has helped to build many ritzy hotel complexes and other lucrative private real estate developments across the country. Developers look to the grants as a way of paying for underground parking garages, adjacent malls and other facilities that the hotels are able to use. Indeed, a House Appropriations Commitee investigative report on who benefits from the HUD grants quoted a real estate developer who said UDAGs were "the gravy in the deal."

"Hotel projects are very attractive investments to the extent that . . . one hotel chain established an office specifically to assist developers or cities with submission of UDAG applications," the report noted. Its multimillion-dollar grants to local governments have helped support building projects for wealthy corporations such as Coca-Cola and big corporate hotel and motel chains like Hyatt-Regency, Hilton, Marriott, and Howard Johnson. The grants, for which more than 50 percent of America's big cities are eligible, have been used to renovate theaters, and help build marina and restaurant developments, shopping malls, skylifts and upper-income housing.

Consider the Riverfront project in Detroit where developers obtained a $19 million UDAG with which to help put up two twenty-nine-story apartment towers. This was not a development for housing-starved low-income familes. The rents were expected to run between $450 and $1,500 a month. Included in this redevelopment project along the Detroit River was a seventy-seven-boat marina and yacht club, a private health spa, an indoor swimming pool facility, rooftop tennis courts, valet parking and fancy gourmet shops. This was a development for the upper middle class and the rich.

A legacy of Jimmy Carter's administration, the purpose of UDAGs is to help cities by giving them funds to help finance various municipal development projects with which to lure businesses and speculators into areas in need of urban revitalization. HUD calls this "leveraging" and says it produces jobs and investments that would not occur were it not for the grants. Wallace Berger, a staff official on the Senate Appropriations Subcommittee on HUD, explains that "The intent was to use [UDAG] in cases where the private sector would not proceed without federal assistance."

But it has not worked out that way in the real world. The General Accounting Office, in fact, has found cases where UDAG-funded development projects were committed to proceed, regardless of whether the grants were available or not. "They were in the bag," an auditor says.

This, it turns out, was the case with Amway's development of the Amway Grand Plaza. According to an early HUD summary of the project, "the funds will be used to build . . . a 700-space parking garage in the complex" adjacent to a dilapidated hotel Amway planned to refurbish.

The corporation's renovation of the rundown Pantlind Hotel turned the graceful 1913 Grand Rapids landmark into a luxurious 390-room hotel, which was completed in 1981. It included a penthouse, a big ballroom, swiming pool, sauna, jacuzzi, tennis courts, concierge service, and a modern convention center, for which the parking gargage is vital.

According to Amway officials, the UDAG to the city was used solely to help build the parking facility, which is linked to the hotel by a pedestrian skywalk over the street. Amway explains that the company lent the city an additional $5.3 million interest free to complete the garage and then Amway planned to buy it back from the city.

When Grand Rapids municipal officials first put together the package deal they persuaded Amway to enlarge upon its original plan simply to renovate the Pantlind. Amway was presented with an offer that, as they say, was hard to refuse. It included a 50 percent cut in property taxes for twelve years on the new construction, worth more than $10 million, plus the authorization of tax-exempt bonds that enabled Amway to borrow at lower interest rates. Approval of the federal UDAG, of course, was part of the deal.

But was the UDAG crucial to enlisting Amway's participation in the big downtown redevelopment project? In other words, would

Amway have proceeded without the grant? When I put this question to Liz Amante, an Amway public relations official, she replied, "I think yes. The project was already under way. The decision [to go ahead] was made before the grant was received."

Thus, the Amway–Grand Rapids UDAG was not necessary for this ambitious and costly redevelopment project to go forward. It was, quite clearly, "the gravy in the deal" for another wealthy special interest.

17

The Imperial Ex-Presidents

Eᴀᴄʜ year America's beleaguered taxpayers are shelling out millions of dollars to maintain a small, elite group of multimillionaires in the style to which they have become accustomed.

We support their lucrative lecture businesses, help to fulfill their million-dollar-plus book deals, pick up the travel bills of their entourage, and chauffeur them to big-paying corporate board meetings and other business and personal appointments. We furnish them with everything from office plants to postage, from personalized stationery to ball-point pens, from speech writers to round-the-clock security guards, from joke consultants to landscaping and swimming pool maintenance. We wash their cars, pay for their magazine and newspaper subscriptions, and foot their telephone bills and cable television fees. We provide them with secretaries, press aides, errand boys, and other special assistants to help them research, write and promote their money-making memoirs, and manage their other business, public, and private affairs.

The tab for these and other services and benefits is $13.1 million annually, and growing. The exclusive group that profits from this relatively sizable government expenditure presently numbers only four people. They are former Presidents Richard M. Nixon, Gerald R. Ford and Jimmy Carter, and Ladybird Johnson, widow of Lyndon Baines Johnson. All are millionaires in their own right. Yet all are eligible for these and other federally paid services and benefits, in addition to generous government pensions, until the day they die.

When the cost of maintaining seven presidential libraries, which is surpassing $15 million a year, is added to the expense of providing round-the-clock Secret Service details, office staffs, stretch limousines, and other special allowances for our former presidents and their spouses, the full bill totals more than $28 million a year.

By comparison, the cost of maintaining the entire White House operation comes to only $22 million.

The rapid growth in support costs for our former presidents has been breathtaking. In 1968 the cost of maintaining the presidential libraries was less than $1 million a year. The office allowances for four former presidents came to $251,000. Secret Service protection cost a mere $390,000. Since 1965 the cost of maintaining the trappings of the presidency for our former chief executives has increased more than fortyfold.

It all started in 1955 when Congress began paying for the maintenance of presidential libraries, and followed that up in 1958 with the Former Presidents Act, which provided an income-pinched Harry Truman with a modest $25,000 pension and $50,000 a year to maintain an office and staff. Up to that time Truman had been answering his own mail, at his own expense, and had refused to accept any of the corporate consulting offers that had come his way. "They were not interested in hiring Harry Truman the person," he said. "It was the former president of the United States they wanted."

But Congress was not content to leave well enough alone. After President John F. Kennedy's assassination, it authorized that all former presidents be given Secret Service protection, and that Kennedy's widow, Jacqueline, and her two children also be protected for two years. The law was amended in 1965 to cover all first ladies for four years, and extended in 1968 to lifetime protection. Thus, over the past three decades the cost of former presidents has skyrocketed from $64,000 to more than $27 million.

Few if any Americans would begrudge providing our former

presidents with whatever reasonable support is needed to handle their public responsibilities (e.g., answering correspondence, serving their country on special assignments) as befits those who have occupied the highest public office in the land. But the outrageously lavish expenditures that have been allowed to take place under the vaguely worded Former Presidents Act goes far beyond what is either necessary or reasonable.

"I do not believe that the taxpayer is under any obligation to see his money being used to make former presidents millionaires," says Senator Lawton Chiles of Florida. Yet that is exactly what has been happening.

Of the total $13.1 million spent annually in behalf of our former presidents, staff payroll and office expenses are the smallest part, though in many ways the most egregiously wasteful. Former President Nixon's office expenses in fiscal 1983 alone totaled $349,000. Ford's came to $340,000, and Carter's, who was still sorting his presidential papers and other White House materials, exceeded $400,000.

According to the General Services Administration, which administers the former presidents' budget, the pensions, personnel, travel, telephones, postage, printing and all other office-support costs for our former presidents and their widows came to $1.1 million in fiscal 1983. This was expected to climb to nearly $1.2 million in fiscal 1984. Included is a $22,000 widow's pension for Mrs. Ladybird Johnson, whose land and broadcasting properties, plus other investments, are worth millions of dollars.

The major cost to taxpayers, however, is the lifetime, round-the-clock Secret Service protection for former presidents, their families and their widows, at a cost of $11.2 million a year. A detail of $30,000-a-year agents was, for example, assigned to Bess Truman twenty-four hours a day until her death in 1982, as they were for Mamie Eisenhower until her death. It continues for our three former presidents and Mrs. Johnson. Inexplicably, pensions and Secret Service protection ends when a widow remarries, thus Jacqueline Kennedy Onassis gets neither.

In an era of high-powered, big-paying book and television deals, lecture tours, and other lucrative business and consulting ventures available to any former president, no chief executive need ever face a life of poverty once out of office. The world of a former president can be a big business, if he chooses it to be. Even if a former president were to forgo such business ventures, a lifetime presidential pension of $80,100 a year is comfortable enough — though former presidents may enjoy even larger pensions due to their military, congressional or gubernatorial service. Ford, for instance, is "a triple dipper." In addition to an $80,100 presidential pension for his two and a half years in office, he receives a $30,000-a-year congressional pension, plus a modest naval reserve pension.

The income and assets of our living former presidents are substantial by any standard. More important, the evidence is clear that much of their wealth was accumulated after they left office. For example, in his last year in office Ford listed his net worth at $323,489. But upon leaving office, he quickly negotiated a lucrative deal for his memoirs, *A Time to Heal,* plus a television contract, which reportedly brought him over $2 million. To this he added income estimated "in the half-million-dollar range" by accepting seats on seven corporate boards, and making twenty to thirty speeches a year at $10,000 to $20,000 a crack.

Newsweek estimated in 1981 that Ford's gross annual income exceeded $900,000 and it has very likely stayed near that sum. He has purchased two homes, one in exclusive Palm Springs, California, and a summer home in Vail, Colorado. He bought two radio stations in Durango, Colorado, in May 1980 and has made other prudent investments. Robert Barrett, Ford's executive assistant, said of Ford's income, "It just keeps rolling in."

After he resigned from the presidency in 1974, Nixon was in debt to the tune of more than $600,000, mostly due to back taxes. However, he quickly recovered financially by earning between $2 million and $3 million from his bestselling memoirs and an additional $650,000 from his televised interviews with talk show host David Frost. His income swelled as a result of several additional book contracts, in addition to the sale of his luxurious properties in San Clemente, California, and Key Biscayne, Florida, for which he made close to $2 million. He made an even handsomer profit from the sale of his four-story townhouse in New York City in 1981, reportedly receiving close to his asking price of $2.9 million. He had bought the building in 1979 for $750,000. Nixon, in other words, became a relatively wealthy man after resigning the presidency. Such wealth was certainly evident when he bought his present home in exclusive Saddle River, New Jersey, which carried an asking price of $1.2 million. The estate included a 900-square-foot swimming pool, tennis court, and 1,000-bottle wine cellar.

On the other hand, Jimmy Carter's wealth was well established in his land and family holdings in Plains, Georgia, before he won the presidency in 1976. Upon leaving office in January 1981, Carter was reported to have $1.9 million worth of land and savings, plus a $1.8 million share in the family farm in Plains, and $600,000 in cash and government Series E Bonds. He sold the family warehouse in March 1981 for $1.5 million, and he and his wife Rosalynn signed lucrative book deals that earned them more than $1 million in advances.

Yet despite their great wealth, our former presidents still receive millions of dollars annually from the taxpayers to surround themselves with the pomp and trappings of the presidency.

Upon leaving office, the president is given up to $1 million in "transition" expenses, and is flown home on Air Force One like a departing monarch — a far cry from that cold winter day in January 1953 when Harry Truman went back to Independence, Missouri, on the train at his own expense. The range of perks and privileges showered on our former presidents is truly remarkable, and so are their unbounded appetites for such benefits. Worse, our former chief executives are not in the least embarrassed that they continue to be a burden to taxpayers long after they have left public office.

Remember when Jimmy Carter sold the presidential yacht, *Sequoia*, reduced the number of executive jets at Andrews Air Force Base, and cut back on the White House limos and color television sets? A different Jimmy Carter returned to Plains, Georgia, where he set up an office in his mother's home, for which she was paid $250 a month plus utilities, and then requested an additional suite of offices in Atlanta for his full-time staff. In 1982 the payroll for Carter's six staff employees totaled $292,800. Office furnishings cost $105,349. His phone bill was $24,800. His staff travel costs came to

$15,000. There was also a one-time transition cost in fiscal 1982 for Carter, which totaled $800,000, to move and store his presidential papers and other belongings.

When Carter moved into his federally paid office in Atlanta he wanted to furnish it with a luxurious $15,000 wool rug and two chandeliers whose price tag was $3,500. Polyester or nylon carpeting would not do for the southern peanut farmer who campaigned in 1976 by conspicuously carrying his own suit bag and wearing double-knit suits. When GSA refused so lavish an expenditure, he managed to obtain the rug for $12,600, and bought less expensive chandeliers for "only" $1,850. Carter also wanted the government to pay for his lunches at Atlanta's exclusive Commerce Club, but Larry Allison, GSA regional chief in Atlanta, turned down the request. "The regulations for former presidents are not that specific, so it takes a lot of judgment," Allison said.

In 1968 Harry Truman was charging the goverment $4,500 for his office space. In 1983 Nixon was ensconced in offices in Manhattan that cost taxpayers $62,651 a year. Carter's Atlanta offices were rented for $58,000 a year. Ford's office, next door to his Palm Springs home, cost $55,698 annually.

An examination of the bills they submit to Uncle Sam suggests that no expenditure is considered too nebulous or too personal to stick the taxpayers with. When the Carters signed their lucrative book deals, they went out and rented two word processors at $12,000 per year and billed the taxpayers for them. When thirty copies of his memoir, *Keeping Faith*, were found water-damaged in his office, Carter was reimbursed for them. When he traveled to London in October 1982 to promote his book, twelve Secret Service agents went with him, staying at the Churchill Hotel at $125 a night each.

Similarly, when Ford needed to spice up his after-dinner speeches with a little topical humor, he billed the taxpayers $42 to subscribe to the humor newsletter, *Orben's Current Comedy*. When one of his official cars got dirty, he put in for $4.99 to have it washed. He also billed taxpayers for his yearly $275 cable TV fee; a pair of scissors, $11.13; a monthly cleaning service, $275; and the landscaping and swiming pool maintenance at his office.

But Ford, who carved out a reputation as president for vetoing "big spending bills," has had no problems running up some big spending bills of his own, except the taxpayer picks up the tab. His 1982 telephone bill was $34,549. His office budget, including a staff of seven, whose payroll is partly financed by a political action committee, was $249,200 in 1983. His staff travel bill for 1982 totaled $25,111, including $12,772.75 for two aides who moved to Vail to be with him during the summer.

In 1982 Nixon's office expenses totaled $236,902, including a $31,000 phone bill, staff travel that exceeded $25,000, $2,826 for newspapers and periodicals, $3,230 for office supplies, and $4,703 for printing.

When Truman and his wife took a trip to Washington one summer, they drove themselves at no cost to the taxpayers. But when Lady Bird Johnson took a thirteen-day vacation trip to Greece "to see the wildflowers and ancient ruins," she was accompanied by ten Secret Service agents at an estimated cost of $25,000.

Former presidents are not totally insensitive to the taxpayers' burdens. GSA officials say Ford often returns $12,000 to $14,000 in expenses each year. Carter gave back $128,000 of his $800,000 in transition funds. Nixon paid out $50,000 of his own money to build a command post at his home in New Jersey for Secret Service agents.

Nevertheless, the majority of these expenditures serve to further enrich or otherwise benefit people of very substantial means. Every lecture appearance, for which former presidents are well paid, is planned, supported and executed by their federally paid staff. "When Ford flies off to earn a $15,000 honorarium, it probably costs the taxpayers $16,000," says the *Washington Monthly*. "It would be cheaper to pay Jerry the honorarium and tell him to stay home."

When Jimmy Carter toured the country promoting his memoirs, his travel and appearances were arranged and coordinated by his federally paid staff. Ford and Nixon received similar staff assistance in the production of their money-making memoirs and other writings. But is this right? "Should taxpayers pick up the tab for Secret Service protection when a former president travels across the country to make a speech for a substantial fee?" asks Chiles. "Should we provide staff to assist with those speeches or memoirs which will produce sizable income for the former president?" Wisely, Chiles answers, "I think not."

Clearly, we have created a kind of presidential aristocracy in which former chief executives are forever cocooned in the comfort and protection of an entourage of secret agents, major domos, and assorted scribes and baggage carriers. We have elevated the presidency to such extra-governmental importance that it ceases to be just a job, albeit a very important one in our nation, performed by a public servant who, when his term is over, simply returns to a private life in which he leaves the presidential life-style behind him. Says Senator William Roth of Delaware, "It is appropriate to ask ourselves whether we are not now in danger of creating an 'imperial ex-presidency.'" Clearly, we already have.

Among the few lawmakers who think the costs of our ex-presidents have gotten completely out of hand, Chiles has introduced legislation that would substantially curb them. His bill would limit Secret Service protection for former presidents to eight years (except in unusual cases in which further protection might be necessary); limit protection for the president's widow to six months after her husband's death; raise widows' pensions from $20,000 a year to $46,000, which is rather difficult to justify, considering Ladybird's great wealth; forbid the use of offices, staff and allowances for partisan political activities or in support of any income-generating ventures or businesses; impose a $300,000-per-year ceiling on office and personnel costs for each former president, gradually scaling it back to a maximum of $200,000; and require that the profits of any books written at government expense be turned over to the Treasury.

Interestingly enough, the budget-conscious Reagan administration strongly opposed Chiles's rather modest reform bill, preferring the status quo. GSA, too, testified that it was satisfied with the current law, and was even opposed to limiting the size of future presidential libraries. The Treasury Department, which administers Secret Service protection, also opposed any diminution of protection for former presidents, their wives and minor children. Chiles's measure, therefore, has gotten nowhere in Congress.

Yet surely among all of the expenditures of government, this one is the ultimate example of bureaucratic excess and abuse. Once out of office, and after a substantial interval of time, there is no need to provide lifetime Secret Service protection, and the portal-to-portal limousine service that goes with it, for these men and their widows. There is, moreover, no earthly rationale for providing financial support to former presidents to write their memoirs and fulfill other book contracts and business engagements that earn them millions of dollars.

Journalist Teresa Riordan, writing in the *Washington Monthly*, agrees that "the safety of former presidents is, of course, of concern to the American people. But one has to question how much protection is necessary and how much is simply an entourage mirage designed to preserve a president's imperial image after he's left office. And if it's that important to protect family members, why did Jacqueline Kennedy suddenly stop needing protection when she remarried, while Mamie Eisenhower needed three Secret Service agents to escort her to church every morning until she died at the age of 83?"

"We seem to have allowed these people to go from working presidents to retirement as royalty," says Chiles. "At a time when we are trying to cut federal spending and asking people in all walks of life to make sacrifices, there is no way to justify the magnitude of benefits former presidents are receiving." Amen.

18

Rewarding the Rich

THE rhetoric out of Washington is not known for making
subtle distinctions about federal expenditures. There is an increasing tendency among the national news media and among the politicians to unintelligently lump the budget into two indivisible
categories: defense spending, much of which, we are told, is bad
and excessive; and social programs, all of which are portrayed as
good and in short supply. The budgetary focus is always on the sum
of its parts, never on the parts or who really benefits from each of
them.

Buried in the budget's megabuck totals is about $424 billion a
year in transfer payments and social programs. Within this sum is
approximately $90 billion in transfer grants to the states and locali-
ties. Buried even deeper within this total is a multibillion-dollar pot
of gold that has been greening America's richest and most solidly
middle-class cities and towns. And it doesn't take a team of accoun-
tants from Price Waterhouse to find out who really benefits from a
lot of it.

Few have bothered to examine these expenditures seriously because they are hidden in thousands of computer entries that defy

easy analysis or evaluation. Their vast numbers alone tend to foster the myth that federal grant-in-aid programs must be bestowing all kinds of good things on needy neighborhoods and deserving constituencies. And in many cases they are. But in many more cases they are not. The latter has resulted in billions of wasted tax dollars.

The federal grant-in-aid dollars flow quietly and relentlessly out of Washington under a variety of easy eligibility formulas — from revenue sharing to community development block grants to urban development action grants. Among the thousands of recipients there are the Newarks and the Akrons, of which there are many. But Washington's largesse also serves another, less needy clientele. These cities and towns almost leap from the computer printouts: Beverly Hills, Palm Springs, Scarsdale, Stamford, Shaker Heights . . . The names flow by in the hundreds, eventually the thousands. What goes on here? How can a government that has run up a nearly $200 billion deficit in fiscal 1983 be giving away money to the nation's richest neighborhoods? This must be illegal.

What is going on, unfortunately, is perfectly legal. An egalitarian Congress set up these transfer programs to make sure that every village, hamlet and town gets a piece of the action — upper class and middle class, old wealth and new wealth, the merely comfortable and the filthy rich. Of course the government is deeply in debt. Of course Washington insists it doesn't have enough money to provide additional housing, health and educational assistance to the truly poor. Yet the checks continue to roll out like clockwork to places where the rich and powerful reside. Washington believes that even a town that drips with Rodeo Drive affluence needs Uncle Sam's help.

Revenue sharing, of course, is the government's $4.5 billion program of no-strings-attached grants that go to every city, town, county and Indian reservation in the country — all 39,000 of them, regardless of need, regardless of the deficit, each year and every year. The money is distributed under a formula based on per capita income, population and tax effort.

Commuity development block grants, totaling $3.5 billion a year, were originally established to help poor and lower-income people for a wide variety of needs — from housing rehabilitation to city parks. But the eligibility formula is so broad that more than 75 percent of America's communities are eligible.

Obviously, many needy communities are receiving funds under these programs. That is not the point. Far more important is the fact that exceptionally non-needy cities, towns and counties, thousands of them, are pocketing yearly checks while federal deficits worsen, poorer communities cry out for needed assistance, and the politicians in Washington insist the budget cannot be cut and that income taxes must be raised.

Here are some typical examples of the communites your taxes are enriching via revenue sharing or community development block grants. As you read the list, bear in mind that the yearly per capita income for every man, woman and child in the United States was $7,298 and the annual median family income was $19,908, according to the 1980 U.S. Census. Per capita income is the total income earned by the population divided by that population. The median family income given is the figure at which 50 percent of the families in the population earn more than this and 50 percent earn less. Revenue sharing and community development block grant sums are for fiscal year 1983.

Palm Springs, California: Heavily populated by wealthy Americans, including multimillionaires like Frank Sinatra and *TV Guide* magnate Walter Annenberg, this lavish resort community has an above-average median family income of $21,206, a per capita income of $11,665, and a municipal budget that is always in the black. Yet in fiscal 1983 its revenue sharing check from Uncle Sam totaled $658,199.

Houston, Texas: A city of big oil, high tech development and enormous wealth, whose city government rarely if ever ends the year without a surplus, Houston's median family income is nearly $22,000. But in 1983 it got a revenue sharing check for $23.7 million and $23.3 million in community development grants.

Beverly Hills, California: A town that has long been synonymous with movie stars, millionaires, outrageously expensive homes and the good life. Though this Gucci-clad community boasts a rich median family income of $40,362, plus a generous per capita income of

$24,387, it was eligible for a revenue sharing payment of $229,793.

Scarsdale, New York: One of New York City's wealthy bedroom communities, Scarsdale has an enviable median family income of $60,524 and a per capita income of $22,950. Yet it received $93,336 in revenue sharing.

Wellesley, Massachusetts: An upper-middle-class to wealthy Boston surburb, its median family income was $36,745 and its per capita income, $12,524. Nonetheless, this Wellesley College town got a revenue sharing check for $271,603.

Palo Alto, California: Despite a median family income of $31,796 and a per capita income of $12,799, this comfortable San Francisco suburb, near Stanford University, got $384,590 in revenue sharing, and $595,000 in community development block grants in 1983.

Shaker Heights, Ohio: This wealthy Cleveland suburb is comforted by a median family income of $34,241, but it was eligible for $150,761 in federal revenue sharing.

Greenwich, Connecticut: An upper-class New York City suburb with a median family income of $35,615 and a very nice per capita income of $16,572, Greenwich still raked in $702,221 in revenue sharing and $708,000 in community development block grants.

East Hampton, New York: This posh Long Island community has a per capita income of $15,451 and a respectable median income of $27,545. Yet it was the recipient of a $30,220 revenue sharing payment.

New Canaan, Connecticut: Trying to make ends meet on a $19,457 per capita income, and a median family income of $49,705, this wealthy New York City suburb reaps a yearly revenue sharing check for $122,000.

Hunter's Creek Village, Texas: An enormously wealthy suburb of Houston's millionaires and oil barons, Hunter's Creek has a princely per capita income of $32,859 and a median income of $68,028. Still it picks up a revenue check for $14,727.

Mission Hills, Kansas: This ritzy Kansas City suburb gets a $14,000 revenue sharing check despite a more than comfortable per capita income of $31,677 — more than four times the national average — and a median family income of $69,727.

Ladue, Missouri: The per capita income in this exclusive St. Louis suburb is a hefty $27,504. Nevertheless, it's eligible for a revenue sharing check of $30,000.

Cherry Hills, Colorado: It's tough struggling by on a per capita income of $30,440 a year, and a median family income of $73,745, yet Denver's suburban enclave for the rich still picks up its tidy $18,289 revenue sharing check.

Aspen, Colorado: The per capita income of this world-famous, upper-crust ski resort is $14,689, twice the national average. Even so, it accepts $95,320 in revenue sharing.

West Hampton, New York: Another of Long Island's wealthy resort communities, it has a per capita income of $12,097, but West Hampton gets a revenue sharing check for $26,253.

Piney Point Village, Texas: A ritzy Houston suburb dripping in oil empires and financiers, its breathtaking $32,026 per capita income is one of the richest in the nation. But it's not proud. Piney Point gladly takes its modest $10,335 revenue sharing payment.

Bloomfield Hills, Michigan: Similarly, this elite Detroit suburb of wealthy business executives and corporate heads enjoys a median family income of $75,000 and a per capita income of $35,129. It still banks a yearly $15,000 revenue sharing check.

Grosse Point Shores, Michigan: Also a wealthy Detroit suburb, with a per capita income of $25,183, and a median family income of $62,819, this handsome bedroom community isn't about to turn down its revenue sharing gift of $11,402.

Sands Point, New York: The per capita income in this comfortable New York City suburb on Long Island is $29,741. The median family income is $75,000. Its revenue sharing check totals $14,500.

San Marino, California: With a per capita income of $21,485 a year, and a median family income of $49,267, what more could this Los Angeles community want? You guessed it. A $57,435 revenue sharing check.

Winnetka, Illinois: The per capita income of this upper-class Chicago suburb is $22,482, and its median income is $55,252. Even so, it got a revenue sharing check for $48,062.

North Oaks, Minnesota: Former Vice-President Walter Mondale

moved into this ritzy Minneapolis suburb, after he had made some big bucks with a prestigious Washington law firm. This town has a per capita income of "only" $18,253, but it still gets nearly $12,000 in revenue sharing.

Kenilworth, Illinois: The per capita income in this wealthy Chicago suburb is $26,662, but it wouldn't think of turning down its $10,000 revenue sharing grant.

Montgomery County, Maryland: Heavily populated by well-paid federal workers, consultants and lobbyists from nearby Washington, it is one of the wealthiest counties in the nation. It has a per capita income of $12,335 and a median income of $33,711. Yet in 1983 its revenue sharing grant totaled $8.8 million and its community block grants were nearly $4.2 million.

Arlington County, Virginia: Another of Washington's suburban counties, its per capita income is a comfortable $12,562 a year, but its revenue sharing take totaled $2.7 million and its community development block grants exceeded $2.3 million.

Westchester County, New York: New York City's upper- to middle-class suburbs enjoy a median family income of $27,278. Nonetheless, the county received over $4.6 million in revenue sharing in 1983 and almost $4 million in community development block grants.

Marin County, California: San Francisco's middle- to upper-class suburbs have a median family income of $29,721, and a per capita income of $12,332. Still, the county cashed revenue sharing grants totaling over $2 million plus nearly $2 million more in community development block grants.

These examples, of course, represent only a small number of the thousands of solidly middle-class and exceedingly wealthy communities that have greedily plugged themselves into Washington's unending pipeline of federal grants. They dramatically illustrate how thousands of America's cities, towns and counties are quite capable financially of forgoing billions of dollars in easy government money. But since the money is there for the asking — in the case of federal revenue sharing you don't even have to ask — why turn it down? mayors and county executives ask. Lawmakers in Washington who

WASHINGTON — CITY OF SCANDALS

earn their political support by feeding such undeserving constituencies are more than happy to keep the pipeline open and gushing.

So the next time our political leaders in Congress go into a predictable tirade over "compassionless" spending cuts, crying that the budget has been "cut to the bone," remember this small but typical list of federal grant recipients, and the billions of federal dollars that continue to flow out to the comfortably middle class and the rich.

184

19

Broken Promises, Forgotten People

Nowhere in government can one find more disastrous examples of wasted resources, program duplication, bloated payrolls and archaic policies than in the Interior Department's scandal-ridden Bureau of Indian Affairs. This is not only an agency that has not worked, it is an agency that has impeded the economic advancement of the American Indian.

The very premise upon which this $1-billion-a-year bureau was established is rooted in bureaucratic duplication and waste. The Bureau of Indian Affairs was created to provide Indians with a range of health, employment, education and management services that other federal agencies are simultaneously providing to non-Indians.

Moreover, it is an agency whose massive problems — vividly detailed in countless government audits — have largely been ignored by Congress as well as by the Interior Department. One hundred and sixty years after this agency was first created in the War Department, the story of the American Indian remains one of national neglect and bureaucratic confusion. Sadly, it is also the story of paternalism and dependency which the BIA has done little to alleviate.

Despite the expenditure of well over $11 billion by this agency since 1960, the social profile of the American Indian remains a national tragedy.

The suicide rate for Indians is almost twice that of the U.S. as a whole. Indian alcoholism is more than seven times that of other Americans. Their accident rate is three times greater than for anyone else in the country. The tuberculosis death rate among Indians is more than six times greater, and their life expectancy is nearly six years less than that of other Americans.

Economically, their plight is equally disastrous. Thirty-nine percent of the Indian labor force on the reservations were listed as unemployed and actively seeking work, according to January 1983 BIA employment figures. On some reservations the jobless rate was as high as 80 to 90 percent in the depths of the 1981–82 recession, though unemployment among Indians is chronically bad. For example, the number of Indians unemployed and looking for work in 1979 was well over 50 percent on many reservations.

Poorly educated and with few marketable skills, the incomes of those who remain on the reservations are among the worst in the country. Only 25 percent of those on reservations who were lucky enough to have jobs were earning more than $7,000 per year.

Typical of the government's neglect for the Indian, few statistics are available concerning the relative wealth and poverty among Indians nationally. According to the 1980 U.S. Census, the median income for all Indian households was $16,643, nearly $3,400 below the national median income. Yet this figure includes Indians who live in urban areas and thus deeply distorts the true income levels of poorer Indians who live on or adjacent to the reservations.

Who is to blame for this tragic state of affairs? Then–Interior Secretary James Watt stirred up a storm of controversy when he blamed their plight on the government. "We have tremendous problems on Indian reservations," Watt said on a radio talk show in January 1983. "I frequently talk about it [by] telling people if you want an example of the failures of socialism, don't go to Russia — come to America and go to the Indian reservation.

"We have 50 million acres of Indian reservations," he continued, "1.4 million American Indians, and every social problem is exaggerated because of socialistic policies, government policies, on the Indian reservations: highest divorce rate, highest drug rate, highest alcoholism rate, highest unemployment rate, highest social diseases . . . because the people have been trained through 100 years of government oppression to look to the government as the creator, as the provider, as the supplier, and they've not been trained to use the initiative to integrate into the American [economic] system."

In the brouhaha that followed his remarks, Watt publicly apologized, "if I have offended anyone," but he did not retract what he had said, which at its very core is unarguable. Despite the expenditure of billions of dollars, many of the problems confronting Indians two decades ago remain essentially unchanged. The government has fostered a life of dependency for many Indians, supporting the reservations where there are declining economic opportunities, and thus segregating the Indian from the economic mainstream.

Based on the 1980 U.S. Census, there are more than 1.4 million American Indians, Eskimos and Aleuts in the United States, 755,201 of whom live on or adjacent to reservations and who comprise most of the BIA's service population. There are roughly 340,000 Indian families in our country.

Thus, the BIA — an agency of over 13,600 employees — has approximately one employee for every fifty-five Indians living on or near reservations, a bureaucrat-to-constituent ratio that must be the envy of every interest group in the country.

The BIA is spending over $1 billion a year on its programs, which was more than $1,200 per capita in 1983, or a hefty $3,000 a year per Indian family, an amount that would lift most needy Indians out of poverty, if we just gave it to them.

Yet BIA's yearly budget does not begin to reflect the total cost of what is spent by taxpayers in behalf of Indians because it excludes other health, education, welfare, employment and income transfer expenditures made in behalf of Indians by other federal agencies.

"If data were available on funds expended on Indian programs administered by all federal agencies, the cost per Indian living on a reservation would be even higher," the GAO says.

As with so many other government poverty programs, the great scandal is that most of this money does not reach needy Indians to the extent that it should. This is because much of BIA's budget is absorbed by a huge social welfare bureaucracy. A 1983 report on Indian programs by the National Tribal Chairmen's Association estimates that 70 percent of the funds appropriated for BIA programs is eaten up by administrative costs.

Beyond the fact that BIA represents a bureaucracy whose mission includes its own self-perpetuation, the continuing scandals within this agency have been documented ad nauseum by the Interior Department's Office of Inspector General as well as by the General Accounting Office. Their reports, whose pages could wallpaper BIA's Washington headquarters, reveal the shocking truth about this agency's continuing mismanagement and abuses.

Consider these examples uncovered by the Office of Inspector General and GAO auditors between 1980 and 1983:

— According to an internal audit, BIA's programs to improve substandard Indian housing "are not being properly controlled and are not effectively progressing toward the program objective of improving the housing of needy Indians."

When auditors examined housing program records at five out of eight locations, they "could not demonstrate that the recipients were selected on the basis of need which is the basic tenet of the program." Instead, they found that "personal and tribal political favoritism were a major influence in the selection of recipients for this congressionally mandated assistance."

Auditors said "serious weaknesses existed in the financial management systems of six of the programs. As a result of these weaknesses, we questioned . . . over $2.5 million of the $5.9 million of costs reviewed."

In each case, they found numerous examples where Housing Improvement Programs (HIP) "were used for unauthorized purposes, or for purposes contrary to HIP requirements."

— An audit of the Individual Indian Money (IIM) system, which is comprised of tribal bank accounts run by the BIA, showed there were "major weaknesses" which had "bureauwide application" to the 240,000 bank accounts and $357 million in deposits for which BIA was responsible.

The audit found that "overdrafting IIM accounts was common" at all of the agency offices examined. Uncovering sixty-six accounts that were overdrawn by about $745,000, the auditors said, "Most of these overdrafts were intentional in order to satisfy the desires of tribal officials."

— Many tribes have incomes some communities would consider enviable, but their funds are not always well managed.

Take, for example, the Crow Tribe of Montana, which earned $11.6 million from federal and state contracts, plus $10.9 million from mineral and grazing leases and interest over a two-year period. In 1982 the tribe declared itself in a state of "technical insolvency."

"The Tribe used whatever cash it had on hand to meet payroll and other expenses regardless of the original purpose of the funds," a BIA statement said.

— This was comparatively mild compared to what auditors uncovered when they reviewed the Field Finance Office in BIA's Administrative Service Center. Poking through the Center's papers and records, the auditors were suprised to discover 406 undeposited checks stashed in file drawers and a safe.

The uncashed checks, dating as far back as 1974, totaled $783,-000. Auditors said other functions at the Finance Office "were in a state of chaos."

— After studying the effect of two decades of federal economic development assistance in South Dakota's Pine Ridge Indian Reservation, auditors could not find much improvement.

"Although millions of federal dollars have been spent," they said, "the reservation's economy is, at best, only marginally better."

The audit found that only one business enterprise "of significance is operating," and even it was "in jeopardy."

— A related audit performed at the Oglala Sioux Community College revealed that the federally assisted school had "purchased items of questionable necessity because it had too much money."

Among other things, the college spent $13,277 on a graduation ceremony for only seventeen students.

— Auditors further discovered that BIA procurement officers were illegally increasing contracts and grants at the end of each fiscal year "with the effect of carrying over and expanding the funds in a succeeding year." This was "an apparent attempt to 'save' funds prior to the lapsing of [year-end] obligation authority," i.e., to keep from having to give unspent money, so to speak, back to the Treasury.

This shady practice "was accomplished by various means, including the backdating of obligation documents, recording no obligations at year-end, and by assigning retroactive starting dates to contracts and grants," the auditors said.

They identified $1.9 million of such questionable funding, which represented 12.5 percent of their sample survey. This, they said, showed "the actions were repetitively taken and are not attributable to isolated or inadvertent procurement decisions."

But there was nothing new to this phony bookkeeping. Such deficiencies "have been identified in previous reports by our office" and by the GAO since 1960, the auditors said.

— An investigation into the multimillion-dollar Indian Action Program, an on-reservation job training program, uncovered so many abuses that auditors called for IAP's elimination.

A twenty-page "Restricted to Office Use" report said IAP funds were being "used for just about anything": building a dog pound, a softball field, developing a radio station, creating a recreation management training program, and sponsoring a seminar for tribal chiefs. Other funds were used "to provide a personal service cadre for tribal members [which was used to] replace broken windows, repair plumbing, pull cars out of ditches and feed cattle."

Over a period of years more than $130 million was dumped into what auditors described as a "vague and ill-defined program." Its effectiveness in improving the lives of needy Indians was "difficult to measure." Auditors visited locations "where IAP was being or had been used to subsidize tribal enterprises by paying all or part of the salary costs of . . . employees. In one case, program funds had kept a profitless, tribally owned concrete company in business for four years. In another case, a subsidized tribal construction company was subcontracting most of its work to non-Indian firms." Auditors discovered job training money was used to build a house for an IAP employee, and in another case build a three-car garage for a tribal president.

Congress finally eliminated funding for IAP in fiscal 1983, but not before it had squandered millions of tax dollars over many years.

— Meantime, GAO auditors have charged that BIA has "lost accountability over hundreds of millions of dollars of grants, contracts and trust funds because its automated accounting and finance system produces unreliable information." BIA officials tried solving its money management problems by spending $15.5 million on new computer equipment, but GAO said "this is not the answer."

The auditors believed the "system deficiencies to be so serious that they present oportunities for improper use of funds and other resources."

— BIA improperly maintained a $17.5 million Indian trust fund which produced $7 million annually, even though the fund's original purpose no longer existed. Instead of abolishing the fund, BIA secretly used it to finance various administrative and travel costs.

In one instance GAO found nearly $4,000 of the fund had been used to ship the household belongings of a BIA official. In another case, a BIA agency used the fund for carpeting, oak conference chairs, resurfacing a road to employee housing, building garages for government-owned housing, and even for employee salaries.

GAO called the fund's use "questionable, because it authorizes using an Indian trust fund for the general purposes of the agency rather than for the benefit of the Indian schools or agencies on whose behalf the trust fund should have been collected." Moreover, the BIA never disclosed the fund's existence to Congress.

Auditors shake their heads in frustration when asked if things have improved at the BIA over the years. "If anything," says one, "they have gotten worse."

In addition to a lack of imaginative, bold leadership, BIA's problems are rooted in the agency's paternalistic, almost feudal structure, dominated by the twelve Area Offices located around the country. It is a multilayered bureaucracy. At the top are BIA headquarters, and the Area Offices which dole out the money and run its many programs. Below them are eighty-six superintendents at the reservation level. The result is an uncontrolled, balkanized bureaucracy in which there is little accountability and even less effective policy.

"The director [of each Area Office] has everything under his thumb," says one auditor. There is little or no separation of duties. The person giving out the grants also monitors them, and thus there is little independent, objective judgment and evaluation.

The BIA's bureaucracy, and its attendant inefficiencies and mismanagement, have been criticized severely by major Indian leadership organizations. The Area Offices in particular have been strongly criticized by the National Tribal Chairmen's Association (NTCA), one of America's major Indian leadership groups, which says the offices are an unnecessary layer of bureaucracy and should be abolished.

"The Indian tribes are of the opinion that the Area Offices generally are of no real practical value and exist mostly to perpetuate the employment of the higher-grade personnel," a draft of an NTCA report asserts. "Area Offices create an unneeded layer of bureaucracy and are roadblocks to efficiency." Ever protective of their bureaucracy, BIA officials of course strongly disagree.

Moreover, the Indian leadership group has charged in a report harshly critical of BIA that 70 percent of BIA's program funds are eaten up by administrative expenses and that much of the agency's budget is not directly benefiting Indians but perpetuating a bloated bureaucracy.

Former Interior Secretary Watt spoke out about the insidious dependency spawned by the BIA. But beyond his rhetoric, and ordering a comprehensive audit of the agency, Watt did little to substantively attack BIA's deep-seated problems. More studies will only confirm what everyone already knows.

In his public comments on BIA's continuing bureaucratic nightmare, Watt looked to the Indian community and to Congress for reform. "There needs to be a change worked out between elected tribal leaders and Congress," Watt said. "And until that change comes about, we're not going to make any progress in Indian Country." He correctly condemned Congress's reluctance to deal aggressively with its own bureaucratic creation, saying, "How can you change the relationship [between Indians and the government] if you can't even get Congress to focus on it." Unfortunately, Watt never recognized the need also to make radical administrative reforms to curb the program's wasteful bureaucracy and refocus its assistance to America's neediest Indian constituencies.

Repeated changes in the agency's leadership have also contributed to some degree to the longstanding problems at BIA. "The top BIA management has changed as much as you change your shirt," says Frank Ducheneaux, chief counsel for the House Committee on Interior and Insular Affairs which has legislative jurisdiction over BIA. Since 1970 there has not been the same head of the Bureau for more than two to three years.

Poor leadership at the top has also been a major factor in BIA's continuing scandals, despite all the investigations that have probed this agency's darkest corners. "Too often in the past, problems in the Bureau or tribal administrations have been identified and then, apparently, ignored," Kenneth Smith, assistant secretary for Indian Affairs under Watt, admitted in a letter to tribal leaders announcing a full-scale audit. "I will not tolerate such non-responses," Smith insisted, but he did not outline what significant changes would be made. "There is lack of will," complains Max Richtman, Democratic staff director for the Senate Select Committee on Indian Affairs. "You need a strong assistant secretary to force reform."

In the final analysis, though, corrective changes will come about only if Congress orders those changes through law. Unfortunately, Congress has been pathetically impotent in dealing with BIA's overwhelming problems. Beyond the congressionally established American Indian Policy Review Commission — which had little substantive impact on BIA's effectiveness — Congress has not comprehensively reviewed BIA's operations and programs with any significant reforms in mind.

GAO, Congress's auditing arm, also believes that nothing will change for the better until Congress acts. One GAO audit concluded that "management alternatives must be legislated by the Congress if Federal activities on behalf of Indians are to be effective."

Yet considering the abuses that numerous audits have uncovered, why hasn't Congress watched the BIA more carefully? Why hasn't it drafted new authorizing legislation and reformed this clearly ineffective, scandal-ridden agency?

I put this question to key officials in the respective House and Senate committees with jurisdiction over BIA. Their responses, collectively conveying the typical congressional attitude of benign neglect, say as much about Congress's continuing reluctance to be accountable for its legislative creations as they do about the worsening problems of the BIA and the American Indian.

"Oversight is a good device, but it has some limitations," says a Senate Select Committee official. "It does not produce major changes. Congress clearly is not going to get into the business of running federal agencies." Says Richtman, "Reform has to come from the administration. We don't have the means to control day-to-day operations . . . the Senate staff isn't large enough to deal with the thousands of BIA employees. It's all we can do to keep up with their budget submissions." Says House Interior Committee official Deborah Broken Rope, "The Bureau to this day still needs to clean up its own act." Another committee staffer says, "I'm not sure the best energy is spent on the BIA. . . . We have stopped trying to come up with bright ideas of our own. The BIA is a swamp, and I don't know what you could get" to change it.

As pointed out earlier, there is deep frustration and anger over BIA's unending scandals within the Indian community itself. A draft of a 1984 report from the NTCA and the National Congress of American Indians bluntly summed up the continuing inability to find solutions to this bureaucratic mess: "The BIA's shortcomings and problems are well documented and can be summarized by stating that, although many people have dedicated entire careers to try to improve its processes, its administration of Indian appropriations is inefficient and its own self-concept of its role relative to Indian tribes is outdated."

Elmer Savilla, executive director of the NTCA, describes the problems at BIA even more succinctly: "The bureaucracy itself has been a roadblock to change." Any deviation from the status quo, any alteration of the size or distribution of its employees and management officials, or any diminution of its authority, is met with furious resistance from its bureaucracy. The BIA's nearly fourteen thousand employees "must depend on the continued non-development of Indian tribes, and for tribes to stay in need of their services, in order for them to keep their jobs," the NTCA bitterly charges in a position paper. The General Accounting Office couldn't agree more. "It is not in the Bureau employees' best interest to encourage tribes to use self-determination contracts since by doing so they may be putting themselves out of jobs," GAO says.

According to NTCA, BIA has failed largely due to a lack of strong leadership within the Reagan administration for reform; the absence of legislative direction and congressional follow-through; tribal indifference, suspicion, or outright opposition; and hardcore bureaucratic resistance within BIA.

To be sure, there has been some noticeable progress in recent years. The gradual development of an Indian leadership cadre bodes well for the future of Indian advancement. Economically, too, there have been modest gains. Significantly, there are now several hundred Indian professionals, e.g., doctors and lawyers.

Still, the fact that the vast majority of American Indians are living in terrible, poverty-stricken conditions is undisputed. That this continues to be true, despite billions of dollars spent in behalf of the Indian, is bitter testimony to the failure of antipoverty programs that try to alleviate the causes of poverty through a range of social services provided by a large and well-paid bureaucracy.

The dominant feature of the U.S.–Indian relationship is still its "schizophrenic" nature. On the one hand, the Indians strongly support the government's trust responsibility for their lands and their people, but as we have seen, they are frequently very critical of the government's use of that trust. Says Richtman, "Indians have a constant struggle of maintaining an identity and then learning to live within a different society. That's not going to change dramatically in a very short time, no matter who's running things."

Clearly the Bureau of Indian Affairs has been an abject failure insofar as the Indians' economic well-being is concerned. Equally clear is that Congress has abdicated any responsibility to take this agency and refashion it in a way that can help integrate the American Indian, and their communities, into the economic mainstream and lead them away from a life of dependency upon government. Moreover, the Interior Department has avoided shaking up the BIA bureaucracy. Its officials say their hands are tied by Congress, but there are numerous programmatic initiatives and personnel changes that could be made to insure that more of BIA's budget goes toward helping provide needy Indians with effective job training, education, and other essential programs.

In the end, however, only Congress can end the bureaucratic nightmare at the BIA. And clearly the best solution is to phase out BIA and in its place establish a small office within the Interior Department to provide block grant assistance to qualified Indian governments under a formula heavily based on population and poverty income levels. Moreover, the expenditures must be limited solely to social priorities — education, housing, health and needed public assistance to the poor — and the grants must undergo regular auditing review.

It does not take a mathematical genius to figure out that, in the absence of the enormous administrative costs being absorbed by a bloated army of BIA bureaucrats, contractors and consultants, much more assistance would get to needy Indian communities under this approach. There undoubtedly will be instances where money will be misspent. But careful auditing, adherence to fundamental expenditure guidelines based on strict social priority and need, will catch such instances early when quick corrective action can be taken. In such instances, a management training corps can be dispatched to insure that nonallowable expenditures are stopped and that proper financial procedures are followed.

This, admittedly, is a radical step, but it can be implemented over a period of time, gradually scaling back grants where Indian reservation economies are improved, or their populations disperse and grow smaller. To some extent, this proposal moves very much in the direction of proposals already offered under a reform plan that was scheduled to be put forth by the NTCA/NCAI in 1984. A draft of that plan ambitiously proposed that Congress decentralize BIA's operations; abolish its functions as a management agency; turn over total control over Indian programs to the tribes; and eliminate BIA's twelve Area Offices along with its costly and unnecessary regulations.

Even so, there is a persistent ambivalence among the Indian leadership between their desire, on the one hand, to control their own affairs and become fully independent, and, on the other hand, to maintain their ties to a paternal government and its public monies. It is time to begin treating the Indians as we would any other American in need, no more and certainly no less. We have broken many promises made to a proud people with a rich historical and cultural heritage, and we have squandered much money on an excessive and wasteful bureaucracy.

The time has come for change that offers necessary assistance for the advancement of the Indian community within the framework of a small but efficient program whose goal must be their economic independence. But such change is not fully attainable until the Indians themselves decide to turn away from government paternalism and toward truly independent, local self-government. There is much evidence that they are ready to do that. More than a century after the last Indian treaty was signed, it is now time for the federally dominated reservation to end.

20

The Firing of Ed Curran

Sometime after Edward A. Curran, the former headmaster of the prestigious Washington Cathedral School, became the director of the government's National Institute of Education, he concluded that his agency was so abysmally wasteful, so unnecessary, so harmful to American education, that it had to be abolished. Yet shortly after he privately communicated these findings to President Reagan, he was fired.

The story of what happened to Ed Curran and the obscure federal agency he headed is an important one — though it was overwhelmingly ignored by the national news media — because it reveals vividly the swift punishment that can befall a public servant who dares to challenge a bureaucracy's very existence. It also shows how an administration elected to eliminate wasteful, ineffective and harmful federal programs can sometimes become the unquestioning defender of such programs; how bureaucratic protocol can become more important than the need to cleanse away a nebulous program that fails every test of performance and effectiveness; and how expenditures, once set in motion, stubbornly defy all efforts to

eliminate them. It is a story that needs to be told and retold —
often.

The story begins with Curran's appointment by President Reagan
and subsequent confirmation by the Senate in 1981 to be director of
the National Institute of Education (NIE), the $53 million research
program within the Department of Education. The slender, mild-
mannered educator was a staunch supporter of Ronald Reagan in
1980 and he took his job as seriously as he took what Reagan said
about reducing waste within the federal government. "I have been
determined to work for the goals which were so resoundingly affirmed in the 1980 election," he later wrote. Thus, it was not long
after he settled into his job that he became convinced that here was
an excellent example of what Reagan was talking about — an
agency whose esoteric, misdirected and marginal research grants
were contributing nothing to the improvement of American education.

NIE has wasted hundreds of millions of dollars over the years on
numerous studies on such subjects as "early American textbook col-
lections," "sex role attitudes in young women and men," "women
facing midcareer changes," "a legal history of American universities," and sexism in school boards, to name a few. While basic
achievement test scores had been plummeting for years, and declining educational standards cried out for a return to basics, NIE
was squandering its resources on such things as a $276,000 "sex eq-
uity in education" project. The grants supported pilot research in
more than two hundred classrooms between the fourth and eighth
grades in an attempt to eliminate sexism in education. No one,
surely, condones sexism in education, but is this what our limited
federal tax dollars should be supporting? Wasn't there a school in
some inner city that could have better used that money to improve
its facilities and educational programs?

NIE's budget has for years been almost routinely approved by
Congress, which rarely questions any research expenditures, though
most members do not have the foggiest notion how its dollars are
really spent. The only significant exception to this occurred when a
powerful senator sharply criticized what NIE had been doing with

our tax dollars and called for its elimination. The attack came from Warren Magnuson, then Democratic senator from the state of Washington and the powerful chairman of the Appropriations Committee. Magnuson was one of the all-time big spenders in Congress, particularly concerning anything having to do with education. Yet he and his staff found NIE's expenditures so "extrinsic to the real needs of our nation's education system" that he proposed eliminating all funding for it in the fiscal 1975 appropriations bill. Bear in mind that this is, in and of itself, a highly unusual step for an appropriations panel which rarely, if ever, eliminates any program, let alone one having to do with education. Surprisingly, the Senate accepted Magnuson's cut, but the House refused to go along, and NIE survived.

Then along came Ronald Reagan, breathing fire about how wasteful the federal government was. Even the panel of experts Reagan assembled during the post–1980 election transition period to study the Education Department suggested that NIE be phased out of existence. But as a respected educator and the former headmaster of a top-notch private school, highly regarded for its educational standards and levels of scholastic achievement, Curran wanted to render his own independent judgment. His study of what NIE was spending its money on soon convinced him that this was an agency that the American taxpayer could well do without. Its only beneficiary was an industry of assorted grantsmanship professionals who made a good living by applying for yearly federal grants to conduct various experimental studies that have had little or no impact on the development of good education.

Convinced of the rightness of his position, Curran submitted the evidence to the Office of Management and Budget and persuaded OMB Director David Stockman to propose in the fiscal 1983 budget recommendations that NIE be phased out by fiscal 1985. Everything seemed to be going well until an eleventh-hour appeal to the White House by Education Secretary Terrel Bell managed to win a reprieve for the agency. Bell's close ally, Edwin Meese, counsellor to the president, overruled Stockman, and the NIE cut in the budget draft was erased. "We came very close to proposing that it be eliminated," an NIE official and Curran ally said at the time.

Frustrated but determined, Curran sought advice from colleagues and friends about how he could overcome the obstacles he faced. How could he convince the administration he was heading an agency that was unnecessary, one that even a prominent, liberal Democrat in Congress once wanted abolished? Congress being the toady supplicant to virtually every special interest in the country, Curran knew that there was little chance of closing down this agency, unless the administration itself called for its elimination in its formal budget requests. With Meese in Bell's corner, only the President himself could make sure that Stockman's next budget carried a zero on NIE's expenditure line. But how could he persuade the President, how could he even reach him?

Curran raised his dilemma with a friend, Lyn Nofziger, a longtime Reagan political adviser, and Nofziger had a simple suggestion: Why not write directly to Reagan and lay out your arguments in a carefully drafted letter of particulars? To insure that the letter would get to Reagan's desk, Nofziger, who had just stepped down from the post of special assistant to the President for political affairs, gave Curran the secret correspondence code available only to top White House and cabinet officials, which would insure that the letter would get through the White House filtering process set up to handle the President's incoming mail.

Curran wrote his letter, and without telling any departmental officials, sent it off to Reagan, bearing the special secret code. Inexplicably, however, the letter did not go directly to Reagan — few letters do — but instead ended up on the desks of Craig Fuller, White House secretary to the cabinet, and Richard Darman, Reagan's liberal special assistant who controls the paper flow to the President. "It's a bit unusual for a letter like this to bear any such code," Fuller told me at the time, obviously surprised that a relatively middle-level department official would have access to such classified information.

Curran's letter has never been made public. The White House refused all requests for its release. Curran, who considered the letter a very private communication between himself and Reagan, has never disclosed it, and has never even discussed it with a member of the press. He did, however, give a copy to Bell right after he had sent it to the President. Bell, a supporter of NIE, was of course furious with Curran's proposal, and even angrier that Curran had gone over his head to the President. To this day, the Department of Education, under strict orders from Bell, has kept its copy under lock and key.

However, I have obtained a draft of Curran's letter, leaked to me by a former departmental official who remains bitter over Curran's mistreatment by the administration. The draft is an almost exact duplicate of Curran's letter, according to this official who read the final version that was sent to the White House. Among the points Curran made to the President were these:

1. NIE is "unnecessary" because educational research would continue without federal funding, particularly among the more then four hundred colleges and universities that have education departments and whose faculties are engaged in research under other grant programs.

2. The agency is also unnecessary because it "is based on the premise that education is a science and that schools are like armies or hospitals in that their progress depends on systematic 'research and development.' . . . this premise is false."

3. "America's schools are in sad shape, not because we don't know how to make them effective, but because we lack the will to apply what we already know. Strong local leadership, orderly classrooms, emphasis on excellence in the basic academic skills, and other ingredients of effective schooling are harder to sustain today than they were before the education programs of President Johnson's 'Great Society.' One reason is that these very programs have modified an army of outside 'experts' with a license to tinker and meddle but with no direct responsibility for actual results.

4. "The agency wastes money," Curran continued. Even Myron Lieberman, an education expert, a former consultant to the U.S. Office of Education, and once a supporter of increased funding for NIE, "became convinced over time that '[NIE's] research is largely useless for any purpose except showing that more research is needed.'

"The taxpayer simply does not need a $99,000 survey on the po-

litical attitudes of college professors, or a $37,000 study of the 1973
New York City School Board elections," he said.

5. "Obviously," he added, "I intend to use my powers as director
to eliminate wasteful projects wherever I can. But at present more
than half of my agency's budget lies outside my direct control, in
the hands of 17 'labs and centers' scattered across the country.

"Like other well-organized special interests," Curran said, these
NIE-funded "labs and centers" lobby Congress "to set aside a protected slice of the budgetary pie for their own well-being. Over the
last 10 years this lobbying has succeeded to the point where the
House and Senate Appropriations Committees treat these institutions as if they were so many dams and bridges — public works
projects which receive favored treatment in Washington as long as
they provide employment back home."

6. Moreover, the agency was "overwhelmingly" tilted toward the
left in the choice of who gets the research grants and the conclusions those studies reach. Nine months after Reagan's inauguration,
NIE "hosted a seminar on tuition tax credits [which Reagan sup-
ports] in which the overwhelming majority of the invited lecturers
were anti-tax credit."

7. As NIE director, Curran said, he had taken "some of the steps
. . . needed to restore balance and objectivity, but I have already
been publicly accused of trying to turn the agency into a conservative propaganda mill."

8. "In the long run, the public interest will be better served if the
federal government simply drops NIE's mission and concentrates
on the mutual collection of factual and statistical data — the mission of the National Center for Education Statistics. The interest
groups would lose, but the values of pluralism, democracy and freedom would all gain."

He further noted that since World War II only two nonmilitary
federal agencies "have actually been abolished," the Community
Services Administration, and the Law Enforcement Assistance Administration, both eliminated under Reagan. "I would be delighted
and honored to help make NIE the third," he told the President.

When Curran showed Bell a copy of his letter on June 1, 1982, the secretary was livid. "How can you head an agency which you think should not exist?" Bell blurted out, without realizing the irony of his statement. Reagan had appointed Bell precisely because he wanted him to preside over the elimination of the Department of Education, a goal never vigorously pursued by the former Utah educator who was an early supporter of creating a separate cabinet-level department in the first place. Bell strongly hinted that if Curran could no longer support the continuation of NIE's existence, perhaps he should consider resigning.

Curran had no intention of doing any such thing, though Bell quickly turned the matter into an "either him or me" situation and pressed the White House to dismiss the staunch Reaganite. Over the next several days Curran fought valiantly to win White House support, to allow him to stay in the post for which he had been appointed and confirmed. He had done nothing to merit dismissal, except exercise his free right to correspond about his deeply held views to the President. Unfortunately, Reagan had not seen Curran's letter and thus subordinates were left to handle the intradepartmental squabble it sparked. That meant that the decision would be up to Ed Meese and implemented by then–White House Personnel Director Helene Von Damm, a longtime Reagan aide.

Initially, the White House hoped a compromise could be worked out between Bell and Curran. To that end the two men held a second meeting on June 8 in the department, at which Bell wanted Curran to recant his views on NIE. But Curran was no Galileo. The future of education did not revolve around NIE, and he was not about to say it did. The next day, after clearing his decision with the White House, Bell called Curran and told him, "I want you to stop functioning as director by the close of business today."

Thus, in the end, the White House chose to side with Bell, and Curran was thrown out. Leaving with him was his trusted aide, Larry Uzzell, who soon set up a national organization, Learn, Inc., to reform federal education policies and lobby for the elimination of NIE.

When it was over, a presidential aide who sympathized with Curran's position in the controversy remarked, "It's a sad day when someone in our administration gets fired merely for suggesting that an unnecessary agency of government be eliminated." To this an Education Department official, one who did not support Bell's action against Curran, said, "One would think that Ronald Reagan's government would be full of people heading agencies they think should not exist."

But for the White House high command, the Curran episode did not concern a wasteful, nebulous federal agency as much as it did a breach of protocol. By going over Bell's head to the President, Curran had "violated good management procedures," said Meese, who gave the final approval to dismiss Curran. "If you are a company commander, you don't write to the commader-in-chief with your problems," he explained to me in an interview. "That's not the way things are done. If every program chief were allowed to do this, there would be chaos."

"Then," I responded, "what you are saying is that if you are a subordinate agency head and you have concluded that your program should be abolished because it is an unnecessary and wasteful bureaucracy, you should never under any circumstances communicate those views to the President?"

"That's right," Meese answered.

There was also Bell's insistence that either Curran leave or he would. "What could we have done?" Meese said. "Keep Ed Curran and let Bell go?" That would not have been a bad idea.

At the end of an interview I had with President Reagan, when my tape recorder had been turned off and we were saying our good-byes, he made an observation that really goes to the heart of what happened to Ed Curran. Shaking his head, and ruminating about the difficulty of getting federal spending under control, Reagan remarked that no matter how hard he tried to curb wasteful spending, it was frustrating "to know that down there underneath is that permanent structure that is resisting everything you're doing."

Edward A. Curran was eventually given another job elsewhere in the administration. Nevertheless, the record shows that when he was down there in that middle-management level bravely trying to eliminate one small corner of a wasteful bureaucracy that Ronald Reagan bemoans, he got fired for it.

21

A Risky Business

CLIFFORD McKenzie's troubles really began in 1980 after he blew the whistle on his fellow workers for pocketing nearly $20,000 in unspent travel advances, and then spilled the beans on $34 million in missing equipment, some of which his supervisors told him to write off.

No sooner had this quiet, self-effacing GS-12 program analyst in the Bureau of Indian Affairs notified Interior Department investigators, than he found himself being harassed by his superiors, and saw his spotless eleven-year work record being smeared with poor, though unsubstantiated, performance ratings. He was given meaningless tasks to perform, and in some cases was ordered to do the same job over and over again. In one instance he was forced to rewrite a report twelve times. His phone calls were intercepted. He was refused visitors at work. A secretary was assigned to "clock me in and out," in an attempt to show he was delinquent in his work habits. He never was.

In desperation, McKenzie, who is married and has two children, tried transferring to a lower-paying position in the Department of Labor in Utah. But BIA officials blocked his escape, saying his job was "critical to the agency." The harassment continued. On his next job performance report, his superiors graded him poor in every category. Then, in September 1981, Clifford McKenzie was fired. His crime: He had told the truth.

A Kiowa Indian with a degree in accounting from the University of Oklahoma, McKenzie worked in the Indian Technical Assistance Center at Lakewood, Colorado, a program run by the BIA. When he discovered that $19,168.88 in outstanding travel advances had been given to sixteen out of the eighteen employees at the Center — some of it had been outstanding for eight years — he complained to his supervisors, though they ignored it. He then filed a complaint with the department's inspector general. He never got a response, but it wasn't long before a copy of his complaint found its way to his supervisors. And that, he says, is when his performance ratings went "from good to bad" and led to his dismissal.

After his firing, McKenzie complained to the Merit Systems Protection Board (MSPB), an agency that was notorious for its failure to stand behind whistle-blowers. After considerable delay, his case was taken up by a regional MSPB hearing examiner in Denver in January 1982, who promptly threw out the government's charges, saying they were flimsy and unsubstantiated. He ordered that McKenzie be reinstated in his job. But the bureaucracy isn't easily defeated. The BIA appealed the decision to the full MSPB board, effectively keeping him out of his job until the board, faced with a huge backlog of air traffic controller cases, could take up the case and render a decision.

In the meantime, McKenzie moved back to Oklahoma and got a job as the administrator for the Cheyenne, Arapaho and Kiowa tribes, while the MSPB kept him twisting slowly in the wind for almost two years. The agency told him at one point that they had lost his records, then managed to obtain a copy from BIA, though McKenzie worried they may have been tampered with. In desperation, McKenzie filed a writ of mandamus in federal court seeking to compel the board to act on his complaint. Finally, on August 24, 1983, the board took up his case, ruling that the Denver hearing officer was wrong in dismissing the BIA's charges, and ordered a rehearing of the entire matter. Thus, as the final months of 1983 approached, there was no end in sight to this honest civil servant's nightmare.

And what of the BIA employees whose delinquencies McKenzie had disclosed, as he was required to do under the Code of Ethics for Government Service? They were simply ordered to repay the money they had been advanced, but no disciplinary action was taken against any of them. McKenzie's supervisor was reduced one pay grade and quietly reassigned to a BIA office in Minneapolis.

Sadly, the story of Cliff McKenzie is not an unusual one. The files of the Merit Systems Protection Board, the agency established by Congress under the Civil Service Reform Act of 1978 to, in part, protect whistle-blowers, are filled with such cases. There are times, such as the George Spanton case outlined in an earlier chapter, when justice is done. But that is uncommon. In most cases whistle-blowers pay a very dear price for their acts. And in most instances their stories are the same: punishment by superiors for their honesty and integrity; failure on the part of the Merit Systems Protection Board to act swiftly and fairly to protect their rights; and deep and sometimes debilitating bitterness over their shabby treatment under the so-called whistle-blowers protection law, which is supposed to protect them but doesn't.

"I do not know how many Mr. McKenzies there are on the federal payrolls," said Congressman Glenn English of Oklahoma when he heard of the BIA employee's struggle. "But certainly instances like this would cause most federal workers to think twice before participating in the 'whistle-blowing' act."

"It's unforgiveable when you look at the effect it has on individuals' lives," Mark D. Roth, acting general counsel of the American Federation of Government Employees, told *Tulsa World* reporter Malvina Stephenson. "We have instances where employees' marriages were broken up, people forced to move out of their homes, and actually leave their home cities to find other employment while awaiting the final decision."

Out of the government's nearly five million officially counted civilian and military employees, the number of whistle-blowers is relatively small. The norm among government workers, as it so often is in the private sector, is to look the other way and keep your mouth shut, if you want to keep your job, or to simply leave and find work elsewhere. Nonetheless, each year some do come forward to blow the whistle and what happens to them afterward is one of Washington's continuing scandals.

There is of course the most celebrated whistle-blower of all time, A. Ernest Fitzgerald, the Pentagon management systems analyst who told a Senate subcommittee in 1968, in response to a question, about the $2 billion cost overruns of Lockheed's C-5 air cargo transport. For his honesty, Fitzgerald paid an enormously high price. He was stripped of his responsibilities, he lost his staff, and he was squirreled away in a small, bare room in the Pentagon without anything meaningful to do. It took a long, costly and personally painful fourteen-year battle in court to get his job back. Yet today, despite the new mechanisms put into place by what he calls the "Civil Service Deform Act" of 1978, Fitzgerald says there isn't "any real change" in the way whistle-blowers are treated. Whistle-blowing is still, he says, "a very risky business."

William Clinkscales, once the chief investigator at the scandal-plagued General Services Administration, knows better than anyone what can happen when you pull back the covers on waste and corruption. You get punished very, very severely. The burly, blunt-speaking career civil servant had helped to expose the scandals that rocked GSA in 1978. Both he and then–chief auditor Howard Davia helped to uncover wrongdoing and mismanagement throughout the government's huge building and purchasing agency through which about $35 billion flows each year. Their efforts — and those of a tiny handful of other brave investigators in the agency, including attorney Vincent Alto — helped spark an investigation and a series of prosecutions that eventually led to nearly two hundred criminal indictments, on charges of contract kickbacks, payoffs and supply store thefts.

It wasn't long, however, before the euphoria that both Davia and Clinkscales felt at the success of their 1978 investigations under GSA chief Jay Solomon turned to frustration and resentment as a new GSA leadership team installed by Jimmy Carter in 1979 quickly turned on both of them. Davia found himself barely clinging to his job as the new GSA administrator, Rowland Freeman, openly criticized his aggressive audits, and Clinkscales found himself being wrongly accused of theft. Both were subjected to harassment and intimidation by their superiors. Then the bombshell hit. Without warning, GSA's then inspector general, Kurt Muellenberg, with Freeman's approval, removed Clinkscales from his investigative job and exiled him to an office, which Clinkscales described as "not much bigger than an elevator shaft," giving him virtually nothing to do. Depressed and frustrated, but determined to fight for what he believed in, Clinkscales filed a grievance with the MSPB, charging he had been punished merely for doing his job, but nothing ever came of it.

Eventually, with the election of Ronald Reagan — who had vowed to put the "whistle-blowers back in charge" at GSA — and Reagan's appointment of Gerald Carmen as GSA's new no-nonsense administrator, Clinkscales and Davia were returned to important assignments where they helped Carmen cleanse the agency of the stain of scandal. Davia was reassigned to Chicago to head GSA's vast Midwest region. Clinkscales was put in charge of a new investigative, trouble-shooting unit that reported directly to Carmen, and in 1983 he was made an assistant administrator.

Yet what happened to Clinkscales remains an ominous warning of what can happen to anyone who dares to open the bureaucracy's locked closets to public scrutiny. But like Fitzgerald, Clinkscales was helped by his tenacity and his resourcefulness, plus an inexhaustible spirit that kept him, in his darkest hours, from quitting and leaving government for good. Others were not so fortunate.

Consider John Breen, a young, conscientious civil servant (whose story was briefly alluded to in chapter 2) who made repeated efforts to tell others in Congress and the General Accounting Office about the mismanagement and abuses going on within the U.S. Savings Bonds Division, an obscure, archaic, $15 million agency within the Treasury Department where he was one of nearly two hundred bond sales promotional representatives. The scandal on which he blew the whistle remains today a still largely overlooked problem that continues to persist within the agency. Among other things, he charged that many bond sales representatives were not calling on all of the corporate executive officers they recorded on their elaborate weekly work reports, though many were making such claims and some were putting in for nonexistent travel expenses as well. But no one would listen to him.

When the story was eventually broken by this reporter, with Breen's assistance, the division's top officials charged that the accusations were "patently false" and a "smear tactic." But an internal investigation conducted by the department's Office of Inspector General in 1981 eventually revealed that Breen's accusations were true, though the price he paid was his own dismissal, along with the dismissal of several others, as a result of his decision to come forward and tell what he knew about wrongdoing in the agency.

Treasury officials made some hurried management systems changes that swept the abuses under the rug and the matter was said to be "cleaned up." But Breen, now looking at the agency from the outside, knew otherwise, as did several others who remained in the division. A subsequent General Accounting Office investigation, ordered in 1982 by Congressman Frank Wolf of Virginia, not only confirmed "the existence of serious abuses," as Breen and I had accurately reported, but went on to say that the "available information shows that some abuses continue despite the division's efforts to discourage them." Among other things, the GAO survey found that long after Treasury officials had insisted the agency's delinquencies were corrected, that possibly up to "50 percent of the sales force was engaged in fraudulent or abusive practices." But instead of being awarded for his bravery in blowing the whistle under very difficult circumstances, John Breen was punished while his superiors who had often looked the other way remained at their jobs.

A similar fate befell Victor McKay, fifty-eight, who blew the whistle on the Agency for International Development. He charged in a memorandum that AID was throwing away millions of dollars educating foreign students who, contrary to the program's requirement, never returned to their homelands. McKay says his memo was tossed into the wastebasket.

McKay's crime was that he told Congress what he knew, specifically that AID was wasting $5 million to $10 million a year to educate students, one-third of whom never went back to their native countries. He was subsequently fired in 1974, succeeded in winning his job back, but was fired again in 1977. The agency denies his charges, insisting that his firing had nothing to do with his whistle-blowing. Today, he works nights at the post office, while continuing to appeal his dismissal, a legal battle that has cost him over $20,000. Yet far more disturbing than the scandal he uncovered, McKay says, is the fact that "to complain about it means you stand alone."

James E. McGarrity, an accountant at the U.S. Bureau of Engraving and Printing, also learned how hard the bureaucracy can hit back after he blew the whistle on lax security and accounting procedures in the Treasury Department agency. McGarrity's disclosures — dealing with a scandal of major proportions that has received little news media attention — led to a 1979 inquiry by the Senate Permanent Subcommittee on Investigations and a congressional commendation from the panel for his cooperation. His testimony resulted in the indictment of two former bureau executives on charges of conflict of interest, along with several forced retirements. A clue that McGarrity knew what he was talking about came in 1982 when two of the bureau's former security guards were arrested in Orlando, Florida, in 1982, thanks to a disgruntled girlfriend who tipped off police that the two men had uncut sheets of money in their possession — money that was to have been burned or shredded at the bureau. The two were later convicted of possessing $117,000 in stolen and unissued currency, and in the summer of 1983 were convicted on charges of participating in a scheme with two other conspirators to "launder" an additional $550,000 through foreign banks.

Was James McGarrity rewarded by bureau officials for coming forward and calling attention to its internal security problems? Not a chance. Following his testimony before the Senate subcommittee, he began getting poor job performance ratings and was eventually swept out of the agency and transferred to another government job. Yet another former bureau employee, Ronald Lewis, was also dismissed from his job when he too blew the whistle on sloppy security at the bureau. Lewis told the subcommittee that security was so poor in the agency that he saw workers gambling in the bureau's locker rooms with unissued money. By 1983 Lewis was still pursuing his appeal for reinstatement at the Merit Systems Protection Board. Bureau officials, of course, have denied the charges.

Will the scandal at the BEP ever be fully uncovered? Not likely. Who in the bureau would dare come forward after seeing what had happened to McGarrity and Lewis?

This was made manifestly clear when the National Taxpayers Investigative Fund, a citizens watchdog organization based in Washington, ran newspaper ads in 1983 calling on "honest federal employees" at the bureau to "stand up" and blow the whistle on who was responsible for the theft of half a million dollars in freshly printed $20, $50 and $100 bills. The NTIF wanted to know who had covered up the theft, and whether it "could still be going on at the bureau."

It did not take long before NTIF executive director Ann Martino began getting a rash of anonymous phone calls from bureau employees who confirmed her suspicions that there had been a major scandal at the bureau that may still exist. "They said they were aware of major theft, fraud or other criminal activity," Miss Martino said, "and that security was lax. One caller claimed he could 'blow the lid off the whole thing.' Another caller said, 'I don't blame you for printing the ad . . . no one will ever know how much money was stolen.' " But it was clear that no one was going to stick their neck out and publicly come forward. "The one thing that each caller had in common was fear of management reprisal," she said.

Yet fear of reprisal sometimes is not the paramount consideration when anger or conscience drive a government worker to spill the beans about an improper or illegal act or condition. That was the case with Shirley Stoll, a nursing instructor at a Veterans Administration hospital who was fired from her job after exposing serious patient abuses at the Poplar Bluff, Missouri, facility in the summer of 1980. The forty-six-year-old professional was branded a troublemaker, harassed by superiors who tried to have her transferred to Wyoming, put into a tiny office for four months where she could make no phone calls and receive no visitors, and eventually was dismissed from her job in December 1981. She took her complaints to the Merit Systems Board in May 1982 and succeeded in winning reinstatement and $7,500 in back pay. But the painful experience left its mark on her and no doubt hurt her career in nursing.

Jake Lapin, an auditor with the Naval Audit Service, was forced to resign when he threatened to blow the whistle on what he testified was an estimated $100 million owed to the government through computer contract payback provisions that federal officials were ignoring. He fought back, spending $30,000 of his own money in his defense, and eventually was rehired, though he still encountered considerable pressure from superiors who wanted him transferred elsewhere. "Multiply my experience by scores of other auditors who have uncovered fraud, waste, mismanagement, and you can understand the huge difference that an effective whistle-blowing law could make," Lapin said.

Meanwhile, David Stith, who was employed by the Department of Housing and Urban Development, advises potential whistle-blowers, "Unless you want to commit suicide, don't blow the whistle." After his transfer to Greensboro, North Carolina, as manager of the Manpower Economic Development program, he found that millions of dollars were disappearing from HUD accounts. "I saw developers in North Carolina walk away with $6 million housing projects for $971 down, out of pocket," he told a congressional committee. But after reporting the delinquencies, Stith became the focus of an investigation during the Carter administration, and the object of harassment. Although his charges of fraud were eventually substantiated by official investigations, he was fired, then reinstated, and eventually transferred to HUD's Denver office. "I don't have any work to do now," Stith has testified. "I sit in a five-by-six office and shuffle papers at a pay scale of GS-14, step 10."

The Civil Service Reform Act of 1978, the centerpiece of the Carter administration's government management reforms, declared that the MSPB's independent, prosecutorial arm, the Office of Special Counsel (OSC) had two primary responsibilities: "(1) to receive and investigate allegations of violations of civil service law, rule or regulation, primarily prohibited personnel practices and to initiate appropriate corrective and disciplinary actions when warranted, and (2) to protect federal 'whistleblowers' from reprisal and refer allegations to agency heads."

Yet by 1980 the consensus of opinion, from whistle-blowers and congressional critics alike, was that the Board and the Office of Special Counsel had done an abysmal job of protecting whistle-blowers as the act had promised. Things did not appear to improve much under the Reagan administration with the appointment of Alex Kozinski whose fourteen-month tenure ended with his resignation in July 1982, to take a federal judgeship. Kozinski had come under considerable criticism from Capitol Hill, particularly from Congresswoman Patricia Shroeder of Colorado whose Civil Service Committee had held a dramatic series of hearings in 1980 on whistle-blower complaints against the agency. Shroeder considered the OCS so useless that she introduced legislation to have it abolished.

All of this may change for the better with the appointment in August 1982 of K. William O'Connor, a hard-nosed, intensely independent former criminal prosecutor of unshakable integrity who went toe-to-toe with the powers of the Pentagon over the George Spanton case and made the Defense Department recoil from their efforts to railroad Spanton out of the Contract Audit Agency. "In my view, when a legitimate complaint . . . is brought to my attention my responsibilities are to insure the protection of the employee," O'Connor told the Senate Committee on Governmental Affairs. The work of his investigators and attorneys throughout 1983 suggested that O'Connor may just rescue the OSC from its sorry image as a shill for the government's managers and administrators and make it work in behalf of honest, accountable government.

Nevertheless, there are some who believe that its small $4 million budget and meager staff are no match for the problem at hand, and some cynics even think that Congress wanted it that way. After all, too many successful, well-protected whistle-blowers could really wreak havoc with all the waste and abuse that exists in their most cherished programs. Significantly, since its inception nine thousand complaints have been brought before OSC, but only forty-three have involved "corrective action," or letters sent to the offending agencies' inspector generals; and only five disciplinary proceedings have been brought against delinquent supervisors, though none thus far has been successful.

Attorney Lewis Clark, executive director of the private Government Accountability Project, which has helped defend many whistle-blowers, says, "Any program that has the scope of OSC's purported mission would have to be at least ten times its current size to make a difference for whistle-blowers. OSC has currently twenty-eight attorneys nationwide. Fitzgerald alone needed the services of a dozen lawyers over a decade to gain vindication . . . the protection offered is less than that of a poor Legal Aid staff." His advice to victimized whistle-blowers? "Avoid OSC at all costs . . . it's the kiss of death to your case."

There is a need to overhaul the law and beef up its protections, but not so shackle program administrators that they cannot make the best use of their personnel and get rid of or transfer unproductive or unwanted workers. Equally important, any reform must change the inequitable tilt in the process by which the original accusations are ignored and the whistle-blower becomes the focus of the proceeding, not the delinquencies and abuses he or she exposed in the first place.

Meanwhile, until that day of reform takes place, the cruel and unusual treatment of whistle-blowers will no doubt continue, though it is likely that we may be seeing less and less of this endangered species. As Cliff McKenzie says, "I certainly would not blow the whistle again. It's not worth it. I personally think it is a phony program. The so-called protection [for federal employees] just doesn't exist."

22

Paying the Lawyers

FOR many years Uncle Sam has been shelling out millions of tax dollars in fat attorneys' fees of up to $350 an hour to lawyers who sue the government, in some instances even when they have lost their cases.

Washington's burgeoning legal industry has grown rich and influential in recent years as America's top law firms have opened up offices in the nation's capital, or expanded existing offices, in order to capitalize on the explosion of laws and regulations that has occurred in the last decade. In numerous cases so-called public interest lawyers are making big bucks by filing lawsuits against various federal agencies under a variety of deliberately complex laws enacted by a Congress dominated by lawyers. Under special provisions in these statutes, federal judges are given the discretion of awarding legal fees whenever they are considered to be "appropriate." And the record suggests that the judges have been exceedingly generous with the taxpayers' money in awarding such fees. In many cases, law firms are making money just handling the fee claim cases for other law firms, and some attorneys advertise that they specialize in such cases. Even when the government thinks the fee awards are excessive and appeals the court's decision, and then loses, the taxpayers pick up the tab for the costs of the law firm's defense in the fee claims appeals process as well.

Laws allowing the payment of such legal fees have been liberally interpreted by the U.S. Court of Appeals in the District of Columbia to mean that legal fees should be paid to attorneys even if they do not prevail in court. Judges have ruled in such instances that even though the complainants have lost their cases, they have "contributed to the public interest" just by bringing the suit into court and should thus be reimbursed by the public for their work, often at the bar's prevailing gold-plated rates.

Consider these examples:

— In 1982, the U.S. Circuit Court turned down the Sierra Club's claims in a Clean Air Act case brought against the Environmental Protection Agency in *Sierra Club* v. *Gorsuch*. The court also rejected the claims of a co-plaintiff, the Environmental Defense Fund. Yet both parties filed for federal attorneys' fees, with the Sierra lawyers asking for almost $100,000, or $90 an hour for 1,100 hours of work. The court decided that $90,000 to the losing litigants was more reasonable, even though the environmental groups had lost every claim in their suit.

— Again in 1982, in *Copeland* v. *Marshall*, a prominent Washington law firm represented some Labor Department women who charged that sex discrimination had barred them from promotions and training programs. A week before the court was to rule, the parties settled out of court and the women received a total of $33,000 in back pay.

Yet even though this case did not go to trial, the attorneys, who had originally sought $205,000 in fees for their work, were awarded $160,000 by the court — or nearly five times what the women received. When the government appealed the award and lost, the attorneys in question demanded additional fees for their time in defending themselves in the appeal, for which the government eventually agreed to settle out of court. In an interview, Assistant Attorney General Royce C. Lamberth, chief of the Justice Department's Civil Division, would say only that "we paid dearly for it."

— In yet another 1982 suit brought by the Environmental Defense Fund against EPA, under the Toxic Substances Control Act, the court ruled in favor of EDF on two issues, but against them on eleven other issues. Nevertheless, the EDF lawyers asked for fees ranging from $50 up to $110 an hour for the 839 hours of time they put into the case. Moreover, they asked that the amount be doubled, citing the high quality of their work and the difficulty they had with the government over their fee claims. The court decided the attorneys should by paid for all the time they spent on the case, and awarded them $77,000 in fees, plus additional payments which brought their total fees to $90,000. The court also granted an additional $9,500 in fees to the attorney who handled EDF's fee claim case.

— In a civil rights action brought against the Department of Transportation, the U.S. District Court approved fees of up to $138 an hour, awarding a total of $17,341.74 to the attorneys who brought the suit. The sex discrimination case, begun in 1979, was eventually settled out of court. The complainants received a promotion and over $4,200 in back pay. But the government opposed the fee award to the attorneys, arguing that two of the lawyers had never argued a case before and that the fees were excessive. On December 1, 1981, the Court of Appeals agreed and reduced the fees to $60 an hour.

— In still another suit, lawyers filed fee claims before the U.S. Circuit Court in the District of Columbia in early 1983, asking the judge to apply a "bonus" to their fees to reflect the complexity of the case they had brought against the Department of the Navy. Attorneys for the Aero Corporation sought $504,815.99 for a total of 932.75 hours of work on the case in which they unsuccessfully challenged the navy's award of a sole-source contract.

The court ruled that the navy had violated the law by refusing to allow competitive bidding in the disputed project, but it also concluded that the contractor in this instance could not be granted any injunctive relief because of overriding defense considerations. However, the judge also ruled that Aero was still entitled to payment of its legal fees because the navy had not acted in "good faith" during the litigation.

The hourly rates for which the attorneys wanted to be paid ranged from $50 for paralegal work to $175 per hour for the lawyers, and on top of this they asked for a 500 percent bonus multiplier of their fee, which would have pushed their nearly $100,000 bill to over $500,000. However, on June 10, 1983, the judge instead awarded them $79,722.25 in fees and nearly $18,000 in expenses, refusing their extraordinary "bonus" request.

— A lengthy federal sex discrimination suit by a group of flight attendants against Northwest Airlines that began on July 15, 1970, and took thirteen years to complete, culminated in what U.S. District Court Chief Judge Aubrey E. Robinson, Jr., called an "extraordinary fee petition." The fee claim, which sought a 200 percent bonus multiplier, asked for over $5 million in fees and expenses. In defense of the fee, the law firm handling the payment petition for the attorneys submitted thirty-six affidavits from what the court called "some of the most prestigious law firms in Washington, D.C." as examples of typical fees charged in such cases.

When the fee claim was awarded on July 29, 1983, the attorneys were given over $3.4 million. Hourly fees ranged from $75 to $175, but the judge had included a 100 percent multiplier which brought the actual hourly rates to between $150 to $350 per hour.

The unprecedented size of the payment led the judge to set forth the following criteria for determining what the hourly rate for future fee awards should be. The standard he set was based on how long an attorney had been out of law school and even their ranking in their law firm:

- "$175 an hour for very experienced federal court litigators, i.e., lawyers in their 20th year or more after graduation from law school;
- "$150 an hour for experienced federal court litigators in their 11th through 19th years after law school graduation;
- "$125 an hour for experienced federal court litigators in their 8th through 10th years after graduation from law school;
- "$100 an hour for senior associates, i.e., 4 to 7 years after graduation from law school; and
- "$75 an hour for junior associates, i.e., 1 to 3 years after law school graduation."

Legal Times said the judge in the case had "unkind words for attorneys on both sides, saying that their extensive filings engendered a waste of judicial resources." Nonetheless, some of the attorneys involved in the suit against the airline were awarded fees that totaled $80 more per hour than they customarily charged. Office of Management and Budget analysts estimate that government attorneys defending the same statutes are being compensated at the rate of $53 an hour, including overhead expenses.

— Another million-dollar-fee case involved a lengthy class action discrimination suit brought against the Department of Energy and its predecessor agencies under the 1964 Civil Rights Act. The case lasted from early 1976 until June 17, 1982. The plaintiffs won the case in a settlement on June 30, 1982, in which the government agreed to pay over $2.7 million in back pay and other compensation. In October 1982 the attorneys for the plaintiffs sought legal fees of over $1.6 million, which represented hourly fees of $25 for paralegals and $125 for the attorneys. The fee petition alone was 135 pages long and represented some of the biggest law firms in Washington.

By late 1983 the Justice Department was still litigating the fee claim case, and engaged in an extensive discovery proceeding in which it was seeking to subpoena the bar association's list of attorneys' fees.

Not only does the awarding of attorneys' fees conflict with the traditionally accepted American rule against fee-shifting — the practice of awarding one party's legal costs to the other party in a suit — but under it public interest lawyers are often being paid more than they would be by their own client.

A perfect example of this was the award of a hefty fee to the government-subsidized, nonprofit New York Legal Aid Society which is funded by federal taxpayers though the Legal Services Corporation, the corps of lawyers set up to provide legal help for the poor. In this fee claim case, *Blum* v. *Stenson,* which the state was appealing to the U.S. Supreme Court, public interest attorneys had successfully litigated a class action concerning persons whose Medicaid benefits had been unfairly terminated.

The attorneys sought payment of $79,312 for the 769.75 hours they had worked on the case. According to the govenment's brief in support of the appeal, these fees represented "$95 per hour for a 1977 law school graduate, $100 per hour for a 1976 law school graduate, and $105 per hour for a 1975 graduate, the most senior member of the litigation team." In addition, the legal aid lawyers also petitioned for a bonus multiplier of 50 percent.

Incredibly, the court agreed to these fee claims, including the bonus, giving the young legal team a total award of $118,968. The fees were upheld by the court of appeals. But as far as the federal govenment was concerned, they were outrageous. "The award of a bonus or multiplier over and above this amount is accordingly suspect; such an enhanced award exceeds the sum necessary to attract competent counsel and thus represents a windfall to attorneys," the Justice Department said in an *amicus* brief to the high court.

"Use of bonuses and multipliers to enhance fees in circumstances that are anything short of extraordinary would effectively negate Congress' judgement that only prevailing parties are to recover fees," the friend of the court brief argued. "Payment of fees at unrealistically high hourly rates is particularly indefensible to the extent that legal services organizations are supported by public funds. Assuming that additional funding of legal services organizations is desirable, it is not appropriate for the court to mandate such funding by awarding fees far in excess of the costs of counsel. This is especially true with respect to public defendants: in that situation fees for non-profit organizations based on market rates essentially represent a public subsidy for legal services groups beyond that voted by the legislature."

The fee payment practice got its start in 1974 when the Supreme Court ruled that fee-shifting could occur only when it is given clear statutory authority. Congress, an institution saturated with lawyers, responded to the high court's ruling by inserting special provisions in well over 120 statutes that specifically authorized federal judges to award attorneys' fees to the prevailing party in a suit brought under the law in question. The idea at the time was to provide broader public access to judicial remedies and to encourage public litigation in areas of various labor, civil rights, equal employment opportunity, environmental and freedom of information laws. Unfortunately, says Marshall Breger, an attorney and visiting fellow at The Heritage Foundation, "Congress and the courts, in their rush to insure access [to justice], gave little attention to the proper limits of encouragement."

Thus, none of the provisions allowing attorney fee payments specify how much the attorneys should be paid. Congress left that up to the courts, whose judges are all former attorneys. Most of the laws under which attorneys' fees are authorized specify only that the fees should be "reasonable," and they leave it up to the courts to apply their own criteria on a case-by-case basis. Many judges rely on the affidavits of local attorneys to determine what the prevailing market rate for legal fees is in a given area, and the objectivity of lawyers who are likely to be affected by a judge's determination has frequently been questioned. As Breger pointed out in an interview, the "present situation requires excessive subjectivity on the part of judges with respect to what is reasonable. It underscores the need for statutory reform."

This was certainly made demonstrably clear when a judge applied the vague language of the Rehabilitation Act of 1973 to a discrimination suit against the federal government, and awarded the prevailing attorneys fees totaling $436,000. The award went to the Greater Los Angeles Council on Deafness, Inc. for their successful lawsuit against a public television station, which charged that it had failed to provide special services for deaf viewers. A "reasonable" fee, in the judge's view, was $175 an hour, but upon further reflection he decided to double it because he thought the attorneys had done an outstanding job on a tough case, resulting in an hourly fee of $350.

Little wonder, then, as some have charged, that fee awards serve as an incentive for the introduction of marginal or frivolous lawsuits, resulting in crowded court calendars. "When lawyers can expect to collect windfalls from their opposition, traditional market restraints on litigation vanish," says Breger. "More money available for fees means more litigation, whether justified or not."

Lamberth, too, believes that many cases probably "wouldn't have been brought," if it were not for the availability of fee payments. The number of suits filed "has increased significantly as fee awards are publicized," he says. "When the court awards $350 an hour [in attorneys' fees], that has to attract lawyers."

Michael Horowitz, a special counsel in the Office of Management and Budget who was assigned the job of "getting control of attorneys' fees," says such awards have spawned a "literal industry" of public interest law in Washington in which "public-sector vendors" have come to regard fee awards as a "permanent financing mechanism." *Newsweek* magazine reports that "public interest groups now rely on fee awards for up to one fourth of their annual budget."

It should come as no surprise, then, that the number of cases involving the payment of attorneys' fees by the federal government appears to be escalating. In 1982, according to the newsletter *Regulatory Action Network*, the legal arm of the Sierra Club was "involved in more than 100 cases — twice as many" as the year before.

State and local governments are also finding themselves under the burden of an increasingly heavy public interest caseload, propelled by federal laws which encourage as well as subsidize such litigation. Senator Orrin Hatch of Utah, a member of the Judiciary Committee, reports that as of January 1983, the state of Florida "paid $778,090 in attorneys' fees while it only paid $211,042 in actual damages during the same period. In other words, the state of Florida has paid 269 percent more in fees to the lawyers than it has in damages to the individual harmed by the government's conduct."

The rise in such cases, and their cost to the taxpayers, has state attorney generals up in arms. John Ashcroft, attorney general for the state of Missouri, told members of the Senate Subcommittee on Separation of Powers just how the public interest attorneys ply their lucrative trade: the "idea," says Ashcroft, "is to file a broad based, ambiguous, shotgun lawsuit against a large state institution, engage in extensive discovery, cause the case to drag on for years [and] gain some relief from the court on a few of the issues raised. . . . Once this strategy is followed successfully by the plaintiffs, plaintiffs' counsel comes into the federal court and seeks an exhorbitant fee for every minute devoted to the case."

No one knows with any accuracy what these attorneys' fees are really costing federal taxpayers. Horowitz calls the special U.S. Treasury account Congress created to pay these bills, "the black hole." He estimates that at a minimum the legal fees are costing taxpayers $20 million a year, but OMB officials say the bill could soon mushroom to $146 million as new legal fee programs enacted by Congress begin to take effect.

The scent of big money has had Washington lawyers lining up for the loot in increasing numbers. Even a new specialization in federal fee claim cases has begun to grow. A letter sent out to prospective clients by the Washington law firm of Trilling & Kennedy advertised that its special knowledge on how to litigate fee claim cases offers "the possibility of substantial financial rewards for your organization."

Meanwhile, a bimonthly newsletter called *Federal Attorneys Fee Awards Reporter* has been published. Each issue includes a virtual shopping list of "Federal Statutes Authorizing the Award of Attorneys' Fees." Also available is a book entitled *Federal Court Awards of Attorneys' Fees: How to Get $ From The Government.* Its author, E. Richard Larson, of the American Civil Liberties Union, acknowledges that there has been a "virtual explosion in federal attorney's fee litigations." Larson says his book "makes this area of the law understandable and easily accessible to all practicing attorneys." For example, he points out that the Civil Rights Attorneys' Fees Act of 1976 is just one of the many fee-providing statutes that authorize "liberal" fee awards.

But the rapidly expanding army of lawyers descending on Washington will have still more information made available on this gold mine that awaits them. According to *Legal Times,* a three-volume textbook on attorneys' fees was in the works, while still another book by Washington, D.C. attorney Joel P. Bennett was also being prepared in 1983. Its title: *Fee Awards Against the U.S.*

The Reagan administration, under the direction of Horowitz's office in OMB, was in the process in late 1983 of drafting legislation with the Justice Department to curb federal attorneys' fees. But going up against the lawyer lobby is not an easy task. When you are talking about attorneys' fees you are talking about some lawyer's bread and butter. When Lamberth showed up at the D.C. Bar Association with a magistrate and a subpoena to obtain a list of the fees maintained by the bar, he was turned away. The bar chose instead to appeal the decision of the judge who granted the subpoena, claiming "an attorney client privilege" as the reason for its refusal. Thus, even though the taxpayers' money is involved, the bar says the public has no right to know how much lawyers are getting paid under this program.

A significant breakthrough was achieved by the government in the summer of 1983 when it appealed to the Supreme Court the 1982 *Sierra Club* v. *Gorsuch* award to public interest attorneys who had lost their case. The high court reversed the lower court's fee award, ruling that an attorney must achieve "some degree of success on the merits" of a suit in order to be eligible for a fee.

Nevertheless, the U.S. Treasury's "black hole" still remains wide open for lawyers to enrich themselves far beyond what most Americans consider fair and reasonable. "There has to be some limit to what the taxpayers have to pay in attorneys' fees," insists Lamberth, to which Horowitz adds, "The notion that government should subsidize discrete segments of the bar for ideological purposes is unjustified and dangerous."

23

Turkey Farming

UNDER an obscure government program tens of millions of dollars have been paid to thousands of federal employees even though they did no work for the taxpayers who paid their salaries.

Congress undoubtedly had good intentions when it passed the Intergovernmental Personnel Act (IPA) in 1970, though it is often difficult in retrospect to understand how Congress rationalizes some of its strange legislative actions.

Nevertheless, the original rationale for IPA was that an exchange of employees between the federal government and local and state governments and educational institutions would be an enriching experience that would make the employees more valuable to their respective superiors and programs.

Unfortunately, as we shall see, it has not necessarily worked out that way. The program has been misused and exploited for far different purposes, while being seriously neglected by the institution that created it. No one in the government is seriously monitoring and evaluating its operation and performance on a government-wide basis. Needless to say, the Congress knows even less about the use to which IPA is being put to. Inquiries to the relevant House and Senate oversight subcommittees were greeted with totally un-informed responses about the effect and use of IPA throughout the government.

In truth, IPA has been pockmarked with abuses and in some cases has been used as a convenient tool to get rid of unwanted federal employees. Federal bureaucrats have been sent off to state and local institutions for up to four years at a stretch, many never returning to the government where their newfound experience was to have been put to use for the taxpayers' benefit.

Consider, for example, the case of Michael Weinberg, a National Science Foundation official who was assigned to the University of Massachusetts for a full four years while remaining almost totally on the federal payroll. Weinberg was a deputy congressional liaison director for NSF who earned nearly $34,000 a year. In 1978 he was transferred to UMass under an arrangement in which the university agreed to pay 10 percent of his salary and NSF continued to pay the balance, along with up to $8,000 in travel expenses.

While at the University of Massachusetts at Amherst, Weinberg worked as a special assistant to the dean of the College of Food and Natural Resources, and also worked with the Institute for Man and Environment, an independent research unit there, apparently pro-viding the university with assistance in obtaining research funding. When UMass originally sought his reassignment from NSF it noted in a letter to the federally funded science research agency that both institutions "have especially strong ties to federal funding sources, and consequently, they rely on a great deal of personal interactions with federal officials." The UMass letter went on to say that "Mr. Weinberg would bring to the university much-needed experience in dealing with these funding organizations. His NSF administrative background, when coupled with his familiarity with federal legisla-tive and political processes, would be a valuable staff resource for the university." The university said NSF would gain from the per-sonnel transfer because the assignment would provide Weinberg "with direct experience in the university administration."

At the end of his two-year tour of duty, Weinberg's assignment at UMass was extended to an additional two years, though the univer-sity increased its share of his salary to 15 percent. Such extensions are considered rare, said NSF officials, but again the rationale was advanced that the experience he gained at the university would be invaluable to NSF when he returned to government. When Weinberg completed his extended leave, however, he never returned to NSF, opting in 1982 to continue as a full-time employee at UMass. His assignment, though highly unusual in terms of is extraordinary length, was completely legal and aboveboard. Nonetheless, it raises legitimate questions about the actual benefits of IPA to the government and whether taxpayers are getting what they paid for.

An unseen rationale behind the IPA program is the extent to which it helps colleges and universities — the biggest beneficiaries of this program — and other local institutions to solicit federal grants and contracts by obtaining the advice and knowledge of federal officials with some expertise in the grantsmanship process. Paul Broglio, NSF's deputy chief of personnel, volunteered in an interview that "the people in the grants office are in great demand" by outside recipients of IPA-funded personnel. When asked if NSF officials loaned to other institutions of higher learning also assist them in obtaining federal grants and other funding assistance, Broglio conceded that "would be a part of it — how to write [grant] proposals," though he insisted this was not the chief purpose of these assignments.

Others are not so sure. "It sounds like the federal government is paying money to teach institutions how to get money from the federal government," said a Senate Appropriations Committee staffer.

Thousands of federal employees have been similarly loaned to various state and local institutions, but government officials who have used the program say it has been abused. In many cases the program is simply a convenient way of getting rid of unwanted federal employees without going through a lot of bureaucratic red tape or costly removal proceedings.

When the General Accounting Office surveyed 115 federal participants, auditors learned that about half of them had either personal or agency problems before their transfer. Indeed, GAO says about 70 percent of those who were experiencing personal or work-related difficulties initiated their own transfers. Many of them never returned to their agencies.

For years after its inception, no one knew what IPA was costing taxpayers governmentwide. In 1982 an ambitious investigation conducted by the *Kansas City Star,* which uncovered significant new abuses, estimated that the government was spending $12 million a year on federal employees assigned to work for someone else.

Since its enactment in 1971, more than ten thousand people have participated in IPA. Of these, thirty-two hundred have gone out to state and local institutions, while more than sixty-three hundred have come into the government. Although the law provides for cost-sharing between the institutions in cases where federal employees leave the government, Uncle Sam usually ends up footing the bill for most of the employees' salaries. The *Star* interviewed seventy-five federal employees who were either on assignment or who had been recently assigned under IPA provisions. Half of those interviewed helped to initiate or arrange their own assignments because they were undergoing some kind of personnel conflict at work or experiencing some other problems with their supervisors. Its survey, the *Star* reported, "indicates the extensive use of the program to solve personnel problems and to create personal opportunities."

Among many program supervisors, using IPA expressly to get rid of unwanted or troublesome employees is commonly known as "turkey farming." The Reagan administration, as previous administrations, has used it to avoid messy, time-consuming and costly transfers, dismissals or reassignments. A Department of Education official, for example, told me that a small group of unwanted employees were swept out of the department in 1983 under IPA. "It's done all the time," he said.

According to Andy Jones, an Office of Personnel Management official in charge of overseeing IPA, 1981 was a banner year for personnel assignments under the program. A total of eleven hundred people participated in IPA governmentwide. This figure dropped to a little less than three hundred in 1982 due to the Reagan administration's budget cuts. In 1983 there were 323 assignments made by the middle of the year.

The biggest user of IPA continues to be educational institutions. Out of 323 assignments in 1983, 234 were between the federal government and colleges. Within this total, there were 129 academicians who took temporary posts in the federal government, and 105 federal bureaucrats who were sent out to the halls of ivy.

The costs of administering IPA totaled $96 million in 1981, declining to $34 million in 1982 as a result of budget cutbacks. In the latter year, the federal government paid 68 percent of the $11 million spent to detail federal workers to nonfederal jobs. At the same time it paid 88 percent of the $23 million it cost to bring nonfederal personnel into the government. Such costs, of course, seriously abuse IPA's "cost-sharing" provisions under which the "gaining agency" should pay 60 percent of the cost of the transfer.

My own sample survey of government agencies reveals continuing abuse of the program, particularly its "cost-sharing" requirements. The National Aeronautics and Space Administration, for example, picks up the entire tab for the dozen or so NASA officials it sends out each year to colleges and universities. NASA officials say there is no monitoring of their work, though "we encourage them to write," says a spokesman.

To its credit, the administration has made some significant reductions in this marginal program. Nevertheless, in a time of national budgetary austerity, while the administration is pursuing some modest reductions in force (RIFs), i.e., dismissals, a competing and contradictory federal program is still sending federal employees away to work elsewhere for up to two years while remaining on the federal payroll. "If we are RIFing people, can we afford to send people away?" asked Rosslyn Kleeman, a General Accounting Office auditor. "You have to question how useful it can be for the government to have an employee absent for four years," adds Tom Vandervoort, a top Democratic staff official on the Senate Appropriations Committee.

Whatever the merits of this program, at a time of stratospheric deficits we should not be paying federal workers who are not working for the federal government.

24

Pay and Pensions: "A National Disgrace"

CHARLES L. MORRIS worked in the federal bureaucracy for forty-two years. When he retired from the Treasury Department in 1965, his annual salary was $7,500. His total contributions to the Civil Service Retirement System during his years in the government totaled $6,000. Yet since his retirement he has received more than $142,000 in pension payments thanks to generous yearly government cost-of-living increases. He thinks his current $17,000-a-year pension is "outrageous."

After thirty-two years as a government economist, James F. Walker retired from the Department of Labor in 1967 at the age of fifty-six, when retirement for most Americans is still many years away. When he left the civil service he was earning $18,000 a year, which provided him with a monthly pension of $820. Over the next sixteen years Walker's pension was tripled by cost-of-living adjustments, pushing it to $2,400 a month, or about $29,000 a year. He has complained to Budget Director David Stockman, saying that federal "retirement checks have been increased by much more than the [actual] cost-of-living increases justify."

William D. Howard was an accountant with the Internal Revenue Service who retired in 1975 at the age of fifty on an annual pension of $23,400. By 1980, just four and a half years later, Howard's pension had jumped to $36,900, again due to cost-of-living raises. By 1981, he was getting $41,496 a year. The Taxpayers for Federal Pension Reform, a public interest group based in Philadelphia, estimates that by 1990, when Howard will be sixty-five, he will be receiving $130,344 a year from Uncle Sam. By the year 2000, when he will be seventy-five, his pension will be $427,536 a year.

Former Congressman Hastings Keith of Massachusetts, whose rapidly rising congressional pension, plus social security and a small military annuity, provides him with a comfortable income of nearly $70,000 a year, calls the federal pension system "a national disgrace." Keith says he has only paid about $36,000 into the pension system that now supports him so handsomely, allowing him to maintain homes in Washington, D.C., and at Cape Cod. His wife, a former employee of the Central Intelligence Agency, also receives over $1,000 a month from her CIA pension. Together, their combined federal pensions give them more than $80,000 a year.

According to the Office of Personnel Management (OPM), one-half of all federal employees retire before the age of sixty, while only a mere 7 percent do so in the private sector. Civil Service employees may retire on a full pension as early as age fifty-five after thirty years of service, while private-sector workers must wait until they are sixty-five before collecting their full retirement pensions.

Early retirement has become exceedingly attractive to federal workers for many reasons, but primarily because thousands of them — like the above examples — have found that they can eventually earn more from their pensions than they have from their paychecks. (See examples of congressional pension excesses in chapter 4.) Approximately 100,000 federal retirees currently earn more from their government pensions than they ever earned from their salaries as a result of annual cost-of-living adjustments.

It should be pointed out that the examples cited at the beginning of this chapter are not typical by any means of the vast number of federal retirees, but they do serve to illustrate the excesses of the system which extend across the board. Out of the 1.8 million civilian retirees getting benefits, "only" 57,470 of them are being paid at least $2,200 a month, or $26,400 a year, according to OPM.

Nevertheless, the average federal pension can cost hundreds of thousands of dollars over the years they are collected. For example, consider the case of a federal worker who retired in 1974 at age fifty-five after thirty years of civil service who was eligible for an annual pension of $27,668 in 1984. Analysts for the Taxpayers for Federal Pension Reform figure that "based on 1984 federal income tax schedules for a family of four paying income taxes on $15,000 a year and taking the standard deduction, it would take 29 families to support" such a retiree. After twenty years of retirement, this retiree will have collected $600,191, 85 percent of which is financed by the taxpayers.

The Civil Service Retirement System (CSRS) now costs more than the federal food stamp and welfare programs combined. Federal civilian retirement payments alone totaled $21 billion in 1983, up from $4.6 billion in 1973. But CSRS is only one of twenty-one major government pension programs, along with thirty-one minor ones, that make up the entire federal pension system. The estimated cost of all federal pensions — civilian and military — in fiscal 1983 was nearly $35 billion. Their unfunded liability — what it would take to pay everyone covered under the system until the day they die — was a stunning $1.4 trillion, almost as much as the national debt.

Over a twenty-two-year period, between 1960 and 1982, CSRS outlays skyrocketed by 2,101 percent, while federal employee contributions to their pension fund increased only 449 percent. The government, therefore, has had to pick up the slack, increasing its contribution by 2,667 percent. Even so, CSRS is going deeper into debt at the rate of $70,000 per minute and presently has an unfunded liability of $515 billion.

According to OPM Director Donald Devine, the pension system's alarming costs are due to automatic cost-of-living adjustments (COLAs) which he calls the "single biggest culprit" in its astronomical growth. "Benefits were increased several times without any consideration of how to pay for them," Devine says, warning that their growth "threatens to overwhelm the American taxpayer."

U.S. taxpayers of course are footing the bill for the bulk of the pension system's rising costs, with each taxpayer paying $256 a year to support CSRS and taxpayers as a whole covering 87 percent of the cost of the program. OPM estimated that the total contribution to the retirement fund in fiscal 1983 was $34.6 billion, only $4.2 billion of which came from employees' contributions, the rest from taxpayers. In fact, the average civil servant only contributes enough to cover eighteen months' worth of future retirement benefits. Moreover, while the average private-sector retirement plan costs 14 percent of total payroll, the federal government's cost is a much heftier 29 percent of payroll. That extra 15 percent the government pays cost taxpayers $9.5 billion in fiscal 1982.

The Military Retirement System (MRS), meanwhile, covers 3 million active duty and reserve personnel and supports 1.4 million retired veterans. Outlays for this pension system alone totaled $16.8 billion in fiscal 1984, its costs having quadrupled between 1970 and 1980. The military retirement fund currently has an unfunded liability of $527 billion.

If you think the civil service pension system is a good deal, consider a retirement plan that allows you to "retire" at one-half your pay after a mere twenty years of service. For our military, that can be as early as age thirty-seven, and in some cases even earlier. Obviously, it is an offer that many find impossible to refuse. Half of all nondisabled officers and enlisted retirees left the military in 1982 after twenty to twenty-one years of service.

"The military pension scheme is not simply generous, it is lavish," says Congressman Les Aspin of Wisconsin who discovered three navy men who retired as early as age thirty-five. Aspin calculated that by the time they reach normal retirement age they will each have received more than one-third of a million dollars in pension payments. "This is straining generosity a wee bit," he believes.

The three military men were born in 1943, entered the navy at age seventeen, and retired at age thirty-five in 1978 with the rank of chief petty officer, pay grade E-7. "Each of these men started getting a pension of more than $117 a week," Aspin said. "Assuming a very modest inflation rate of 5 percent, each of these men can expect to draw more than $380,000 before they reach the normal retirement age of 65. Yet all of these men are able bodied, nondisability retirees who are able to move into second careers." Nevertheless, for the next twenty-four years they will be getting their regular civilian pay plus their navy retirement checks.

While twenty years is the minimum amount of military service time required for a pension, the three servicemen benefited from an old provision of the retirement law that permitted navy and marine corps enlisted men to receive credit toward retirement for reenlisting early. In their cases, all had accumulated two years of credits and thus they were able to retire before age thirty-seven.

Retiring at age thirty-five is a bit unusual, but military retirement for servicemen in their late thirties has in fact happened rather frequently. Indeed, during the very year these three navy men retired they were joined by 121 thirty-six-year-olds, 645 thirty-seven-year-olds, 1,931 thirty-eight-year-olds, and 3,893 thirty-nine-year-olds. All of them will be receiving retirement checks for the rest of their lives.

Meanwhile, pay-scales and other ancillary benefits in the federal civilian workforce remain as comfortable as ever, despite unceasing complaints from the bureaucracy that federal workers remain underpaid. The average bureaucrat earns anywhere from 11 percent (according to the Office of Personnel Management) to 35 percent (according to the U.S. Chamber of Commerce) more than his private-sector counterpart. Over sixty thousand civil servants earn more than $50,000 a year, while even mail carriers and postal clerks for the U.S. Postal Service can now earn a maximum $24,000 a year, far more than the average salary paid to public school teachers, college instructors, nurses, or policemen. Federal blue-collar workers generally are much better paid than their counterparts in the private sector.

Benefit for benefit, the government far outshines private-sector jobs, and federal salaries have made the Washington, D.C. area one of the most affluent areas in the country. Yet a Labor Department survey of pay-scales in the private sector insists that federal workers are deeply underpaid by anywhere from 17 to 36 percent. If bureaucrats are to catch up to their private-sector counterparts, this 1983 survey maintains, federal civil servants must be given a 21.5 percent raise. How can this be?

The truth is that the Labor Department's Professional, Administrative, Technical and Clerical (PATC) survey, which is the tool the government uses to set federal pay-scales, is inherently flawed. A General Accounting Office investigation discovered in March of 1983 that the employment categories PATC surveyed "contained disproportionate numbers of jobs which were highly paid in the private sector." Equally important, the PATC survey does not bother to survey state and local government jobs, nor does it look at businesses of less than 250 people. These crucial exclusions, says the President's Private Sector Survey on Cost Control, "eliminates over 96 percent of the firms in all major sectors" from consideration in determining federal pay-scales. This kind of selective pay-scale comparison means that the PATC survey "is skewed upward," says the Private Sector Survey, and has allowed the government to shove its pay-scales way beyond what their occupational counterparts are earning out in the Real World. For example, between 1967 to 1980 federal pay went from being 25 percent greater than average state and local government salaries to 42 percent greater, according to the Office of Personnel Management.

Another method the government uses to determine its salary levels is to compare federal *job descriptions* to *actual work* performed in a comparable private-sector position. But does the avereage bureaucrat do everything his job description says he does? Not always. Former federal employee Leonard Reed says that "anybody who has ever worked in a government agency knows that job descriptions will endow a file clerk with responsibilities before which a graduate of the Harvard Business School quails." Little wonder then why the average salary for a typical white-collar Washington bureaucrat is now over $30,000 a year and why the total federal payroll is now over $100 billion a year.

In its 1983 study of the federal personnel system, the President's Private Sector Survey found that by reducing the pay and benefits of federal workers to levels comparable to the private sector, the government could save a total of $35.6 billion over a period of three years. The study, among other things, revealed that "compensation systems for the federal government . . . have become seriously flawed through both Congressional and Administrative action"; that the federal white-collar payroll is "overly costly because of maladministration," which has resulted in overgrading; and that from 1949 to 1981, the number of employees in the higher pay grades had doubled and the number of lower pay grades had been cut in half.

A July 1982 study by the Office of Personnel Management, titled "Federal White-Collar Position Classification Accuracy," also found that thousands of federal workers were holding positions whose official job description for pay-grading purposes were vastly exaggerated. Based on a sample survey, OPM estimated that 14.3 percent of the government's 1.3 million white-collar positions were overgraded. While 188,000 federal employees were occupying more highly paid positions than they deserved, only about 20,000 civil servants were estimated to be undergraded or classified in lower positions than they should have been. In all, this misclassification — "when the official titles, occupational series or grades do not match the way the employees are actually operating in their positions" — was costing the government $682 million a year.

At the same time, "in-step" pay raises have become virtually automatic in the government. Basically, when you strip away all of the civil service procedural gobbledygook, the only real criterion for such raises is longevity on the job. Currently, OPM uses a five-level appraisal system to measure a civil servant's performance for a possible raise. The highest rating is "outstanding," followed in declining order by "exceeds fully successful," "fully successful," "satisfactory," and "unsatisfactory." In order to qualify for an "in-step" raise, or the next pay level to which an employee is entitled within his grade, a civil servant need only receive a rating of "satisfactory," the second lowest rating possible. OPM, which has been trying to upgrade the rating level required to qualify for a raise, says the government has "a personnel system that straitjackets initiative."

There are other, less tangible benefits afforded federal workers, which are rarely mentioned. Perhaps none ranks so high as job security. Depressions or recessions come and go, business bankruptcies and layoffs rise and fall, but the civil service largely escapes them all. For all their complaining, civil servants can take comfort in knowing that they are far more secure in their jobs than the rest of the workforce. True, about nine thousand federal workers were said to have lost their jobs during fiscal 1982, but twelve million other Americans also became unemployed that year. Compared to an overall unemployment rate of 10.8 percent, that rate for civil servants was just .3 percent, and new openings elsewhere in the bureaucracy soon restored most of those lost jobs.

Finally, despite the commonly heard argument that the government cannot keep qualified civil servants on the federal payroll because federal pay is so low, the truth is that competition for federal jobs is fierce. In 1980, the ratio of inquiries to job placement was 61 to 1, according to OPM, and government officials say that ratio remains high. The *Wall Street Journal* reported in March 1983 that the government had nine persons actually filing applications for every job it has available — twenty-two for each professional and administrative position and thirty for each senior manager position. Over one million persons tried to find work at the Postal Service alone in 1981.

To be sure, there are many conscientious, capable and hardworking employees at all levels of government, just as there are many retired civil servants and military personnel who have served their country well, often under the most difficult of circumstances. But the record is clear that an uncoordinated, inequitable and dishonest system of federal pay and pensions has been created whose abuse and wasteful exploitation is a national disgrace.

25

"Home, James"

E_{VERY} administration and each new Congress condemns the excessive and improper use of government cars and federally paid drivers to chauffeur bureaucrats to and from their homes and to other personal social engagements, but each year this practice continues, as costly and wasteful as ever.

While this relatively minimal expenditure obviously does not compare in cost with an $88 billion synfuels extravaganza or a $4.5 billion revenue sharing binge, it is still an important government abuse for us to examine and evaluate. For it is within these seemingly harmless bureaucratic comforts and perquisites that one truly comes to understand how our "public servants" have been able to justify so easily the steady expansion of special privileges, benefits and programs that have grown into the multibillion-dollar burden we are all forced to support. An undisputed axiom in government spending is that very few civil servants spend our money as if it were their own. It becomes so easy to squander someone else's money on less-than-vital activities, even among those now in power who once condemned such expenditures from outside the government. The use of chauffeured automobiles is a case in point.

Except for a handful of cabinet secretaries and a few other top federal officials who are specifically granted this perquisite, the use of chauffeurs to drive federal employees to work is expressly prohibited by law. Yet year after year the law has been conveniently ignored to the detriment of the American taxpayer.

Nearly two years after the Reagan administration had come into power vowing to cut wasteful spending throughout the federal government, Senator William Proxmire of Wisconsin discovered that the problem had in fact grown worse. A governmentwide survey conducted by Ron Tammen, one of Proxmire's chief investigators, found that 190 government bureaucrats were being given door-to-door chauffeur service at an average annual cost of $32,000 per official, or a total cost of $3.4 million a year. Moreover, Proxmire discovered that the number of government officials who were benefiting from this service had risen by fifteen, an 8 percent increase over the Carter administration, according to a previous Proxmire survey. Among this latest survey's more interesting findings:

— Housing and Urban Affairs Secretary Samuel R. Pierce headed the list of big spenders in 1982, when the survey was taken, with an Oldsmobile 98 Regency, which HUD was leasing for the princely sum of $8,088 a year. With gas and maintenance, Pierce was squandering $9,588 annually for his luxury car. Under the glare of Proxmire's scrutiny, Pierce ended the leasing arrangement in March 1983, and instead leased a ritzy 1983 Lincoln Town Car under a more favorable deal (worked out by the GSA with the Ford Motor Company) for $3,075 a year. With $1,550 in maintenance, that brought his bill, not including chauffeur, down to $4,625.

The then Energy Secretary James B. Edwards was second, with a car costing nearly $8,000 a year; his successor, Donald P. Hodel, turned in Edwards's overpriced 1981 Oldsmobile four-door Delta 88 and leased a 1983 four-door Lincoln Continental instead — also for $3,075 a year.

Third on the most extravagant list was Interior Secretary James Watt, who resigned in October 1983, and who was using a car that cost a little over $7,000 per year. Watt also recoiled from Proxmire's withering blast, canceling the lease for a Buick Electra in

April 1982 in favor of a 1983 Lincoln Town Car for $3,089 a year.

— As far as the number of officials provided with chauffeur services, the Defense Department is clearly the worst offender, giving sixty of its top brass this most sought-after service.

— The award for most overtime costs for a chauffeur went to the Central Intelligence Agency. CIA Director William Casey's chauffeur earned $20,000 a year but, thanks to $26,000 in overtime, made more than $46,000 in 1982.

Meanwhile, consider the case of Donald I. Hovde, who as undersecretary of Housing and Urban Development was caught in early 1983 using his government-leased Buick Le Sabre and a chauffeur to drive his family about on personal errands and to get to and from work from his home in nearby McLean, Virginia. Hovde also used the driver and car to take his parents on a sightseeing trip to the Capitol, bring his daughter to school, squire his wife about on errands, pick up his laundry, get himself to the airport for personal trips, and attend a wedding and other private social engagements and dinners. HUD Inspector General Charles Dempsey figured that Hovde's use of chauffeur and car cost taxpayers $6,845 in overtime and gas costs. The undersecretary bitterly disagreed with the estimates and, after some wrangling, the inspector general cut the bill by more than half, to $3,149, which Hovde paid.

Hovde, the former president of the National Association of Realtors, insisted that he was unaware of the restrictions against using government cars for personal use. However, the IG's investigation found that Hovde had been warned by other HUD officials that this use of his driver and car for personal trips could violate HUD regulations. Hovde, who said his misuse of his car and chauffeur was "just an honest error, inadvertently made," was subsequently appointed by President Reagan to the three-member Federal Home Loan Bank Board.

Four other HUD officials were also found to have used their government cars for unauthorized purposes. Among the abusers was Stephen Bollinger, HUD's assistant secretary for community planning and development. Bollinger later agreed to pay $2,611 for the cost of using a government car to get to work. Dempsey's investigation discovered that the HUD officials had used the government cars for commuting over two hundred and eighty times and had used chauffeurs more than eighty times to have themselves driven to Washington's National Airport during off-duty hours when they could have taken taxis at much less cost. The chauffeured service cost $15.73 per trip compared to $5.75 for a cab ride. Investigators said HUD's motor vehicle staff, who knew about the unauthorized trips but told no one about them over a two-year period, had collectively earned $111,000 in overtime pay during this time.

Or consider the story of Robert P. Nimmo, Ronald Reagan's administrator of the Veterans Administration who faced numerous charges of wrongdoing, including the redecoration of his offices, improper first-class air travel, and the personal use of a government chauffeur. The wealthy California rancher had ordered a government-leased, four-door Buick Electra for $708 a month and had himself driven to and from home even though an internal report advised him that this was in clear violation of the law. Nimmo subsequently reimbursed the government for the $6,441 the inspector general said he owed for his misuse of the government car, then later resigned on October 4, 1982, under a storm of criticism.

It is difficult to understand why these and other abuses of government chauffeurs occur, because the law is certainly clear: Title 31, Section 638(a) of the U.S. Code forbids the use of government cars except for "official purposes," which in no way includes being driven to work. The exceptions are the President, the vice-president, cabinet secretaries, diplomatic personnel abroad, government doctors on out-patient duty, and federal personnel in the field. Congress also assigns chauffeurs to its congressional leaders and the Architect of the Capitol. But for everyone else, it is illegal.

Of course, lower-level government officials can find a loophole in any provision if they try hard enough, and this was the case with Dr. Edward N. Brandt, Jr., the assistant secretary of Health and Human Services who was appointed by President Reagan to head the Public Health Service. Brandt has a rationale for being driven to his office at HHS headquarters near Capitol Hill in a four-door sedan, but it is one that congressional oversight staffers find questionable at best. When asked for the statutory authority that allowed the doctor to be driven from his home to his office, HHS spokeswoman Shirley Barth said it was perfectly legal because "Dr. Brandt is being transported from one government facility to another." How can this be? Well, the law allows officials in the course of their duties to be driven from one government facility to another to attend meetings, testify before Congress, and fulfill other official responsibilities. Because Brandt is provided with a government-owned home on the grounds of the National Institutes of Health, he considers his domicile to be a "government facility," which it is in a manner of speaking since Uncle Sam owns it, and in this way he justifies his door-to-door chauffeur service.

No one in Congress has been more of a stickler about the abuse of government chauffeurs than Bill Proxmire who, besides his celebrated "Golden Fleece Awards" for wasteful federal spending practices, is perhaps best known for his habit of running to work. Proxmire has seen more than his share of government limousines pass him in the morning as he jogged to Capitol Hill, noticing the little reading lamp in the backseat along with that ultimate status symbol, the car telephone. Yet he wondered why he often did not recognize the backseat occupants as being members of the cabinet then in power. The reason, of course, was that they were not cabinet officials and their ride to work was in violation of the law.

When Proxmire conducted his survey in late 1982, it stirred up all of the legendary excuses that attempt to defend this needless and frivolous luxury:

Excuse Number One: "A chauffeured automobile enables me to conserve my valuable time and be more productive."

Excuse Number Two: "I must often attend early-morning and late-night meetings, and public transit is often unavailable."

Excuse Number Three: "Our offices are in a high crime precinct."

Excuse Number Four: "My use of a chauffeured automobile is in the government's interest."

On the contrary, says Proxmire, "The only interest being served here is the personal convenience and desire for status of the federal official. There is no government interest." This was also the view of the Justice Department's Office of Legal Counsel in an opinion issued in 1979, which ruled that such excuses were invalid. The department's attorneys said that despite every excuse ever used, "Nothing in [the law's] text, background or prior interpretation supports a reading so contrary to its plain meaning." The Justice Department had this advice for government officials who argue that chauffeurs give them more time to do their paperwork and thus make them more productive public servants: "A senior official may lengthen his or her working day, if necessary, by coming earlier, leaving later and living closer to the office. Using government transportation instead is a matter of personal convenience."

Nevertheless, despite a clear prohibition, the figures show that dozens of high-level bureaucrats are thumbing their nose at the law and the taxpayers. At the Defense Department, for example, only Secretary Caspar Weinberger, and the secretaries of the army, navy, and the air force can legally be afforded this privilege. Yet sixty officials were receiving this door-to-door service, twelve regularly and forty-eight others on an intermittent basis.

Second to the Pentagon with the most chauffeurs is the Department of Transportation, with twenty-two top-level officials getting the royal treatment, fourteen on a regular basis, and eight administrators who have cars exclusively at their disposal.

Congress is third in the limousine sweepstakes, with eleven congressional officials getting the aristocratic service. In the Senate they are South Carolina Senator Strom Thurmond, the Senate President Pro Tempore; Majority Leader Howard Baker of Tennessee; Assistant Majority Leader Ted Stevens of Alaska; Minority Leader Robert Byrd of West Virginia; and Assistant Minority Leader Alan Cranston of California. In the House they are Speaker Thomas P. "Tip" O'Neill of Massachusetts; Majority Leader James Wright of Texas; Majority Whip Thomas S. Foley of Washington; Minority Leader Robert H. Michel of Illinois; Minority Whip Trent Lott of Mississippi; and the Architect of the Capitol.

Among other federal agency heads given the luxury of a chauffeur-driven car is the president of Amtrak; the president and vice-president of the Overseas Private Investment Corporation; the president and chairman of the board of the Synthetic Fuels Corporation; the Postmaster General; the director and deputy director of the U.S. Information Agency; the administrator of the Agency for

International Development, the foreign aid agency formed to help the world's poor; the chairman of the Merit Systems Protection Board; the chairman and director of the Federal Deposit Insurance Corporation; the chairman of the Federal Communications Commission; and the chairman of the Federal Reserve Board.

What is all of this costing the taxpayer? Like so many other government costs, the figures are unreal for this line of work. The average salary of civil service drivers for thirty-three major departments and agencies surveyed is $28,145 a year. Yet this figure sharply contrasts with the average pay for the Defense Department's civilian drivers, which the Pentagon says is $35,290.

When overtime pay is added to these salaries the income becomes even more substantial. The average annual overtime payment for government chauffeurs was $11,205. In fact, Proxmire's survey, completed September 30, 1982, found three agencies where chauffeurs were being paid overtime in excess of their yearly salary. At the CIA the total salary for Director Casey's chauffeur came to $46,625. At the Commerce Department, Secretary Malcolm Baldrige's chauffeur earned $41,660, the same as then Secretary of State Alexander Haig's chauffeur.

No one would begrudge providing our cabinet secretaries and a few other top executive branch officials with this service. But in a government where nearly two hundred mostly non-cabinet-level bureaucrats are being driven to official and nonofficial functions, being squired to work in the morning and home in the evening, and having their families carted around on routine personal errands and appointments, this red carpet service has become an unmitigated scandal.

"Let them ride the bus to work to study how effective our transportation system is," suggests Proxmire, "or run to work to consider the value of federal health programs, or car pool to save on energy consumption as they urge everyone else to do."

On June 6, 1983, the General Accounting Office's comptroller general issued an opinion that found the use of the government's chauffeur-driven services was clearly "exceeding the limits of the law." The GAO said there was much confusion over the statute's implementation because it was overly vague, and it suggested that

Congress rewrite the law. Clearly, the excessive and continued abuse of government drivers calls for tougher prohibitions and penalties, placing them, if necessary, in each appropriations bill Congress approves for every agency of government. For many top-level bureaucrats the chauffeur-driven car is the ultimate symbol of power and prestige and luxury, but it is a luxury that America's hard-pressed taxpayers and depleted Treasury can no longer afford.

BOOK III

THE REAGAN ADMINISTRATION

26

Reagan's Report Card

W E were saying our goodbyes after a rather wide-ranging discussion about his administration and the difficulties of the presidency one year after he had taken office when Ronald Reagan asked, "You haven't any suggestions, have you, of more places that we can find to cut the budget?"

The President had read a book I had written in 1980 that investigated federal spending practices and specifically detailed where one hundred nonessential federal agencies, programs and expenditures, totaling over $25 billion, could be cut from the budget. He referred to the book in speeches and in interviews during his 1980 presidential campaign as proof of his contention that government spending was loaded with waste, fraud and abuse. After his inauguration, he passed out copies of the book to department heads and top White House aides at one of his first cabinet meetings, urging the new managers of his administration to read it. "If Lambro can find this much waste in the federal government, why can't we?" he told his cabinet secretaries, according to an aide who was at the meeting.

On this particular day I had walked into the Oval Office prepared to ask Reagan a number of questions. I was not, however, expecting any questions in return, particularly one so difficult to answer in so short a time. I remember Jimmy Carter being asked by a flighty talk show host during his 1976 campaign to explain, in the thirty seconds that remained in the program, what could be done about inflation. Since Carter didn't have the foggiest notion how to combat inflation, as the 17 percent inflation rate during his administration so graphically revealed, his answer was understandably briefer than his allotted time. But my interview was over and Reagan's aides were impatiently waiting to get the President on to his next appointment, though he seemed to want to talk a little longer. "Well," I replied a little sheepishly, "those hundred programs and agencies I discussed [in my book] are still there. That's a good place to start. You've gotten rid of one or two of them, but the rest are still there."

"Yes," Reagan responded, rather noncommittally, pausing to think a bit. "You know, just between us, one of the hardest things in a government this size — no matter what our people way on top are trying to do — is to know that down there, underneath, is that permanent structure that is resisting everything you're doing." He spoke of the bureaucracy as if most of it were several stories beneath the surface of the earth and he had only broken through to the first strata. Shaking his head, he remarked on how difficult it was to "get the management going and how long it takes to get clear down there."

Reagan, of course, was not voicing an unusual presidential complaint. John F. Kennedy once confessed that it was easier talking about what he wanted the government to do than to get the government to do it. There were, Kennedy learned, two governments: one that is temporary and elected, and one that is permanent and implacable — i.e., the bureaucracy, which receives its life-giving sustenance from Congress and its public support from the special interests it serves, forming an Iron Triangle that has never been broken. Like his predecessors, Reagan has learned this too, much to his frustration.

Yet to hear the screams of the bureaucrats, the Washington news media and the special interests, one would think that Ronald Reagan had killed Big Government. In truth, though he has slowed its growth in some areas, government overall has been growing under Ronald Reagan by every measurable criterion — in terms of dollar expenditures and in terms of its percentage of the Gross National Product. The fiscal 1981 budget in Jimmy Carter's last year in office accounted for a little over 24 percent of the GNP. The fiscal 1982 budget Reagan inherited from Carter, even with the minor spending reductions Reagan achieved, still ended up representing 24 percent of the GNP. However, Reagan's first full budget, for fiscal 1983, lifted federal spending to nearly 25 percent of GNP, and while his fiscal 1984 budget was expected to decline slightly as a percentage of GNP, it was still falling within the previous 24 percent range. The same was expected for his fiscal 1985 budget, presented in February 1984. This is hardly the "Reagan revolution" we have heard about.

Contrary to the public perception that Ronald Reagan and his brilliant budgeteer, David Stockman, had slashed the budgets of federal departments and agencies from one end of Washington to the other, nothing could be further from the truth.

The Defense Department, of course, was clearly one that Reagan had no intention of cutting. He had, in fact, campaigned and was elected to the presidency on a pledge to strengthen America's weakened military capabilities. Under his administration, Pentagon outlays went from $183 billion in fiscal 1982 to $205 billion in fiscal 1983 to $231 billion in 1984, pushing military spending to about 29 percent of the total federal budget. Yet at the same time, it should be borne in mind that military spending as a share of the GNP had been declining for decades while spending for social programs rose significantly throughout the 1960s and 1970s. Between 1975 and 1981, social welfare expenditures increased by 4.7 percent annually after inflation, while the real yearly increase in military spending over this same period was only 1.8 percent.

Yet contrary to Reagan's exuberant budget-cutting rhetoric, and his deep, private frustrations about slowing the growth in federal expenditures, he has frequently pushed for major nondefense budget increases throughout the government. The Washington news media has kept this side of his spending requests largely secret because it did not fit in with their characterization of Sir Ronald, the ax-wielding Black Knight of the Woeful Countenance, driving federal programs back to the Middle Ages. In fact a closer reading of Reagan's budget proposals show that despite the rising deficit and the need to curb spending, there were numerous exceptions where Reagan proposed sharp spending increases or, at the very least, recommended that existing spending levels be preserved. In every case, of course, the administration had a rationale for demanding more money from Congress, just in case anyone should ask. As it happened, no one ever did, at least not from the news media. After all, the story was Reagan's budget *cuts*, wasn't it? Or was it?

In truth, while his proposed increases in defense outlays and some modest curbs on social programs were grabbing all the headlines, Reagan was seeking spending increases left and right. His fiscal 1984 budget requests, for example, sought to increase the Justice Department's $2.9 billion annual budget by $400 million, citing a renewed emphasis on fighting organized crime. He requested a similar $400 million rise in the State Department's $2.2 billion budget even though many of its embassies are notoriously staff heavy and little had changed in the world's problems to merit so huge an increase. He also asked for a $200 million increase in the National Aeronautics and Space Administration's $6.7 billion yearly allowance, and a $1.3 billion hike in the Veterans Administration's $24.3 billion budget.

Still further Reagan requests for fatter budgets included the Agency for International Development, a core agency in our foreign aid program, which sought a $100 million raise in its $1.1 billion annual budget; the scandal-ridden Farmers Home Administration, whose budget Reagan wanted increased from $3.5 billion to a hefty $4.5 billion; the Transportation Department, whose coffers were swollen by the extra five-cent-per-gallon gasoline tax hike Reagan sought and got from Congress, proposed that its budget be boosted by a whopping $3.2 billion from its spending level of $21.2 billion; and even the darling of the multinational corporate subsidies, the Export-Import Bank, wanted its lending authority punched up by an additional $1.4 billion.

Reagan went along with all of this and much, much more in his fiscal 1984 money requests to Congress, including a panoply of budget increases for smaller agencies such as $128 million more for the $581-million-a-year U.S. Information Agency, headed by his friend Charles Zwick; a nearly $200 million increase for the National Science Foundation's $1 billion yearly checking account, despite substantial evidence that many of its grants fund nebulous or very low priority studies; the National Endowment for the Arts put in for a $10 million raise for its waste-ridden $140 million budget; the Federal Emergency Management Administration requested over $100 million more for its $444 million budget, saying it needed to beef up civil defense programs; and HUD's urban development action grants, used to help finance big commercial real estate developments, sought to increase the previous year's $488 million in outlays by $24 million.

Even the Department of Energy, that caliginous collection of dubious energy industry subsidies and payoffs, which Reagan vowed to dismantle in 1980, was still at full throttle in February 1983 and in fact was asking, over the President's signature, for an additional $100 million above its bloated $8.7 billion budget.

Reagan's fiscal 1984 spending recommendations also sought to keep many agencies and programs exactly where they were, spending-wise. The Department of Education, which he promised to turn into a subcabinet agency, saw no real reduction in its budget. It was a little over $14 billion in fiscal 1981, when Jimmy Carter left office, and three years into the Reagan administration its budget had actually been increased by about $300 million more per year. True, in 1983 Reagan sought to cut DOE's budget, but it was a relatively undramatic $900 million reduction that the administration did not fight vigorously to obtain. Meanwhile, the White House had all but abandoned any pretense of seeking to dismantle the department that Jimmy Carter and Vice-President Walter Mondale had presented to the National Education Association, the huge teacher's lobby, in payment for NEA's political endorsement in behalf of their reelection.

Similarly, and regretfully, Reagan's fiscal 1984 budget sought no significant cuts in dozens of other federal programs such as the Rural Electrification Administration's $230 million budget, even though his own Office of Management and Budget admits that REA's job of bringing electric power to America's rural areas was virtually completed long ago. Reagan asked for no diminution of the Agriculture Department's $41 million Economic Research Service, even though its services are primarily benefiting major agricultural industries and markets. Not a penny was cut from USDA's $470 million Agricultural Research Service, whose research often benefits wealthy agribusinesses. The Bureau of the Census, whose only job under the Constitution is to conduct a census every ten years, still wanted a robust $83.6 million a year to keep its life-support system going, and Reagan agreed. The U.S. Travel Agency, which even Jimmy Carter wanted abolished, is now called the U.S. Travel and Tourism Agency, and Reagan was right up there arguing that this ludicrous government program should get $5.1 million, which it did, to keep its tourism programs alive.

And all those regulatory programs that Reagan was going the slay? The Civil Aeronautics Board, a fossil of the airline regulatory age that we will never see again, still got $71 million even though it should have been phased out of existence long ago.

The Federal Trade Commission, an agency that among other things keeps smoking machines going year-round to test the tar content of cigarettes so that the tobacco industry can use the statistics in its advertising to sell more cigarettes, still sits sassy and contented as ever near Capitol Hill in its Roosevelt-era building. Despite the complaints of only a few negligible Naderists, the FTC is barely pared down. Reagan sought a meager $8 million cut out of a $68 million bureaucracy that has done little if anything to help the consumer.

Similarly, the Interstate Commerce Commission, the oldest and most unnecessary of the federal regulatory agencies, still requires trucking entrepreneurs to come hat in hand, with an expensive ICC-approved lawyer, to get certification from the United States government in order to haul freight in interstate commerce. In payment to the Teamsters Union, which supported him in 1980, Reagan named Reese H. Taylor, a former Nevada trucking industry attorney, to the ICC chairmanship, and deregulation initially slowed to a crawl. Admittedly, that changed when the balance of power was tilted at the ICC in favor of deregulation with the appointment by Reagan of two deregulators. Still, Reagan sought a mere $5 million cut in the ICC's $43 million yearly budget, and ambitious legislation pushed in 1983 by Transportation Secretary Elizabeth Dole to further deregulate the agency was put into the deep freeze by the White House, once again bowing to the Teamsters in preparation for the 1984 campaign. A golden opportunity to eliminate an unnecessary regulatory vestige of the FDR era has been lost.

Even the most hated agency in Washington, the $200-million-a-year Occupational Safety and Health Administration, symbol of federal nannyism at its worst — and one that Reagan himself railed against in his speeches, syndicated column and radio broadcasts — received a modest increase in Reagan's fiscal 1984 budget requests.

In expenditures both large and small, the administration's requests for budget increases speckled the Reagan budget, seemingly oblivious to the mounting $200 billion deficit that was shedding its gloom over the fiscal 1984 horizon, and threatening to worsen in fiscal 1985. But a strange psychology seemed to take place in which it was argued that the deficit was so huge anyway, what's a few more million dollars? Thus, as the budget's debt climbed higher, exceeding 6 percent of GNP in 1983, Reagan's fiscal 1984 budget had the temerity to ask for a $6 million increase in the budget for the Executive Office of the President. Even David Stockman, that arch-budget-cutter himself, was asking Congress to increase his office's $3.8 million budget by another $2.2 million, while the Reagans wanted their executive residence budget upped from $3.8 million to $4.5 million.

A Reagan revolution? In some spending areas, yes, but in many other expenditures, both large and small, far from it.

Significantly, the thick budget documents Ronald Reagan sent to Capitol Hill in February 1983 and again in 1984 did not propose the true elimination of any government department or major agency and in fact not one has occurred as a result of his administration.

Even the two agencies — the Community Services Administration and the President's Council on Wage and Price Stability —

that Reagan was instrumental in "abolishing" were not really and completely eliminated. There were numerous news stories late in 1981 about the shutting down of the Community Services Administration, the core agency of the antipoverty program begun under President Lyndon Johnson's Great Society. Stories appeared in the *Washington Post* about how the agency was "closing its doors." But if, two years later, you were to visit the building in downtown Washington where CSA had its offices, you would find that they are still there, their bureaucracy sharply pruned back, of course, but still in business. The agency has not been abolished, as you and I would define that term. It was merged into the Department of Health and Human Services, its name changed to the Office of Community Services, and its workforce slashed from two thousand employees to about fifty-five people. But the agency is still spending $31 million in discretionary grants, and $317 million in funding for local Community Action Programs, which is simply being block-granted to the states. Meanwhile, the office itself still has an administrative budget of $4.3 million a year to spend, including several millions of dollars more in funds for public service jobs and a rural development loan program. Thus, two years after it had been "abolished," the agency, such as it was, still remained alive, a testament perhaps to the miracle of bureaucratic immortality.

In the opening days of his administration, the Council on Wage and Price Stability, whose monumental ineffectiveness was self-evident during the 17 percent inflation under Jimmy Carter, was also closed down by Reagan, in a manner of speaking. However, Reagan abolished only that part of the program under his discretionary authority, which had monitored wages and prices in the economy. The other part of the agency, which monitored government costs that threaten to fuel inflation, was also closed down though much of its personnel was shifted to some statistical-gathering corner of the Commerce Department to live on in perpetuity.

Much, too, was written about the "elimination" of CETA, the Comprehensive Employment and Training Administration program within the Department of Labor, which spent a stunning $58 billion since its inception, $24 billion of which was poured into public service jobs around the country. A total of thirty-two million people participated in CETA, six million of whom were provided with temporary public service employment. But CETA became one of the most scandal-ridden programs in the government, with its funds largely politicized by state house and city hall bosses who saw that their political cronies and supporters got a lot of the jobs.

While Reagan has boldly phased out CETA as we have known it, in its place he has substituted another big, new, nearly $4 billion program called the Job Training Partnership Act, which came into existence on October 1, 1983, needing of course another bureaucracy to run it. However, instead of CETA's focus on make-work or dead-end public service jobs, this program's emphasis is on job training in cooperation with the private sector through business-led advisory councils, shifting responsibility away from the federal government to state and local officials. In fact, 70 percent of its funds must go directly into employment training.

At its height in fiscal 1978, CETA was a $9.5-billion-a-year program. Though it was formally "eliminated" in September 1983 in a programmatic sense, it still had $3.6 billion left in its budget at the end of 1983 and most of its huge bureaucracy, both in Washington and out in the field, remained in place to take over running Reagan's equally ambitious substitute program. Yet while CETA's wasteful public jobs program per se was being "eliminated," Congress rarely gets rid of any program entirely. Bureaucratic vestiges often remain. In this case, Congress quietly stuck $25 million in public service jobs funds into its 1984 "emergency jobs" program for the Office of Community Services.

Early in 1981, as the administration was taking over the reins of government, David Stockman, director of the Office of Management and Budget, issued a brief, four-page appendix to the President's budget recommendations, which outlined programs it was recommending for termination between fiscal 1981 and fiscal 1986. A careful review of this administration's wish list, though, shows that by 1984 Reagan had succeeded in eliminating few of the major programs on the list: the Juvenile Justice and Delinquency Prevention Program, solar energy programs, Legal Services Corporation, Volunteers in Service to America (VISTA), mass transit operating subsidies, and many more, continued to exist by 1984.

One can argue, as the administration does, that even though the President seeks little or no money for these programs, Congress goes ahead and funds them anyway. But a measure of any administration's success is its ability to lead and to persuade, to extract concessions from Congress. Strong arguments for the elimination of these and other agencies have not been aggressively carried up to Capitol Hill in a full court press, as they were during Reagan's dramatic assault on Congress in 1981 with the full blush of his 1980 election mandate freshly behind him. Thereafter, the administration did not really push to keep the burden on Congress to defend the continuation of marginal, wasteful and unaffordable federal programs. Somewhere along the way, after its successful 1981 budget assault, the administration abandoned legislative confrontation with the congressional power structure as a means of achieving its fiscal goals.

Early in 1983 David Stockman admitted that despite all of the brouhaha in the media over the "Reagan budget cuts," relatively little had actually been cut. He suggested that critics were so microscoping the budget that they were missing the larger and more relevant reality of how federal spending, especially social welfare spending, had risen enormously in the last decade. Totally ignored was the fact that the administration had achieved only very modest reductions in budget growth.

Also overlooked in the midst of legitimate concern for the plight of the needy was the fact that Reagan's fiscal 1984 budget proposals contained one-half trillion dollars in nondefense spending, exclusive of interest. "In constant 1983 dollars that is down 4 percent from 1981, but it is 95 percent higher than in 1970," Stockman told the National Press Club on February 10, 1983. "A budget which spends nearly twice as much as in 1970 after adjusting for inflation can't be neglecting domestic welfare entirely," he said.

Yet still the news media were inaccurately portraying Reagan cruelly slashing programs for the poor and the hungry. White House reporter Lesley Stahl, for example, told *CBS Evening News* viewers on May 1, 1983, that the number of people getting food stamps was "considerably fewer than a couple of years ago, before cutbacks." CBS later admitted she was wrong. Food stamp recipients had been climbing under Reagan, largely due to the recession. In 1980, 19.3 million people were getting food stamps, according to the Agriculture Department's Food and Nutrition Service. By 1983, however, the number of recipients had ballooned to 22.2 million people, costing nearly $12 billion a year.

Food stamps, though, is only one of many programs that make up that one-half trillion dollars in yearly nondefense spending, which includes a total of $424 billion in annual income transfer payments and social welfare programs. Head Start for children, supplemental nutrition for women, infants and children (WIC), supplemental security income benefits for the elderly, blind and disabled, handicapped education, employment training, housing assistance, aid to education — funding for all of these programs was up in fiscal 1984 over the previous year. When compared to 1970, Reagan's 1984 budget makes Lyndon Johnson's Great Society spending "appear positively antediluvian," said Stockman.

Ronald Reagan came charging into Washington with two big campaign promises in his saddlebags: the dismantlement of the departments of Education and Energy. The promises never went anywhere because of Congress's resistance to eliminating anything it creates. But they also failed because the White House, and the men Reagan chose to head these two nebulous departments, neither aggressively nor imaginatively championed and pursued their dissolution. As noted above, the budgets of these two relatively new cabinet departments have suffered no diminution under Reagan and have, if anything, enjoyed slight dollar increases. The administration argues it did not have the votes in Congress to make good on either of these promises. Yet even if one were to buy that argument, which I do not accept entirely, Reagan still had the power of the veto and, by using it, could have forced significant reductions in each department's expenditures and thus their activities. Yet, for whatever reason, he chose not to exercise presidential power and leadership vigorously to achieve goals he set forth in his campaign and on which he was, after all, elected.

Of course there are deeper, more politically physiological reasons for Reagan's failure to make any headway on two major planks in his campaign platform. Education Secretary Terrel H. Bell, an education careerist of a generally liberal persuasion, had moved in and out of federal education posts prior to his taking the cabinet post in the Reagan administration. He was never a Reagan enthusiast and thus was ideologically unsympathetic with Reagan's deepest goal of reducing the meddling federal hand in local education and returning the entire department back to some subcabinet level, with some serious reductions in its less-than-vital activities, particularly in areas of research and low-priority federal grants.

Bell's halfhearted proposal in 1982 to move the entire department into a government-funded foundation, virtually lock, stock and barrel, hit a stone wall on Capitol Hill. Not surprisingly, Bell never lobbied aggressively for it. "Don't forget, he was one of the early boosters for establishing a Department of Education in the 1970s," a top-level department official pointed out. "Why would anyone expect him to fight for getting rid of a bureaucracy he fought so hard to achieve?"

Similarly, then–Energy Secretary James B. Edwards, a dentist by profession and a former governor of South Carolina with no real background in energy matters, was ill equipped from the beginning to argue articulately for the department's dismantlement. Thus, a poorly conceived legislative plan to divide the department's programs between the Interior and Commerce departments fell apart — largely because DOE was not headed by someone with the credentials and credibility to fashion and sell a legitimate and salesworthy dismantling plan to Congress and to the energy industry. That the White House never swung aggressively behind the idea of doing away with the Energy Department betrays a failure of leadership both by Reagan and his weak domestic policy staff, all of which led to the unfulfillment of a major campaign promise.

The administration's failure to win even the most modest curtailment of these two departments or the elimination of other major programs is dramatically reflected in the infinitesimal reduction in the federal workforce during the first three years of Reagan's presidency. There were 2,843,404 executive branch employees (including Postal Service workers) in January 1981, Jimmy Carter's last month in office. By May of 1983, the Office of Personnel Management reported that the total number of federal workers stood at

2,833,183, or a reduction of a little over 10,000 employees, representing a meager decline of only four-tenths of one percent. Most of
the reduction came as a result of normal attrition through retirements and career changes, and a relatively small number of dismissals. Overall the total federal civilian workforce still hovered near
2.9 million. The ranks of the federal bureaucracy have hardly been
scratched under Ronald Reagan.

Despite all of my misgivings, however, the Reagan administration's performance has been several notches above any administration in recent memory in many significant respects. Reagan has at
least kept the focus on the need for spending restraint, and thus has
changed the entire domestic policy debate in Washington to one of
limiting the growth of government. While only a few years ago,
lawmakers were coming forward with ambitious plans for new
spending, now the only serious discussion in Washington's legislative and executive branch councils is over how much that growth
should be curtailed.

Reagan has moved forward significantly on deregulation through
his Task Force on Regulatory Relief headed by Vice-President
George Bush, but not nearly as aggressively as candidate Reagan's
1980 political rhetoric suggested he would, though the little no-
ticed, but welcome, news is that there have been no major new regulatory initiatives of any significance thus far in his presidency.

Still, decades of unnecessary labor, transportation, and commerce
regulations remain untouched by this administration — regulations
that have become obstacles to business expansion and job creation.
A government in which it remains a federal crime for jobless men
and women to sew apparel in their homes, among a number of
other for-profit cottage industries still forbidden by the Labor Department — and that continues to price uneducated and unskilled
minority youths out of the job market through an inflexible minimum wage — has still not delivered on the free market beliefs of
Ronald Reagan.

Reagan has also been relatively effective at trying to improve the
management of government by getting tougher on rooting out
waste, fraud and abuse, though there has not been nearly enough
investigative and prosecutorial resources applied to this problem as

is needed. The inspector generals have largely delivered a mixed performance, and in most cases hardly have earned the White House's description of being "meaner than junkyard dogs." They need beefing up, a few replacements, and a broader mandate.

Without question, however, the shining centerpiece of Ronald Reagan's administration has clearly been his three-year reduction of the personal income tax rates, which rescued the economy from its precipitous decline to near-depression levels and proved so many of the economic soothsayers, doomsayers, pundits and Big Spenders wrong. As the tax reduction plan moved through Congress, Democratic lawmakers and the voodoo economists they listen to predicted that cuts in the marginal tax rates would spur inflation, sharply aggravate interest rates, and lead to higher unemployment. In each case they were wrong.

To be sure, inflation, even at its much more modest levels under Reagan, continued to push taxpayers into higher tax brackets, and social security taxes continued to rise significantly. These events plus a number of legislated tax increases virtually canceled out the tax cuts for most taxpayers. Nevertheless, it certainly can be argued that the President's unprecedented tax rate reductions gave America's beleaguered taxpayers, and the economy, significant relief from the much more oppressive levels of taxation they would have paid had no tax cuts been passed at all.

Although he did not originally propose it, Reagan also deserves credit for defending another major tax reform enacted under his administration — the indexing of personal income taxes. Due to take effect by 1985, indexing will keep Americans from having to pay higher tax rates simply because their incomes kept abreast of inflation. That's bad news for Congress, which has been able to sit back and reap increasingly larger revenue dividends without having to change a single digit in the tax code, merely by letting the inflation their big spending had spurred push workers into higher tax brackets. But it is good news for taxpayers who are simply trying to stay ahead of inflation — benefiting those on the lower-to-middle end of the income scale most.

Nevertheless, Reagan's overall record remains a mixed one on national domestic policies. He has gone farther than any president in recent times in seeking to limit the incredible rate of growth of government, and for that he is to be applauded and supported. At the same time he has seen even his relatively modest budget limitations, and his attempts to focus social welfare programs more narrowly on the truly needy, maligned as draconian and lacking compassion. That such modest reductions can trigger such an outpouring of bitterly exaggerated rhetoric serves to illustrate how severely bloated and excessive federal expenditures have become in a broad range of public programs.

Sadly, however, Ronald Reagan's bold attack on the federal bureaucracy in 1981 has been followed by a long reign of fiscal timidity, one that deeply underestimates the willingness of the American people to cleanse a government that remains overbudgeted, overemployed, overextended, and overinvolved in a range of activities in which it has no business. The federal government remains as obese as ever, and a policy of merely trying to reduce the rate at which its obesity is growing is doomed to failure. The task ahead for Ronald Reagan, or whoever comes after him, is not just to limit, but actually to roll back the size of government.

27

Balancing the Budget

"ANYONE who thinks he can balance the budget in one year or even two is absolutely crazy," Edwin L. Dale blurted out over the telephone.

It isn't that Ed Dale, the former chief economic reporter for the *New York Times* who became the Reagan administration's spokesman at the Office of Management and Budget, doesn't believe that eventually the budget can be balanced. It's just that there are all those political obstacles to overcome, the enormity of the budget, the great girth of the deficits, the special interest groups, plus all those so-called uncontrollable entitlements, not to mention the administration's resistance to any sizable defense cuts, well . . . "it just can't be done that quickly," Dale persisted.

This unimaginative, almost paralytic attitude toward the budget is a typical one in Washington. The establishment view is that cutting federal spending to any significant degree, let alone balancing the budget, is virtually impossible. It is a goal devoutly to be wished, of course, but not one that bears any realistic chance of being achieved. The root causes of this fiscal coma stem from many things, but especially from a false perception of federal spending it-self — one that sees the budget as a huge, monolithic juggernaut that cannot be stopped, never mind rolled back. Thus, the popular mythology in the capital city is that when you examine the budget's major components, there is in the end little that can be cut without destroying a lot of programs and agencies which the political-media-bureaucracy axis equates with saving humanity.

The intelligent and always readable Washington journalist William Greider composed perhaps the classic version of this impregnable view of the budget, which he included in his now-famous *Atlantic Monthly* piece on "The Education of David Stockman." It went like this:

When you discount 48 cents of every federal dollar for social security, military and civilian pensions, welfare and health care payments, plus veterans costs, then take away 25 cents for the Pentagon and 10 cents for interest payments on the debt, you're left with "seventeen cents for everything else that Washington does." Then account for programs like the FBI, national parks, county agents, the Foreign Service and the Weather Bureau, he continued, and that leaves a meager eight cents out of each federal dollar. But that's eaten up by grants to state and local governments, aid to handicapped children, and highway construction. Sure there is waste, sure there are programs that are "unnecessary and ineffective, even crazy," but after acknowledging that, we cannot "escape those basic dimensions of federal spending," Greider tells us.

Greider is not alone in his myopic view of the budget. The Washington news media to a large degree have been aggressive perpetrators in this ongoing deception over the budget's harmful realities. When Jimmy Carter's OMB director, James McIntyre, briefed reporters on one of Carter's budgets, I remember him holding the thick budget book aloft and declaring with a perfectly straight face, "I've looked through this budget again and again for something I could cut without our country suffering adverse consequences and I can't find it." To this day I will never understand why McIntyre was not laughed off the podium by the usually cynical White House press corps. But he wasn't, of course, because we have allowed our political leaders to con us into thinking that everything Washington does with our money is vital and essential to our national survival. More often than not, it isn't.

The figures are grim. The gross federal debt reached $1.4 trillion in 1983, and is expected by the Congressional Budget Office (CBO) to hit $1.8 trillion by fiscal 1985, and surpass the breathtaking $2 trillion mark by fiscal 1986, absorbing increasingly larger and larger amounts of the nation's available income and savings. Borrowing to finance this debt — whose rapidly rising interest payments were running about $100 billion a year — as well as to finance spending by off-budget lending agencies was projected to stay at 6 percent of GNP over the next four years, about twice what it was during the recovery of 1975–1979. "This level of borrowing means," CBO has told Congress, "that the federal debt held by the public will grow faster than GNP, rising from 31 percent of GNP in 1982 to 50 percent by the end of 1988." By contrast, the ratio of total outstanding debt to GNP had been dropping from the end of World War II to the early 1970s when it remained about level through that decade. The last time it had hit 50 percent of GNP was in 1959.

Equally disturbing, the one-year budget deficit climbed to just under $200 billion in fiscal 1983, after having ballooned to $111 billion in fiscal 1982, which was nearly twice the $60 billion deficits run up in each of the two previous years under the Carter administration. Unless further spending cuts were made, or federal revenues increased dramatically, OMB Director David Stockman was predicting yearly $200 billion deficits "as far as the eye can see."

Since 1981, administration critics have been screaming about Ronald Reagan's budget cuts, but knowledgeable observers of federal spending continue to ask, "What cuts?" Before he left office, Jimmy Carter proposed a fiscal 1982 budget of $739 billion. Much to his credit, Ronald Reagan succeeded in cutting that budget by $11 billion. But Reagan's next (fiscal 1983) budget, with much help from Congress, reached $830 billion, or $13 billion higher than Carter's original spending estimate for that year. Thus, in the space of just two years, the budget rose by $102 billion, $24 billion higher than even Carter's excessive budget figures suggested it would.

The administration's fiscal 1984 spending proposals came in at

$848.5 billion, a seemingly modest increase, but when all was said and done the real budget total for the year was headed toward $868 billion. Spending in fiscal 1985, which was to begin October 1, 1984, was projected by the Congressional Budget Office in the $928 billion range. The budget Reagan would submit in January 1985 was estimated by budget analysts to be very near the unprecedented $1 trillion mark. In other words, Ronald Reagan, the Budget Slayer, had presided over four years of significant budgetary growth — with yearly federal outlays rising from $728 billion in fiscal 1982 to over $928 billion in fiscal 1985, representing cumulative increases well over $200 billion in estimated outlays.

In terms of deficits, however, the Reagan administration, again with most of the spending impetus from Congress, scaled new heights in the annals of federal debt accumulation. Between fiscal years 1982 and 1985 the government will have run up yearly budget and off-budget deficits, the difference between spending and incoming tax revenue, exceeding $700 billion.

. Could Reagan and the Congress have done better? Could the budget have been substantially reduced in size without enacting major new increases in taxes? I firmly believe that it could and that it still can. Contrary to the conventional wisdom about an "uncontrollable" federal budget, we can have a balanced budget any time we want. And it can be done without raising taxes, savaging the poor, or gutting our needed military defense buildup. Here's how:

1. Revenue Sharing: Thousands of well-heeled cities and towns like oil-rich Dallas and jewel-drenched Palm Springs, not to mention merely comfortable middle-class communities, are wastefully reaping billions of dollars from this massive no-strings-attached giveaway program. Regardless of need, federal checks are being sent each year to 39,000 local governments, thousands of which deposit tidy budget surpluses in the bank, or regularly balance their budgets. The states were expected to compile $60 billion in budget surpluses in fiscal 1985. The federal government, meanwhile, must borrow the money to give it away. Eliminate it. Annual savings: $4.6 billion.

2. Community Development Block Grants: Though originally designed to help only poor and low-income people, these grants

have also been heavily benefiting wealthy and middle-class cities and towns that are more than able to pay for their own community development. Zero it out. Savings: $3.5 billion.

3. Foreign Aid: Uncle Sam spends nearly $12 billion a year on foreign assistance of all kinds, much of which never reaches the world's poor, according to internal audits. In a time of fiscal crisis that threatens the economic health and security of our nation, is it too much to suggest that we reduce our foreign aid expenditures by 50 percent until we get back on our feet economically? I think not. Estimated savings: $6 billion.

4. Department of Education: A national Roper public opinion poll found that 83 percent of those surveyed in the U.S. think education should not be a function of the federal government. Despite more than three quarters of a trillion dollars spent on federal aid to education in the past ten years, test scores have plummeted, a decline halted only in 1982. Clearly, the key to better education is not more money but better teaching. It is equally clear that the Department of Education, whose grants provide less than 7 percent of all elementary and secondary education expenditures in the U.S., cannot produce good teaching. Education, including higher education, is a state and local responsibility. I would abolish the entire department with the exception of its approximately $1 billion a year expenditures for the handicapped, which I would double. Savings: $14 billion.

5. Bureau of Indian Affairs: The BIA essentially duplicates existing federal health, education, welfare and job programs being provided to non-Indians. As revealed in chapter 19, it is hard to find a more scandal-ridden program anywhere, most of whose resources are consumed by an overpaid, bloated bureaucracy. If BIA's budget were simply divided up among America's 340,000 Indian families, many of whom are not poor by any means, it would be enough to give each family $3,000 a year, or more than enough to lift most poor Indians out of poverty. It's time for the Indians to be treated like everyone else, while providing a safety net of assistance to the truly needy. Close down the agency, but provide block grant assistance to needy Indian governments from out of the Interior Department's remaining budget. Savings: $1.2 billion.

6. Mass Transit Assistance: Billions of dollars in federal grants are being given to localities for mass transit operating costs, planning activities, demonstration projects, and even managerial training and research. Private systems operate more efficiently than government ones, but in any case, Washington should not be responsible for mass transit. OMB analysts say, "Primary responsibility for mass transit should remain with state and local governments." Stop the grants. Savings: $3 billion.

7. Military Retirement: Military pensions cost taxpayers $15 billion in 1982, $16.5 billion in 1983, and an estimated $17 billion in 1984. As with other entitlements, indexing pensions for inflation has been a costly mistake, one that private pensions cannot afford to provide. Eliminating yearly cost-of-living adjustments (COLA) could save an estimated $650 million in fiscal 1984.

8. Civil Service Retirement: It was also a mistake to peg civil service pensions to inflation. Pensions have not only been rising faster than federal pay but, again, they are providing federal retirees an unjustified benefit their counterparts in the private sector do not have. Suspend the COLA. Estimated savings in 1984: $880 million.

9. Nonnuclear Energy Research and Development: The Energy Department is supporting private-sector research on new fossil fuels, solar and geothermal technologies, as well as energy conservation and storage. Meanwhile, spending on research and development programs among U.S. energy corporations is up, dwarfing the total federal effort. Thus, getting the government out of this field will not significantly affect private energy R&D spending. Savings: nearly $1 billion.

10. Economic Development Administration: There is very little evidence that EDA grants to economically depressed areas have significantly alleviated unemployment. That nearly 80 percent of the country was eligible for grants when President Reagan came into power shows how EDA had been turned into the ultimate pork barrel. The Reagan administration has emptied EDA's barrel considerably but Congress continues pouring in more money. Now it should be sealed closed for good. Savings: $224 million.

11. Extension Service: Maintaining extension offices in every county in America is a vestige of a bygone era when we were a

heavily agricultural country and communications was still in its infancy. Today, with a declining farm population, these county offices are turning to servicing nonfarm constituencies with advice, counseling and literature on lawns, backyard gardening, hobbies, home economics, etc. Shut them down. Savings: $332 million.

12. Maritime Administration Subsidies: This program has been subsidizing the U.S. shipping industry for nearly fifty years, but with little effect on our decaying maritime fleet. If U.S. commerce is being shipped on cheaper foreign flag ships, so much the better for our trade costs. Vigorous deregulation, not more federal subsidies, is needed to make our maritime industry competitive with the rest of the world. Savings: $400 million.

13. Amtrak: The government's heavily subsidized passenger rail service is burdened by antiquated work rules, excessive pay scales, and poor management practices. For example, on Amtrak's Phoenix–to–Los Angeles run passengers pay only $66 for a one-way trip whose real cost is $280. Sell the lines or close them down. Savings: $716 million.

14. Soil and Water Conservation: These programs have not been effective, according to various government budget analysts. A study by the Department of Agriculture found that only 21 percent of federal erosion-control aid went to areas that accounted for 84 percent of all serious erosion. Less than 4 percent of water-conservation aid went to lands where water use was highest. An indefinite moratorium on these programs is needed until our budget is in better shape. Savings: $917 million.

15. Bureau of the Census: The 1980 census needlessly squandered over $1 billion. Much of the census data it gathered, e.g., how many bathrooms, air conditioners, and telephones we have, is primarily used by big business. In a time of austerity, this program should be mothballed until 1990 when the next census can be conducted on a far less epic scale. Savings: $168 million.

16. National Oceanic and Atmospheric Administration: In addition to environmental satellites, fisheries and oceanic research and development, NOAA runs the Weather Service and provides the shipping industry with charts and maps. The Reagan administration sought a modest reduction in its budget, plus a program of fees for

industries using its services. But there is no reason why many of NOAA's lower-priority research projects cannot be postponed indefinitely. Significantly higher user fees than those proposed should be established to fund its most vital services, including the Weather Service, which provides a valuable, marketable service to broadcasters and newspapers at very little cost. Estimated savings: $500 million.

17. Nuclear Energy Research: Ronald Reagan wanted to shift these research and technology programs to the Commerce Department as part of a proposed dismantlement of the Energy Department, but that idea went nowhere.

A better idea would be an indefinite moratorium on funding these projects, along with elimination of further funding for such programs as the Clinch River Breeder Reactor. Encouraging the nuclear energy industry's development by streamlining federal regulatory policies would more than make up for the government's withdrawal from current R&D funding and would set nuclear energy on a free-enterprise basis to begin meeting our energy needs for the future. Savings: $815 million.

18. Urban Development Action Grants: UDAG gives grants to communities to subsidize commercial developments and thus "create jobs." But government audits and my own investigations (see chapter 16, The Gravy in the Deal) reveal that in many cases UDAG-subsidized developments were committed to be built anyway. Moreover, UDAG money is being used to build ritzy hotel complexes and upper-income housing projects. Dry up this gravy train. Savings: $440 million.

19. Social Security: Indexing social security for inflation, which in large part has contributed to its past insolvency, can no longer be afforded. The 7.4 percent cost-of-living adjustment granted in 1982 cost taxpayers a crushing $15 billion. If the 5.7 percent COLA for 1983 had been eliminated, it would have saved an estimated $9.8 billion. Estimated savings for fiscal 1984: $4.4 billion.

20. Military Pay: The military payroll is costing taxpayers about $40 billion a year. Annual raises and promotions continue to push the figure higher. It is certainly reasonable to ask our well-paid military personnel to take a pay freeze in order to help restore this

country's economic security. Millions of people in the private sector have done so. Estimated savings: Nearly $2 billion.

21. Civilian Pay: Federal civil service paychecks will total nearly $60 billion this fiscal year. As with the military, it is difficult to justify giving further pay increases at the present time while the government continues running severely high deficits. Civilian federal workers can take comfort in knowing that whatever happens to the economy, most of them will have job security, an incomparable pension, early retirement, plus other benefits not available in the real world. Estimated savings: $2.6 billion.

22. Consultants: Uncle Sam spends about $4 billion annually on consultants, better known as "beltway bandits" in Washington. Congressional hearings and investigations, internal audits, and GAO reports have shown that much of what the government is buying in the way of consulting reports, studies, program evaluations and a range of other consultant services is of little or no value. A 50 percent reduction would hurt only the con artists, make-work specialists, and lucrative consulting businesses and organizations in Washington, D.C. and elsewhere. Estimated savings: $2 billion.

23. Military Commissaries: With better military pay, it is no longer necessary — if it ever was — to provide cut-rate groceries and other goods at military commissaries for our active-duty and retired defense personnel. The stores should be eliminated except in remote areas where needed by military servicemen. Savings: $850 million.

24. Postal Service: The elimination of Saturday mail delivery was suggested by the Carter administration, but the idea died after heavy lobbying from postal employees. It still remains a good idea. Of course, the government's monopoly on first-class mail delivery should be broken, opening up the business to the private sector, as Federal Trade Commission Chairman James Miller has wisely suggested. In the meantime, taxpayer subsidies for the ever-inefficient Post Office can and should be reduced. Eliminating Saturday delivery is a good place to start cutting costs. Estimated savings: $588 million.

25. Corporate Welfare: There is, according to an internal analysis in the Office of Management and Budget, an estimated $30 billion

in "corporate welfare" scattered throughout the budget, much of it buried in off-budget accounts. It runs the gamut from credits and subsidies to trade assistance, loans, loan guarantees, federally backed insurance policies and other forms of federal assistance for a variety of industries — from travel agents to aircraft merchants. Uncle Sam's corporate sugardaddies include the Export-Import Bank, the Small Business Administration, the Rural Electrification Administration, the Synthetic Fuels Corporation, the Overseas Private Investment Corporation and many more.

If Congress were to do nothing more than eliminate or substantially curb many of these unnecessary expenditures, it could make a major dent in the budget deficit.

26. National Highway Traffic Safety Administration: Anyone who has taken even a cursory glance at the highway death toll in the last decade knows this agency has been a joke. Years of costly research, experiments with the ill-fated seat-belt interlock system, and billions doled out to subsidize state and local highway safety programs have not curbed the fatality rate. Increased gas costs, the 55-mile-per-hour national speed limit, changing driving habits, a more exercise-conscious population, a crackdown on drunk drivers by local authorities, among other things, have done much more to reduce highway fatalities. For all its bumper bashing, research and costly regulations and recalls, the NHTSA has accomplished little if anything.

The enforcement of local highway safety laws is not Washington's responsibility. Close the agency and institute a federal highway assistance bonus system which would significantly reward states with lower per capita highway accidents and fatalities. Savings: $200 million.

27. Occupational Safety and Health Administration: If performance means anything in government programs anymore, then surely this agency is a failure. Despite billions spent on a huge bureaucracy, this program has had little effect on workplace accidents, the large proportion of which are due to carelessness and inexperience.

OSHA's workplace inspectors should be eliminated, and its worker health programs consolidated into the Environmental Protection Agency, which should have the responsibility for handling serious occupational health problems caused by harmful chemicals, or other substances. Savings: $212.6 million.

28. Grants-in-aid: Grants to state and local governments have increased from $7 billion in 1960 to more than $90 billion today. But as we have seen with revenue sharing, there's no money to share. An across-the-board reduction of $10 billion in grants-in-aid would still leave an $80 billion pot that could be more efficiently turned over to the states and localities through block grants. Savings: $10 billion.

29. National Science Foundation: Several years ago then–Senator Henry Bellmon of Oklahoma shocked NSF officials by asking them at an oversight hearing what would happen if Congress decided to "totally end" NSF's funding for five years. The officials were so surprised that anyone would even suggest such a thing that they asked to respond in writing. They predicted all sorts of bad things for enlightened research, but the true answer, of course, is that America would survive. Although NSF is Congress's favorite sacred cow, the agency has not produced many stunning scientific breakthroughs. Defunding this agency would hardly end scientific research in the United States. On the contrary, much of the work it subsidizes would go forward anyway under the auspices of universities and corporations and dozens of other federal research programs. Even with NSF's demise, the government would still be spending a mind-boggling $43 billion a year in research and development. Savings: $1.3 billion.

30. Defense spending: There is room for substantial spending cuts and budget savings in the Pentagon's expenditures without gutting the readiness and strength of our armed forces or abandoning our needed military buildup.

Those who oppose any spending restraint in the Pentagon argue that it is impossible to cut the defense budget in the short run, except in the areas of pay and benefits, because of long-term contractual obligations. Yet I believe we can make relatively modest cuts in defense programs and practices that can lead to a tighter, tougher, and more efficient military machine that has grown bureaucratically fat, lethargic and wasteful. Many contracts now in the Pentagon pipeline can be renegotiated to modestly reduce or stretch out some procurement levels. Substantial savings can be achieved through selective base closings, more competitive procurement practices, service consolidations, longer tours of duty, a cutback in unnecessary travel costs and recreational facilities, pay and pension reforms, plus other management changes, auditing provisions, and spending cuts which I list in greater detail in chapter 11. Estimated savings: Between $10 and $20 billion.

31. Step up the collection of $38 billion in outstanding delinquent loans and other long overdue payments out of the $250 billion presently owed to the federal government.

32. Cut $1.5 billion from the abuse-ridden $3.5 billion Farmers Home Administration loan program.

33. Save $289 million by mandating workfare for welfare recipients able to work.

34. Withhold $300 million from the civil defense program, a collection of make-work activities of dubious effectiveness and value.

35. Eliminate $700 million spent to run the U.S. Employment Service which unfairly and ineffectively competes with private and other local government employment services.

36. Cut $300 million from the Agriculture Department's yearly $460 million research program.

37. Reduce the $11.5 billion highway assistance program by a modest $1 billion.

38. Pick up about $800 million a year in various coast guard user fees from commercial vessels and private yacht and boat owners.

39. Phase out $500 million in school lunch subsidies for middle-class and wealthy schoolchildren, but preserve the reduced-price and free lunch programs for the needy.

40. Roll back the budgets of the departments of State, Justice, Interior and Labor to fiscal 1981 levels for a savings of $8.4 billion.

41. Curb the Veterans Administration's $24.8 billion budget by a modest $2 billion, including ending payments to veterans with "10 percent disability."

42. Postpone $225 million in building and maintenance projects by the General Services Administration.

43. Cut $1 billion from the Environmental Protection Agency's $2.4 billion in yearly construction project grants.

44. Slash $1 billion from overfunded federal housing programs. The government is already obligated to spend $363 billion on housing programs, and of that amount, as of mid-1983, an awesome $263 billion had not yet been spent. "If Congress did not commit another single dollar to housing," says Senator Bill Armstrong of Colorado, "another 300,000 units are already authorized to be provided by 1988." At present, housing assistance is going to 13 million Americans in 5.6 million housing units.

45. Phase out all farm subsidies — costing taxpayers $21 billion in fiscal 1983 — which prop up commodity prices at artificial levels in order to keep an overabundance of crop and dairy farmers in business. Meanwhile, government warehouses are bulging with produce for which billions more are spent in storage costs. Eliminating the subsidies and target prices would allow farm products to reach real market levels and thus make America's food more competitive on the world market.

46. Scale down the National Aeronautics and Space Administration's $7.2 billion annual budget by $1 billion, and require private investors and foreign governments to pay more for the use of the space shuttle and other NASA facilities and services.

47. Save an estimated $1 billion by declaring a temporary moratorium on all ongoing Army Corps of Engineers public works construction projects.

48. Close down these nonessential federal agencies: the Federal Trade Commission, the Civil Aeronautics Board, the Interstate Commerce Commission, the National Endowment for the Arts, the National Endowment for the Humanities, the Legal Services Corporation, the Securities and Exchange Commission, the Federal Election Commission, and the Corporation for Public Broadcasting. Savings: $978 million.

49. Eliminate the government's $1 billion-a-year press and public relations operations, including all promotional filmmaking, broadcasting and publishing activities — except in areas vital to human health and safety.

50. Cut at least $1 billion out of the bureaucracy's $9 billion-a-year transportation bill through a moratorium on all nonessential

and low priority out-of-town travel, substituting teleconferencing wherever possible.

51. Raise up to $10 billion by selling off unneeded federal properties, buildings and unused equipment.

52. Eliminate the scandal-plagued Small Business Administration, which has helped less than 1 percent of the nation's small businesses. Reducing business tax rates would do far more to help America's small business community than a program ten times the size of SBA. Savings: $576 million.

All of this totals over $200 billion in potential spending cuts and budget savings, and thus far exceeds the present yearly deficit. Obviously, there is room here for disagreement over spending priorities and need. But even if my budget-cutting proposals were to be cut in half, that would still wipe out the structural deficits of about $100 billion, which even the most optimistic level of economic recovery would not eliminate.

Of course, the spending cuts and savings I have listed cover only a relatively small number of potential programs, agencies and expenditures where budget reductions and savings can be achieved. A fuller examination of spending programs would yield much larger savings. The point that they serve to make, however, is that the budget is not some monolithic fiscal entity that defies reductions and budgetary controls. Even among entitlement programs, I do not propose cutting benefits, but simply placing a moratorium on future cost-of-living raises until the government can slash the deficit, catch its fiscal breath, and give the economy a much-needed boost by allowing it to nurture itself on the newly freed savings that would become available.

True, my list contains some very controversial spending reductions. Yet it eliminates the deficit without touching some of the government's biggest and most costly social programs, such as food stamps, aid-to-dependent children, Medicare and Medicaid, and other major components of the social safety net for the needy. It does not weaken our basic defense establishment, nor does it weaken applied medical research.

What my list seeks to do is to show that the budget is filled with many expenditures that are not necessarily vital to the health and safety and defense of our nation — spending that can be cut. Non-essential agencies can be zeroed out. Automatic cost-of-living adjustments can be withheld. Low-priority expenditures, unproductive research, and no-strings-attached grants to undeserving communities can be reduced or eliminated.

So Ed Dale is wrong. The federal government's budget could be balanced in one or two years, if we really wanted to do it that quickly, without harming the sick, the old, the poor, the jobless, the search for the cure for cancer, national security, or our efforts to clean up the environment. On the other hand, it probably wouldn't be very prudent to undertake so Herculean a task in one or two years. After all, it took decades for the government to become this fat, and it would be dangerous to the nation's health to attempt to shed that many pounds so quickly. The shock of a sudden withdrawal of federal funds from hundreds of subsidies and grants-in-aid programs and the resultant spurt of unemployment among federal, state and local bureaucracies would have a cataclysmic effect.

But it certainly can be done through a prudent, multiyear program of gradual spending reductions and program eliminations. All that is required is leadership, determination, political courage, and a national will to bring the federal budget into balance with its income, and thus give America's still-anemic marketplace the medicine necessary to regain the full health and vigor that is essential for future economic growth and prosperity.

28

Facing Reality

W HEN Ronald Reagan was sworn into office on January 20, 1981, he was presented with a proposed fiscal 1982 budget left behind by Jimmy Carter, which Reagan managed to cut ever so slightly — actually by only 1.5 percent — to $728.4 billion. By January 1985, after four years in office, according to projections by the White House Office of Management and Budget, Reagan will be proposing a budget for fiscal 1986 that will call for outlays of $992.1 billion, or nearly $1 trillion. If that projection holds true, and there is no reason to doubt that it will not, federal budgets compiled under Reagan will have skyrocketed by a stunning $263.7 billion during his four "budget cutting" years in office.

This is not to suggest for a moment that Carter, who preached limitations in everything but federal spending, did any better during his one-term presidency. On the contrary, his record was a great deal worse. When the former Georgia governor came into office in 1977, he began with a fiscal 1978 federal budget of $451 billion, which seems relatively modest to us today. When he departed Washington, he left behind a proposed fiscal 1982 budget of $739.3 billion. Carter had compiled budget expenditures totaling nearly

$290 billion over his four years in office. Moreover, had he stayed in office, according to his own administration's estimates, he would have pushed yearly expenditures close to the one trillion dollar mark by fiscal 1985, one year earlier than Reagan.

Now, clearly Reagan has had a great deal of help in pushing federal spending up so dramatically over such a relatively short period of time. I pointed out in an earlier chapter the enterprising extent to which his own administration has sought significant budget increases in dozens of departments and agencies, while simultaneously demanding that Congress cut spending elsewhere. For himself, Reagan argues that all of this increased spending has to be laid at the doorstep of Congress whose appetite for more and more spending is insatiable. As far as Reagan is concerned, it is Congress that is spending far beyond the country's ability to pay, and he is happy to provide anyone willing to listen with a little civics lesson to explain what he means.

The President did just that in an Oval Office interview* in preparation for this book in which he distilled, perhaps without really knowing it, the dilemma that faces us all as government continues to absorb unacceptable levels of the nation's income. For example, when I asked him if he accepted any blame at all for the unprecedented federal deficits that his administration was racking up — which were expected to total an estimated $700 billion over his four years — he swiftly and emphatically replied:

"No, not a bit. They keep calling it the President's budget. It isn't the President's budget. Under the Constitution there is only one branch of government that is authorized to spend money. That is the Congress of the United States. And if the Congress had given the President in these last few years the cuts in spending that the President had asked for, the deficit would be $40 billion less than it is right now.

"I think it's time . . . [to] instruct the people of this country a little bit as to just how all of this comes about and who is responsible," Reagan continued.

"The most practical way to reduce the deficit is to get economic

*The interview took place in the Oval Office of the White House on October 6, 1983.

recovery, to get those people that are out there now [who are] being helped by the government financially because of their unemployment, to get them back working, earning and paying taxes again is what will make the biggest drop [in the deficit].

"More than half of the present budget deficit is structural," the President said, meaning of course that it is simply the result of the government's spending more than it takes in. "The other half is cyclical, that is, caused by this recession. So you can deal with one half of that deficit through the economic recovery. You deal with the rest in getting the spending of government down, and that means Congress having the courage to do what they haven't done yet, and that is to deal with the entitlement programs. And they haven't made one change in those, and they are the principal cause of the other half of the deficit."

"Nevertheless," I responded, "Ronald Reagan, not the Democrats in Congress, has sent budgets to Capitol Hill for fiscal '83 and fiscal '84 which called for deficits of $91 billion and $189 billion respectively. If the President is submitting spending requests that actually propose such huge deficits, how can you dare ask Congress to do any better?"

"Because," he answered, "it is apparent, and was apparent from the beginning, after almost fifty years of this kind of economics, that you could not in one jump pull the rug out from under people who are totally dependent on many government programs. You had to bring this down in a way that would preserve a safety net for the people in need.

"So what we aimed at was to get us on a declining pattern of deficits to where . . . we could foresee the day of the balanced budget. And I might also point out that the sincerity of those who want or don't want deficits I think is exposed also in the fact that I have been asking for, pleading for, a constitutional amendment requiring a balanced budget. And it has been mainly the majority party in the House that has refused to even consider this. And I doubt that any of those candidates for president want such a thing."

Still, I argued, "if you don't propose" the deeper cuts needed to effectively eat into the structural deficit, how can you hope to persuade the Congress to do so? Only "the full weight of the chief exec-

283

utive" behind formally proposed budget reductions can hope "to steel them to make those cuts." I then recalled how Ed Meese, counsellor to the president, having seen an article I had written about erasing the deficit, had dropped me a note saying he found my cuts "very interesting," but added, "Now just tell us how we can get Congress to agree to them." I wrote back, I told the President, "Ed, first you have to propose them."

"Well, now wait a minute," the President interjected, "you also first have to face the reality of whether you can get [the budget cuts] or not. Now, even with the reductions that we asked for, we couldn't get all of them. As a matter of fact, the budget that I sent up for [fiscal] 1984, Congress wouldn't even consider it. Now I have to be aware of that. I don't sit here all alone with this. We meet with the congressional leadership of both parties. We talk with committee chairmen and the leadership on the budget that we are proposing, and we have to face up to what are the realities. And we still ask for more than they are willing to give us in cuts.

"But it doesn't do any good to just send a budget up there that would not even be considered," Reagan went on. "We did in [the fiscal] '84 [budget], as I say, and even though it was not as drastic as what you were earlier suggesting, as I say, they simply refuse to even consider it."

"But isn't that sort of passively giving in to [Congress's] appetites and their excesses?" I asked.

"No," the President said, "I think there is a recognition of reality since the Constitution says they are the only ones who can authorize and appropriate money to spend.

"Now, there is nothing I can do about this," Reagan said, seemingly throwing up his hands, "except one thing," and he went on to explain, as he has before, that he would veto spending bills that exceeded the spending levels he had agreed to. Unfortunately, Reagan has rarely used the veto, accepting clearly excessive spending bills that fell generally within the administration's spending targets, even though those targets were based upon projected deficits of over $100 billion in fiscal 1983, and nearly $200 billion in fiscal 1984 and 1985.

There is, of course, nothing wrong with facing "reality" except

284

when it gets in the way of achieving your objectives. The reality that Reagan characterized as supporting a safety net for the needy certainly does not square with the deeper reality, outlined in preceding chapters, of a federal spending machine that is spewing out billions of dollars, not just for the needy, but for the middle class, for the upper class, for the corporate welfare class, and for hundreds of government programs of dubious effectiveness, efficiency and value. Moreover, Reagan's curiously un-Reagan-like acquiescence to "the reality" of Congress's resistance to truly substantive spending reductions — in sharp contrast to his thus-far much tougher posture against significant tax increases — is strange when one considers that it is the very reality of Congress's spending that has in fact brought America to its present fiscal catastrophe.

"This is a situation that is unacceptable," complains businessman J. Peter Grace, chairman and chief executive officer of W. R. Grace & Co., and the chairman of the President's Private Sector Survey on Cost Control which in late 1983 recommended a three-year total of $424 billion in budget reductions and savings. "Not only" are current spending levels unacceptable "on the grounds of fiscal responsibility," Grace says, "but even more compellingly on grounds of moral responsibility toward future generations that will bear the heaviest burden."

Peter Grace is right. The fast track on which government spending remains fixed and about which the President says "there is nothing I can do" is clearly unacceptable. However, there is something that can be done about it. But the President has to resolve that instead of accepting "reality," he intends to change it, or in the very least vigorously challenge the kind of irresponsible reality that has been practiced for too long by the Congress, particularly by the congressional committee barons from whom Reagan insists he must first receive a kind of budgetary benediction before sending his recommendations up to Capitol Hill. These of course are the very people who have spent the government into its current state of indebtedness and against whom Ronald Reagan ran for the presidency.

But what can he do about it?

First, Reagan can begin by more aggressively using the power of the veto to force deeper spending cuts. Sadly, despite his tough, gunslinger rhetoric about keeping his veto pen ready to shoot down big spending bills, Reagan actually used his veto authority only five times during 1983, none of which was against those big appropriations bills he scorned for so many years. In the entire two previous years he used the regular veto a mere seven times and the pocket veto eight times, of which only two were overridden. Yet he vetoed only three funding bills in 1982 and only one in 1981. In sharp comparison, President Gerald Ford used the veto sixty-six times over the two and a half years of his presidency against a totally Democratic Congress and only twelve were overridden. Seven of Ford's vetoes were against excessive appropriations bills.

By failing to exploit the combined potential of his Republican majority in the Senate with his Republican and conservative Democratic allies in the House, Reagan wasted a unique opportunity to pound the budget into submission and force Congress to tame its appetites. On at least two separate occasions during the summer of 1983 letters were signed by House Democrats promising to uphold spending vetoes by Reagan. On June 9 a sizable group of seventy-nine conservative Democrats — more than enough to give Reagan the votes he needed to make his vetoes stick — wrote to House Speaker Thomas P. "Tip" O'Neill, balking over the then-pending Democratic budget while strongly indicating that they would be ready to back possible presidential vetoes supporting "judicious" budget cuts. A second letter sent to Reagan in July, and spearheaded by Congressman Philip Gramm of Texas, the former Boll Weevil Democrat who switched to the Republican Party, was signed by an impressive bipartisan group of 146 House members who pledged to back the President's vetoes of excessive spending bills. Thus, the President had an extraordinary chance to pursue a much more ambitious budget-cutting offensive during his first three years in office. Unfortunately, Reagan chose to keep his veto pen, which he said he kept under his pillow at night, under his mattress, using it very rarely in support of his war on the budget.

Second, as long as presidents who get elected by promising to curb the growth of government dare to submit only budgets assured of winning congressional approval, then there is little hope of ever significantly curbing federal spending. The only way that Reagan can show a recalcitrant Congress that he means business about significantly curbing the growth of spending is to back up his tough rhetoric with concrete, no-nonsense spending proposals. The idea that only budget proposals guaranteed to "win" enactment should be sent to Capitol Hill accedes to the prevailing media mindset, which is also prevalent among Reagan's chief aides, that budgets that fail to win approval from Congress must therefore be bad budgets. On the contrary, just the opposite may be true. Reagan would be better advised to submit a budget that goes significantly beyond what Congress would like to cut from nonessential and low-priority programs, taking his lumps in whatever Congress chooses to do with the budget, and then fight for his own set of lower spending figures through skillful and vigorous use of the veto. It would be a battle waged on principle, for fiscal sanity, and in behalf of good economic policy. And I suspect that it would be a struggle that the American people would enthusiastically support.

To a significant extent, Reagan is no doubt correct in saying that every budget is in the final analysis Congress's budget. The annual charade that the Congress and the media go through over the President's spending recommendations tend to overlook the fact that no presidential budget ever emerges totally intact from the Byzantine authorization and appropriations process which Congress has constructed. No matter who occupies the White House, Congress always works its own will on each president's budget through the Rube Goldberg congressional budget-making procedures that lawmakers have inflicted upon themselves and the country.

Despite Congress's media-hyped image of having imposed some self-restraint on its spending habits through the so-called budget control process, in reality its record on spending is actually worse under the Budget Act of 1975 than it was prior to its enactment. According to an internal economic study prepared for the Senate Labor Committee, federal budgets have in fact been going up faster than when Congress operated under no congressional budget act at all. During the seven-year period prior to the Budget Act, fiscal years 1969 to 1975, total outlays experienced an overall growth of 18.7 percent. But during the seven-year period after enactment of the Budget Act, between fiscal 1976 and 1982, federal outlays grew by a robust 30.1 percent. So much for Congress's ability to control the government's purse strings!

All of this provides a compelling justification for Ronald Reagan, or any future president determined to get control of federal spending, to begin using vigorously every constitutional tool at his disposal to do battle with Congress in the name of restoring fiscal common sense to our national government. There are those who may dismiss this approach as confrontation politics and suggest that government by veto is a nasty business that must be avoided at all costs. But the alternative is the politics of acquiescence and compromise which usually end up preserving the status quo — by which federal spending continues to soar upward, the government plunges ever deeper into debt, the economy worsens, and a bloated and wasteful bureaucracy remains a national scandal.

Index

Addabbo, Joseph, 120, 134
Administration Committee, House, 23, 58
Aegis System, navy's, 118
Aero Corporation, 219
Aerospace Guidance and Metrology Center, 110
AFL-CIO, 82
Age Discrimination in Employment Act, 68
Agency for International Development (AID), 211, 245–246, 254
Agricultural Research Service, 256
Agricultural Yearbook, 50
Agriculture Committee, House, 23
Agriculture, U.S. Department of: Animal and Plant Health Inspection Service, 150; extension services, 271–272; and import duties, 148–151; research funding, 256, 277; soil and water conservation, 272
Air-Defense Gun, Army, 83
Air Force: Aerospace Guidance and Metrology Center, 110; "black bag" accounts, 51; and C-5B lob-

bying, 131–140; contractors' wages, 104; 89th Military Airlift Wing, 51–52; Office of Legislative Liaison, 134
Air Force Academy, U.S., 113
Air Logistics Center, 126
Air Products & Chemicals Co., 160
Albert, Carl, 63, 65
Alberta Tar-Sands, 157
Alexander, Andrew, 69
Alimanu Military Reservation, 113
Allis-Chalmers, 145
Allison, Larry, 174
Alto, Vincent, 209
Amante, Liz, 168
American Bankers Association, 61
American Enterprise Institute, 15, 87
American Indian Policy Review Commission, 193
American Indians, 185–197. *See also* Bureau of Indian Affairs
American Mining Congress, 61
American Petroleum Institute, 61
American Standard, Inc., 146
Amtrak, 74, 245, 272